Harold Taylor and
Sarah Lawrence College

Praise for *Harold Taylor and Sarah Lawrence College*

Harold Taylor was an artist of his own life, forever experimenting and investigating, creating, tasting and testing, sipping and savoring—always living his life with a distinctly forward lean, on-the-move and in-the-mix. In *Harold Taylor and Sarah Lawrence College: A Life of Social and Educational Activism*, Craig Kridel dances the dialectic, arm-in-arm with Taylor, illuminating both a time, and a life—part chance, part choice—in all its messy contradictions. Kridel describes himself as an editor, but a more accurate description is also more capacious: comrade in arms, dramaturge, soulmate, and choreographer.

—William C. Ayers, formerly Distinguished Professor of Education and Senior University Scholar, University of Illinois at Chicago

Imagine being close friends with both John Dewey and Duke Ellington, being accused of communist activity, being an unofficial advisor to Adlai Stevenson, and being president of Sarah Lawrence College. Harold Taylor is such a man, and his expansive life of intrigue and intellect is on full display in a new memoir brought together—posthumously—by educational historian Craig Kridel. The memoir is vivid, beautifully-written, humbling, timely, and provides a window into the life of one of the nation's most interesting leaders and thinkers.

—Marybeth Gasman, Samuel DeWitt Proctor Endowed Chair in Education and Distinguished Professor, Rutgers University–New Brunswick

This delightful book resurrects for a new generation of readers the sharp eye, keen wit, and good humor that made Harold Taylor one of the bright lights of American higher education in the mid-twentieth century. His lively posthumous memoir reveals how after leaving Sarah Lawrence in 1959, he endured as a principled, perceptive commentator who held his own in political controversies while at the same time writing accounts that leave us a legacy of perceptive observations about key figures from colleges, foundations, Congress, and even candidates for the US presidency. The result is an autobiographical anthology that reminds us today that about a half century ago higher education leaders such as Harold Taylor provided a refreshing alternative to a business model of executives in charge of the university.

—John R. Thelin, University Research Professor,
University of Kentucky

Unless tragedy befalls them, university presidents blend in with the institution's furniture. But Harold Taylor is the exception that will, for me, prove the rule. This beautiful, intellectual autobiography not only helps readers to know Taylor's professional persona but to understand how he grappled with significant issues that still define higher education today: academic freedom, free speech, privacy, patriotism, and how to serve as a public intellectual. The insider dramatis personae are worth the price of admission. Taylor will not be relegated to hidden archives if this fascinating narrative has the effect it had on me, showing me this leader's life, hidden in plain sight all along.

—Michael A. Olivas, Wm. B. Bates Distinguished Chair in Law (Emeritus) at the University of Houston Law Center

A true renaissance man, Harold Taylor was erudite, elegant, and exceptional in all his endeavors and the epitome of what an intellectual should be—curious, concerned, and reflective. His dedication to whatever he took on was stellar. Seeing him strolling about campus with his large English sheepdog and tiny cairn terrier whilst smoking his pipe is one of my favorite memories, and reading this book took me back to the wonderful feeling of being young again and learning in the stimulating progressive environment of Sarah Lawrence, led by the brilliant and memorable Harold Taylor.

—Harriet Pogul Wohlgemuth,
Sarah Lawrence alumna, 1959 and 1979

Harold Taylor and Sarah Lawrence College
A Life of Social and Educational Activism

Compiled and edited by
CRAIG KRIDEL

Foreword by
LEON BOTSTEIN

EXCELSIOR
EDITIONS

Cover image: Harold Taylor meeting with the Sarah Lawrence College Student Council, 1945. Sam Shere/The LIFE Picture Collection/Shutterstock

Published by State University of New York Press, Albany

© 2022 State University of New York

All rights reserved

Printed in the United States of America

No part of this book may be used or reproduced in any manner whatsoever without written permission. No part of this book may be stored in a retrieval system or transmitted in any form or by any means including electronic, electrostatic, magnetic tape, mechanical, photocopying, recording, or otherwise without the prior permission in writing of the publisher.

For information, contact State University of New York Press, Albany, NY
www.sunypress.edu

Library of Congress Cataloging-in-Publication Data

Names: Taylor, Harold, 1914–1993, author. | Kridel, Craig Alan, editor. | Botstein, Leon.
Title: Harold Taylor and Sarah Lawrence College : a life of social and educational activism / Craig Kridel, Leon Botstein.
Description: Albany : State University of New York Press, 2022. | Series: Excelsior editions | Includes bibliographical references and index.
Identifiers: LCCN 2022009660 | ISBN 9781438490632 (hardcover : alk. paper) | ISBN 9781438490656 (ebook) | ISBN 9781438490649 (pbk. : alk. paper)
Subjects: LCSH: Taylor, Harold, 1914–1993. | Sarah Lawrence College—Presidents—Biography. | College presidents—New York (State)—New York—Biography. | College teachers—United States—Biography. | Education, Higher—Political aspects—United States—History—20th century.
Classification: LCC LD4881.S45 T39 2022 | DDC 378.1/11 [B]—dc23/eng/20220520
LC record available at https://lccn.loc.gov/2022009660

10 9 8 7 6 5 4 3 2 1

Contents

Foreword: Harold Taylor in Retrospect   vii
   by Leon Botstein

Acknowledgments   xvii

Preface   xxi

1   The Day Duke Died   1

2   A Student's Journey   17

3   Coming Down from Cambridge   35

4   The Wisconsin Years: A Serious Concern for the Relation of Thought to Action   55

5   Sarah Lawrence Remembrances: A Community in the Making   63

6   Assault on a Small College   89

7   On Being Written About: Mary McCarthy and Randall Jarrell   107

8   Dewey, Meiklejohn, and the 1950s   125

9	Thoughts on Leaving Sarah Lawrence and Life Thereafter	145
10	Adlai Stevenson and the 1960 Presidential Campaign: Putting the Public Interest above His Own	155
11	The Student Revolt Revisited: Students in a Stormy Time	173
12	Unbegun Chapters: Hubert Humphrey, Plagiarism, and Albert Barnes	195

Epilogue: Luck, Fate, Commitment, and Change   211

Postscript: The Play of Ideas   229

Appendix: Sample Schedule for Harold Taylor, May and June 1965   233

Notes   237

Index   265

Foreword

Harold Taylor in Retrospect

If history can be said to have shadows, or dark recesses, it would be a fair assumption that the name Harold Taylor has receded into them. However, his posthumous fate, already predictable at the time of his death in 1993, may not be irretrievable, as the welcome publication of this book, Taylor's memoir (elegantly edited by Craig Kridel), suggests. Taylor was a prominent college president who was covered extensively (unlike most of his peers) by the national news media. He became a highly visible personality in the post–World War II American education scene. He was regarded throughout the nation as a key representative of the "progressive" movement in American education, particularly in higher education.

In the 1960s and 1970s, having resigned the presidency of Sarah Lawrence College in 1959 and elected not to assume a second presidency in higher education or at a comparable cultural institution, Taylor remained on the scene as a freelance public intellectual. He pursued writing, and speaking. He hosted a television show, sat on the boards of not-for-profit ventures, taught and consulted for public agencies, particularly the United Nations. To attempt to make a mark exclusively as a purveyor of opinion was a risky choice. But Taylor believed the recognition he had achieved at Sarah Lawrence gave him momentum sufficient for his future.

Legend has it that a curious counterfactual claim was made in defense of Taylor's conception of his future in 1959. Had Taylor become president of Lawrence University in Appleton, Wisconsin, another fine small undergraduate institution, and not Sarah Lawrence College, a more notorious progressive women's college just outside of New York, his life and work would have gone unnoticed and he certainly would not have been able to gain the fame and recognition that enabled him to pursue a career in the public realm. This speculation may not be all that apt, since Nathan Marsh Pusey went from being president of Lawrence in Wisconsin directly to being president of Harvard during Taylor's presidency of Sarah Lawrence.

Unfortunately, the fact that Taylor, who was in his mid-forties when he left Sarah Lawrence, never went on to a position of leadership at a major institution from which advocacy of the causes he believed in might have been pursued is never fully explained in his memoir. Indeed, Taylor's foray into autobiography is more descriptive than confessional. Taylor dabbled in politics a bit through the Democratic Party, advising Adlai Stevenson in 1960. He became a sort of elder statesman and self-appointed guide to the rebellious younger generation of the 1960s best represented by Tom Hayden and the Students for a Democratic Society of the now-legendary Port Huron Statement. The generational confrontation in the years surrounding the historic student rebellions of 1968 helped sustain Taylor's presence in the public eye. He became something of an interpreter between adversaries, a person of stature whose sympathies were with the rebels but whose manner, language, and framework of values gave him empathy for skeptics, critics, or the confused among his contemporaries who watched the civic unrest and violence with horror.

Taylor's star, although dimmed, still shone brightly enough to sustain him through the 1970s and 1980s to the end of his life. However, during that time the world of American higher education changed at a dizzying rate. So too did domestic American politics, particularly after Watergate, as would America's place in the world after Vietnam and toward the end of the Cold War.

Above all, higher education expanded dramatically during the 1960s. There was a decisive shift in emphasis within public policy and debate away from the content and structure of the undergraduate curriculum and the pedagogical approach to learning, toward graduate education, the teaching of science, and issues of access. The debates during the 1940s and 1950s about curriculum quickly seemed the parochial obsessions of a very small and privileged segment of society. When Taylor arrived at Sarah Lawrence in 1945, the educational philosophy of a college of four hundred women—overwhelmingly wealthy and upper-middle-class white women—mattered to the nation. By the time Taylor entered his second decade as president and began to contemplate his departure from Sarah Lawrence, radical discontinuities between past and future were visible on the horizon. Consider the events that took place between 1955 and 1965. John F. Kennedy was elected and assassinated, the Hungarian Revolution of 1956 was suppressed, and Sputnik launched; Fidel Castro's revolution in Cuba achieved its goal, and a civil rights movement took off in the aftermath of the 1954 *Brown v. Board of Education* decision ending legal segregation. The nation's attention regarding education turned away from small cozy colleges to universities, away from disagreements about how and what to teach in philosophy and literature, to a focus on training scientists, people of business, and engineers.

Taylor abandoned the career of leading an institution of higher education just as the type of institution he led was becoming marginal. If Taylor and private small undergraduate colleges had been at the center of public attention in 1945, by 1960 the nation's interest had shifted elsewhere. Clark Kerr, president and chancellor at the University of California, now commanded the public stage. He concerned himself with large-scale public systems of higher education designed to serve the broad public and structured to flourish as research centers. Kerr's 1963 Godkin Lectures at Harvard (they appeared in book form as *The Uses of the University*), in which he made the term "multiversity" famous, placed him at the center of the debate about the connection between higher education and democracy in America.[1] Kerr displaced the heated controversies between Robert Maynard Hutchins and self-proclaimed followers of John Dewey about the college curriculum, core requirements, and approaches to general education for undergraduate students (in which Taylor took part). He crafted a new vision of a utilitarian, large-scale public university system, defined by research and graduate education.

Nonetheless, there were three central and controversial matters regarding colleges and universities that had preoccupied Harold Taylor and that remained unresolved and yet crucial to the vision and new realities in higher education articulated by Kerr. These basic issues have not lost their urgency in the twenty-first century, particularly in the context of the overwhelming dominance of large-scale universities and the striking expansion—still incomplete—of American higher education (primarily through community colleges) in terms of access and democratization.

First is the issue of academic freedom and freedom of expression in higher education, particularly the right to dissent from majority views without fear. As Taylor never tired of repeating, freedom of inquiry and expression in the classroom and in research is basic and necessary to the mission of higher education. Academic freedom also defines a key connection between institutions of higher education and the actual practice of democracy as defined by the principled protection of minorities and the nonconformist individual.

In Harold Taylor's time the challenge to academic freedom came in the form of the wave of anti-communist sentiment of the late 1940s and early 1950s. Taylor defended individual faculty and Sarah Lawrence as an institution from public pressure exerted by the American Legion and political scrutiny by congressional committees. He presided over a college during a period of hysteria marked by suspicion, witch hunts, loyalty oaths, blacklisting, and dismissals. Taylor defended academic freedom with uncommon courage and clarity. He understood that academic freedom is essential to the university. Its pursuit and protection are obligations in the politics of a free society. Insofar as the university educates both the leaders and citizens of the nation, freedom of inquiry—the unfettered pursuit of disciplined skepticism, the rules of evidence, and reasoned critical argument—defines the processes of democracy, the protection of rights, and the way we shape our ideal of justice.

The second issue on which Harold Taylor focused and that bedeviled the rapidly growing world of higher education in the 1960s was how best to fulfill the teaching mission of the university and serve its students, especially as enrollments grew. Taylor never wavered from his allegiance to the ideas and practices advocated by John Dewey and Alexander Meiklejohn. Taylor objected, however, to the crude and widespread association of Dewey with what came to be labeled "progressive" education in the 1960s. Sloppy thinking and thoughtlessness prevailed in the 1960s, in schools of education, public policies, and classroom practices; they were routinely justified by association—purely through rhetoric—with Dewey and the progressive innovations of the 1930s.

Taylor observed, during the 1960s and the 1970s, that the quality of education in America was declining just as access was expanding. This discouraging and ironic reality triggered widespread dissatisfaction with public education and a neoconservative critique of American education that unfairly placed blame on the progressive legacy in school curricula and pedagogy. This defined the policies of the Reagan administration. In response, Taylor pointed out the lack of rigor and intellectually vacuous character of popularized versions of progressive educational ideals and practices. Taylor offered a progressive alternative. He emulated Dewey by articulating high expectations and standards within his notion of active learning by doing. Excellence emerged from properly forging the link between theory and practice. For Taylor, knowledge and the love of learning came not from student respect for the authority of the teacher as expert but from the need to know of the learner.

The anti-authoritarian and anti-canonical stance Taylor celebrated in a so-called "student-centered" curriculum was premised on the belief that this was the best and perhaps only way to cultivate allegiance to the highest standards in the conduct of education and discovery and to achieve the dissemination of knowledge through schooling in a democratic society. Taylor's opposition to a lecture system and a curriculum defined by fixed content and requirements was based in the way he construed the connection between education and politics. In totalitarian systems, both fascist and communist, authority, passivity, and uniformity in education prevailed. In a free society, however, participation, innovation, and experimentation needed to be nurtured in schools and colleges. As the country faces a public discourse in politics where agreement regarding the criteria of truth seems impossible to obtain, and the technological capacity to falsify reality and tell lies that masquerade as the truth has made propaganda even more powerful than it was in the 1930s and 1950s, the independence, rigor, and effectiveness of education in preparing citizens to take on active roles as critical, informed participants with a profound respect for learning and science have never been more crucial to the future of democracy.

Taylor asked, over and over again, what kind of learning experience should be provided in America that inspires the most people. His question has never lost its pertinence. After all, in the years between 1959 and Taylor's retirement in the 1980s, one could hardly call American education a success. High school graduation rates, after rising between the mid-1930s and the mid-1960s, began to falter in the 1980s. The standards represented by the high school diploma remained inadequate. Fewer than 50 percent of those who finished high school and entered college ended up completing their undergraduate degrees. And throughout the nation there was an increasing sense of a cultural decline despite more years of schooling by a higher percentage of the population. In the 1960s and 1970s Taylor asked how the nation might do better.

Taylor's third major preoccupation was the arts, not only in the university but in society as a whole, particularly in American democracy, whose economic foundation was and remains a marketplace economy. This aspect of Taylor's career is less well known. But it fits in closely with his interest in Dewey, for whom the arts were an essential part of his theory of knowledge and its acquisition. The arts were distinct forms of life in which doing and making led to theories and norms, not the other way around. They were exemplars of inductive thought. Furthermore, Taylor identified with being a musician. He had considerable experience as a jazz musician, both in North America and abroad. Improvisation and refinement in the development of musical ideas through actual practice—for example, revisions by an ensemble preparing a particular performance whose temporal dimensions were agreed upon—seemed to vindicate the progressive approach toward learning. Making art in the public realm, for Taylor, was an ideal example of freedom and participation, two central virtues in Taylor's ideal of democracy.

Given the prominence Harold Taylor achieved and the significance of the issues he engaged, why has Harold Taylor been as forgotten, except by a very few? (It should be said that most of his peers who were presidents of colleges and universities never aspired to being remembered in any broad historical narrative). From his era, only James Bryant Conant and Robert Maynard Hutchins retain some glimmer of posthumous prominence. The answer lies largely in the fact that Taylor's leadership was limited to a very small single-sex undergraduate college. Under his leadership it certainly reached a level of prominence in the news rarely achieved by small institutions; but that does not compensate for the absence of the scale and range of endeavor of Harvard and the University of Chicago.

Furthermore, Taylor was at his best as a speaker, not a writer. His books and articles are all elegant and refreshingly free from jargon, but no single piece of writing has yet been rediscovered and found a new audience. Nothing Taylor wrote on education and society competed with the impact of three books that spanned the crucial years of his career, one by a Sarah Lawrence colleague, Erich Fromm's 1941 *Escape from Freedom*; David Riesman's 1950 *The Lonely Crowd*; and Paul Goodman's 1960 *Growing Up Absurd*.[2] Taylor's contribution to his academic field, philosophy, was respectable, but minor and, after leaving Sarah Lawrence, he paid scant attention to the academic discipline of philosophy. As far as music was concerned, despite his professed identification as a professional musician, the fact was that he was not, talented as he may have been. None of his books became a "classic" of its time.

The uncomfortable truth was that Taylor's commanding quality was as an advocate and leader. He was possessed of remarkable gifts—

including musical—that made him multifaceted and charismatic but vulnerable to the accusation of dilettantism. He was apparently considered quite handsome. He was exceptionally at ease in small and large groups. His incredible youth as a college president (he began when he was only thirty), his abundance of charm, and his capacity to converse intelligently on a startling range of subjects made him a natural target for skeptics with sharp tongues. Had Taylor taken responsibility for another cultural or educational institution subsequent to his tenure at Sarah Lawrence, the caricatures based on him in novels by Randall Jarrell and Mary McCarthy would have been overshadowed by his subsequent institutional achievements.

It is not at all certain that apart from any future account of the history of Sarah Lawrence or the history of anti-communism of the late 1940s and 1950s—the domestic cultural politics of the early years of the Cold War, before the Cuban missile crisis—that Harold Taylor's career and legacy will be subjects of interest to readers in the twenty-first century. The monumental and tireless efforts of Craig Kridel represented by this book now are the only source of hope that Taylor will retain his proper role in history. With painstaking care and considerable ingenuity Kridel has rescued and augmented Taylor's own memoir and given scholars and practitioners an invaluable primary source for understanding and evaluating Taylor's life and work. Kridel has put Taylor back into view and made it possible for future historians to take his role in this history of American education into account.

Kridel's contribution is vital not only because Taylor was an influential figure and highly visible from the past, but he was also exceptionally courageous on the matter of academic freedom. Taylor, as his memoir indicates, anticipated the direction institutions of higher education would take in choosing their leaders, their presidents. When he resigned in 1959, Taylor saw the proverbial handwriting on the wall. Presidents would no longer be expected to influence the intellectual direction of an institution and therefore the character of teaching and research. They would become professional administrators and managers. Their primary responsibility would shift from ideas to money and, most importantly, to the raising of money, from public and private sources. They would increasingly resemble and become indistinguishable from either corporate executives, in commerce and industry, or ambassadors to nations abroad. Kingman Brewster, the eminent president of Yale in the 1960s who became the American ambassador to Britain, was reputed to have quipped, with evident sarcasm and some resentment, when asked what qualified him to be America's ambassador, that he had been a university president in the United States and therefore was adept at speaking persuasively at length about nothing.

Taylor deserves to be remembered because he helped fight a battle that still has not been won in the ongoing struggle for academic freedom. Anti-communism, as framed during the Cold War, has vanished but the pattern of governmental intrusion into the pursuit of teaching and research has not. Censorship of books by school boards is on the rise and legislation to forbid certain content is still with us, as is the use of public platforms, particularly internet-based social media, to shame dissenting faculty, administrators, and students, and drive them out from their communities. Ostracism has made an ugly comeback. A climate of fear inhabits many of our finest schools, colleges, and universities. It inspires self-censorship and a reluctance to take public positions that challenge reigning cultural and political orthodoxies. Universities should protect dissent and minority opinions based not on mere slogans but on reasoned argument and rigorous research. In the context of contemporary iterations within the public realm—social media and internet journalism—and their impact on the conduct of government, the principles and practice of academic freedom that Taylor believed in remain under siege, not only from radical conservative quarters but from radical progressive movements. And in the polarized world we now live in, there is little appetite for reasoned debate, patience, empathy, compromise, or reconciliation.

Taylor's life and work remain relevant as well to the question of the effectiveness and quality of American education. Our elementary and secondary schools continue to perform poorly, both for the privileged and especially the underserved in our society. Teaching within higher education is still woefully deficient, even in explicitly utilitarian fields, such as medicine, law, engineering, and education. If that were not enough, there has been a precipitous decline in the level of general education among undergraduates; the place of the humanities and the arts in the curricular and extracurricular life of institutions of higher education has never been quite so tenuous. Apart from their achievements in semiprofessional sports, universities are less influential and respected than they were when Harold Taylor was active as a leader in higher education.

Last but not least, in the wake of the unprecedented COVID-19 pandemic, the noncommercial performing and visual arts that Taylor believed in and fought for remain at risk as a result of declining financial support from government and leading foundations and philanthropists. The caricature of America as driven by an obsession with material values—money and wealth—that prevailed in the late nineteenth century has not lost its plausibility in the twenty-first century, especially in our era of unprecedented economic inequality.

This memoir, a volume of opinions and experiences from the second half of the twentieth century, could not, therefore, have appeared at a better moment. Its protagonist, Harold Taylor, stood for the centrality, in a democracy, of freedom and personal autonomy. He foregrounded the importance of the liberal arts, and the necessity for an approach to teaching in classrooms that inspires and motivates students. He championed the role of colleges and universities in furthering a public culture that advances social justice. He promoted civil critical public discourse marked by empathy and tolerance across all forms of difference. He never tired of underscoring the indispensable place of the arts in aiding citizens to locate and formulate a sense of personal meaning in a modern pluralistic democracy.

Harold Taylor's book, literally resurrected by Craig Kridel, may help us remember what might still be possible to achieve in education for the public good in a free and just democratic society.

—Leon Botstein
President and Leon Levy Professor in the
Arts and Humanities
Bard College

Acknowledgments

I met Harold Taylor (1914–1993) in the 1970s, began helping him with his autobiography in the 1980s, and found myself archiving his papers, including this unpublished memoir, in the 1990s. Our friendship lasted for sixteen years; however, my involvement with this manuscript has lasted for over four decades. I assumed as a friend and curator of his professional materials, I would assist the efforts of biographers who sought to research the life of an important midcentury educator. Maxine Greene and Louise DeSalvo suggested otherwise, insisting that my extensive knowledge of the Taylor papers placed me in an important position to serve if not as biographer then as compiler, arrayer, editor, and "closer" for a posthumous memoir. I remained reluctant, in part, recognizing that my role with these materials was not as researcher but as curator, seeking to serve and help others. Yet, with the recent decision to deaccession and transfer the Taylor collection to another archival repository, I felt that in good faith I could accept the responsibility to complete the memoir rather than allow the manuscript to wallow in obscurity. I now see that my familiarity not only with the papers but with the author himself allowed me to work through the many ethical if not moral issues of completing another's work.

I had moments of doubt, however, about this project—never of the significance of Taylor's career but, rather, whether his many insights and the timeliness of Harold's voice from the past would be recognized and appreciated today. For perspective, I turned to colleagues since my main concern was not editing the story of a life but, instead, deciding what should actually appear. Tone and taste as well as timeliness became crucial and somewhat difficult for me to ascertain after years of "smelling the archival dust" from the Taylor papers.

I am quite grateful for the help from these candid readers who viewed my rough drafts as final copy and who became particular and precise with their suggestions and comments. They voiced their beliefs and confirmed my hopes that Harold's life and writings offer profound insights for today's students, administrators, professors, and activists during this time of aimlessness in higher education. All brought great expertise and, with good fortune, one reader who has been a music mentor for decades was also, coincidentally, a renowned Randall Jarrell scholar. Others contributed with directness and thoughtfulness in their respective areas of biographical research, secondary and higher education, history of education, British music, and social activism. I thank all who came to my aid: William Ayers, Clifford Bevan, Robert Bullough, Lauren Cook, Louise DeSalvo, Suzanne Ferguson, James Finkelstein, Maxine Greene, Avni Gupta-Kagan, Kate Rousmaniere, William Schubert, Wayne Urban, and Alan Wieder.

This project could not have been undertaken without the permission of Jennifer Taylor Tuthill and Mary Taylor Lehner who kindly allowed me to complete their father's manuscript. Abby Lester, former archivist and head of research services at Sarah Lawrence College, has been a comrade during these past years, providing assistance quickly and always with good cheer. The ultimate placement of the complete collection of the Taylor papers at Sarah Lawrence is a testimony to her great expertise and sensibilities.

As a photo-archivist I have enjoyed the great copyright chase for permission-to-publish and delighted in those property rights oddities that occur when one seeks consent. I am thankful for the thoughtfulness of Martha Tenney, director of archives and special collections at Barnard College, and the kindness of Susan Greenburg Wood, Gary Gladstone, Deirdre Brennan, Pauline Moffitt Watts, and the Taylor family who granted permission for the use of photographs. Grace Wagner of the Special Collections Research Center at Syracuse University Libraries, Nora Reilly and Christina Kasman of the Sarah Lawrence College Archives, and Valencia Morton of the University of South Carolina College of Education were helpful in searching for and preparing fugitive materials. Reference librarian Mary Bull provided invaluable assistance, for many drafts and for many years, with all matters related to all aspects of the Taylor professional collection and this memoir. Crafting a posthumous memoir would have been nearly impossible without drawing upon Taylor's oral history sessions conducted by Kenneth Duckett, Michael Rossman, and Carole Nichols in 1966, 1974, and 1985, respectively. I applaud their efforts.

I greatly appreciate Leon Botstein's willingness to write a foreword; he has crafted an insightful, thoughtful, honest examination of both Taylor's career and his memoir and has done so without being sentimental or harsh. Harold would have been quite pleased, especially since he knew Botstein and admired his leadership and work at Bard College. I extend my great thanks to William C. Ayers, Marybeth Gasman, Michael A. Olivas, John R. Thelin, and Harriet Pogul Wohlgemuth for preparing public statements on behalf of this publication. I remain astonished at how they were able to capture the essence of Harold Taylor's life in a mere few sentences. Within moments of our first conversation, SUNY Press's Excelsior Editions editor Richard Carlin recognized the importance of Taylor's career and, without his support, this project would not have come to fruition. I appreciate the great precision of Dana Foote and the efforts of Kate Seburyamo, Eileen Nizer, and Alicia Brady, all of SUNY Press.

I hope Harold would be relieved with the appearance of his memoir, and I believe he would be pleased with most—albeit, not all—of my editorial decisions and comments. I often asked myself "what would Harold do" as I read various fragments and passages of the manuscript. Now, I suspect he would sit back, pour himself a glass of Old Taylor bourbon, on sentimental grounds, and begin reading the next page.

—Craig Kridel

Note: Italic is used in those chapters by Harold Taylor to designate the editor's comments.

Preface

> Whatever may be true about one's actions and commitment to political and social change, it is a question of how you deal, one day at a time, one week at a time, one year at a time, with individuals and groups of people. What really counts is how you lead the life you are living, and the obligation that I feel is to do whatever I can to help improve whatever situation I am in.
>
> —Harold Taylor, interview with Michael Rossman, 1974

Harold Taylor found himself in many different situations and with many different individuals and groups of people and, through the decades, he enjoyed various unexpected opportunities—serving as president of Sarah Lawrence College, becoming an unofficial advisor to Adlai Stevenson, coordinating various peace organizations, and developing international programs and progressive education projects at colleges and universities. Yet, he remained steadfast in his efforts to improve whatever situation—program, project, or institution—he was in. Coming to national attention in 1945 with his hiring, at age thirty, as president of Sarah Lawrence College, Taylor would distinguish himself as one of the few spokespersons for progressive education and educational experimentation during the 1950s, underscoring the importance of the arts and humanities, and would emerge in the 1960s as one of the country's leading public intellectuals and campus speakers, addressing issues related to student activism, peace education, and international studies. In his role as president of Sarah Lawrence, he became an outspoken critic of secondary and postsecondary education and wrote for the general public as well as for higher education administrators, faculty, and students. Complications arose, however. Taylor would become the target of anti-communist attacks during the 1950s, would be publicly humiliated as a character in two well-known academic novels, would learn that a designated biographer withdrew from the invitation to write his biography, and would receive criticism from colleagues as well as the common sniping among academics toward their college president.

One of the more unfortunate aspects of Harold Taylor's career occurred toward the end of his life as he sought to write an autobiography. Health issues, certain professional responsibilities, and an odd incident with his professional papers impeded efforts and, while he drafted four of ten essays with some degree of ease, new chapters and revisions proved difficult. In correspondence with Jessica (Decca) Mitford in 1982, he bemoans this struggle as she would advise him to write just one publishable page a day and, after one year, the manuscript would be finished.[1] The memoir remained uncompleted.

With this publication, Harold Taylor may now begin to receive the attention that he deserves, even as interest in mid-twentieth-century white, male, higher education administrators has waned, and reenter the professional literature of postsecondary education. In Taylor's memoir, now titled *Harold Taylor and Sarah Lawrence College: A Life of Social and Educational Activism*, he writes for the general (informed) public with wit, irony, insight, and self-deprecating humor. He seeks not to prepare a primer for the aspiring college administrator nor does he introduce the reader to the specifics of his professional work. Yet, what appears is more than the standard memoir of self-discovery or reverie. Taylor allows us to witness the development of a now rare species in postsecondary education—the college president who, guided by his cultural, political, and educational beliefs, accepted responsibility for social and educational action. Taylor believed that his role and that of the American university was to address and attempt to resolve social issues, and he willingly confronted McCarthyism and the American Legion in this role as social activist. He did this not as an ideologue with predefined solutions but, rather, with an interest in seeking answers to problems while guided by philosophy, literature, and the arts. And, with the company of colleagues, he recognized the importance of educational activism—experimentation as a way of life—encouraging faculty and students to reexamine and reconsider their pedagogical settings and to explore and experiment with new practices.

Few college administrators could boast of knowing the names of every student and faculty member at their institution, as Taylor did in the late 1940s. Today's university presidents, bound by the political beliefs of boards of trustees and the funding from state legislators and private donors, are often political appointees or business types who do not typically forge their values from the historical writings of philosophers. Most higher education leaders, reticent to take political stands and instead guided by either an institutional context of consumerism or the threat of litigation, do not turn to the writings of David Hume, John Dewey, or Alexander Meiklejohn for advice. The career of Harold Taylor, however, suggests that higher education would be a much different and better place if they would.

~

No life history represents a complete portrayal of an individual, and this memoir—now taking the form of a montage—was never meant to represent a traditional autobiography nor, most certainly, an intellectual biography. Much is missing, intentionally as well as unintentionally. From the outset, Taylor did not set out to write a comprehensive birth to late-career personal history or, as he said to me once in passing conversation, "writing about what I had for breakfast." Rather, he intended to prepare episodic essays related to if not prompted by specific events and professional roles.

As a friend and colleague of Harold's during the last years of his life, I was aware of many of these events and roles. I helped Taylor with his memoir beginning in the early 1980s through the early 1990s when I visited him at his summer home, Brushwood, in Holderness, New Hampshire. During what became annual summer sojourns, he would talk about the chapters at hand and plans for other topics. I worked as a research assistant, organizing papers, locating published works, serving as a fact finder, and typing portions of the manuscript. As curator of his professional papers during the years since his death, I became quite familiar with the details of his life and career while cataloging boxes of personal and professional correspondence, project reports, and diaries as well as assisting those visiting researchers interested in examining his career. In compiling this manuscript, however, I did not review his writings in search of an "inner self" or intimate details, which were, at times, brought up in our conversations and subsequently appeared in documents and scraps of archival ephemera. Nor did I seek to prepare a celebration of life or, unwittingly, a hagiography of his career. I admired as well as questioned if not, at times, criticized Taylor as he certainly did me.

With enthusiasm as well as a degree of sadness, I watched Harold struggle while helping organize versions of this manuscript, to be titled "A State of Mind."[2] I supported him through many events—some unanticipated and some tragic—and now complete this project after having saved and preserved his professional papers, originally archived at the University of South Carolina's Museum of Education and now housed at the Sarah Lawrence College Archives.[3] I have not interpreted Taylor's writings but, instead, allow him to speak for himself while serving as an arrayer as well as an editor. My efforts have been as much an act of synthesis as documentary editing since I have supplemented this manuscript with excerpts from interviews, other autobiographical essays, correspondence, speeches, and publications. Chapter introductions, succinct to the verge of being cryptic, are just that—mere introductions providing contextual information for the authenticity of Taylor's voice. As Harold speaks, readers may interpret, imagine, and wonder as they wish.

Taylor began drafting ideas for an autobiography as early as 1975, yet a full undertaking did not begin until much later.[4] A setback occurred in November 1988 when, recovering in the hospital from a hip operation, his quite cluttered and dusty West Village brownstone underwent an unsupervised cleaning during which time original papers and manuscript pages—drafts, important and carefully selected private correspondence, and irreplaceable photos—were thrown away. Taylor was despondent after what he called "the purge" but managed to return to his writing. Upon his death in 1993, the unfinished manuscript sat for years among his professional papers at the University of South Carolina's Museum of Education. Interested researchers appeared and many read portions of his memoir; however, none fully committed to writing a biography and, thus, no one drew from this unpublished work.

~

This collection evolved from a chapter about Taylor's professional relationships with John Dewey and Alexander Meiklejohn, different draft versions of an essay centering on his friendship with Duke Ellington, written fragments about his early life and academic studies, and a somewhat completed draft, "On Being Written About," which discusses his representation as a character in Mary McCarthy's *The Groves of Academe* and Randall Jarrell's *Pictures from an Institution*. One partially written chapter, "The Student Revolt Revisited," describes Taylor's participation in the 1968 Columbia University counter-commencement and other activities with campus activists and Students for a Democratic Society. Another essay, "Assault on a Small College," was completed but lost, presumably, in the November 1988 purge.

Taylor had planned three other chapters; yet, these were never begun. "Hubert Humphrey's Visit" would have portrayed his involvement in the peace movement and a visit to the White House in 1966 with a group of authors to meet with Humphrey. "Plagiarism" was to describe events surrounding the 1951 inaugural address of Cornell University president Deane W. Malott, who was accused of plagiarizing portions of a 1949 speech by Taylor and, I assume, Harold was going to critique

Photo of "A State of Mind" manuscript, 1989. Courtesy of Craig Kridel.

the changing nature of higher education administration. "Three Dancers" would have discussed his friendships and professional activities with Agnes de Mille and the Agnes de Mille Dance Theatre, Martha Graham and the Martha Graham School of Contemporary Dance, and Sarah Lawrence College faculty member Bessie Schonberg where, no doubt, he would have stressed the importance of the arts in his life. By drawing upon interviews and correspondence through the years and the official 1985 oral history conducted by Sarah Lawrence College, I have provided a semblance of Taylor's thoughts and reflections on certain of these themes in "Unbegun Chapters." In addition, I constructed three other chapters, "Sarah Lawrence Remembrances," "Assault on a Small College," and "'Adlai Stevenson and the 1960 Presidential Campaign," as well as two interludes, "The Wisconsin Years" and "Thoughts on Leaving Sarah Lawrence and Life Thereafter," drawn from an assortment of reflections and other materials from his archival files. The collection concludes with a biographical vignette that introduces important projects and experiences that had not yet been mentioned.

∽

Taylor's manuscript has been reviewed for consistency and contemporary punctuation conventions; a few alterations, inconsequential, were made to the original text with no change to meaning or tone. Endnotes have been added to document text and provide additional information about people and events. During Taylor's time, gender-free and gender-inclusive writing was uncommon, and some of the pronouns in the memoir remain sexist in their usage. In keeping with standard memoir disclaimers, Taylor's accounts of specific conversations throughout the chapters are not, obviously, taken from actual transcripts but, rather, represent dialogue that he felt evoked the meaning and mood of what was said, as faithfully retold by him. My editing decisions included, on occasion, shifting text to endnotes and, at times, drafted material has been omitted altogether. On rare occasions, text originally deleted by Taylor has been reinserted.

Knowing that certain portions of the text would have received Taylor's further editing, I have wondered whether it is fair to present this work publicly when only one abridged essay had been officially deemed by its author as completed and ready for publication. Harold Taylor never was afforded the opportunity to polish these chapters, and my unease remains as I wish I could have included further revised and extended versions of many of his essays. Any concerns toward editing practices do not compare, alas, with those ethical issues that I faced. There is much additional content that I could have included; however, my role has been to complete another's work. Aware that Harold did not wish to address or confront certain topics and accepting an oath of fidelity to his wishes in my role as scribe rather than biographer, some personal details, if not rumors, about his life do not appear. I have tried to honor original drafts while also recognizing that the manuscript was indeed a work-in-progress and, sadly, as a posthumous publication will always remain as such.

As Taylor was being advised of the "one-page-a-day" plan by Decca Mitford, he admitted questioning whether a memoir was the proper book to write at that time in his life. Mitford noted that "writing is the bugger of all time" and went on to say that her best-selling exposé about funerals, *The American Way of Death*,[5] could have easily been dismissed on such grounds. She advised him that a "better scheme is to write the interesting bits (meaning, of interest to oneself) and then hope to string them together into a book of general interest."[6] I, too, hope that this assortment of "interesting bits" will be intriguing and will encourage readers to reexamine the writings of Harold Taylor. Higher education needs college presidents who accept the role of public intellectual and who see the importance of the university as an agent for change in a democratic society. The career of Harold Taylor offers insight for university leaders, professors, and students to reconsider educational practices today, and his life provides much for those who are exploring the world of ideas and who, guided by faith in democratic discourse and a belief in social and educational activism, are searching for meaning and ways to do whatever they can to improve and to build their own thoughtful and humane communities.

Chapter 1

The Day Duke Died

While the essays in this memoir could be sequenced in a variety of ways, Taylor designated "The Day Duke Died" to be the opening chapter, and it was the first essay he began writing in order to consider whether he would prepare an autobiography. In correspondence with his close friend and former Sarah Lawrence College faculty member poet Alastair Reid, he makes reference to "starting on the Ellington episode to see what it turns out to be."[1] The chapter was never officially completed, and the original draft includes different versions. Yet, as the most unstructured chapter among the collection, "The Day Duke Died" may best represent Taylor's vision for this publication and, I suspect, would have become the pattern for subsequent chapters, capturing the unfolding narrative style that he sought with nonchronological reveries meandering in various directions and then concluding with personal insights.

Taylor's friendship with Duke Ellington began in 1939 when the Ellington band found themselves idle in England due to the (British) Musician's Union ban on performances by American instrumentalists.[2] Taylor spent a week showing Ellington around London. Jazz was much more than a mere avocation for Taylor, and his decision to pursue a life as an academic and then college president can be placed in juxtaposition with his achievements as a clarinetist and music critic. Taylor noted that playing jazz could have as easily become a career since, as he later recalled, "a Canadian musician with an American style could do quite well in London" during the 1930s.[3]

The specific anecdote in this chapter about Taylor's own level of playing may not accurately indicate his abilities and, most likely, was included in jest. Taylor once mentioned to me that Ellington, on another occasion, said that *while he would not have been hired as a band member, he would have been invited to sit in on post-performance jam sessions. Taylor's role as a music critic should not go unnoticed. After the completion of his doctorate in philosophy at University of London, he served as full-time news editor and columnist for the British jazz magazine* The Melody Maker *(at what he described as an exorbitant salary for the times), and his writings are cited in the professional musicological literature as recently as 2015.*[4]

Taylor begins "The Day Duke Died" by describing Ellington's funeral on Memorial Day, May 27, 1974, and throughout the chapter affirms his belief in the importance of open-ended, improvisatory experience as a fundamental aspect of learning in what will become a reoccurring motif for the entire memoir.

We drove in the rain of a spring day in 1974 in a cortege of black limousines though the streets of Harlem, past the Apollo, past Duke's old apartment on St. Nicholas, on a last trip with Duke through a territory drenched in the memories of where he had been and what he had done. The people in the streets turned to look at the cortege and the carloads of flowers, without knowing it was Ellington on the way to his funeral. When we arrived at the Cathedral of St. John the Divine, there were ten thousand people inside and another ten thousand in the rain on the streets. It was an open-hearted, full-scale celebration of Duke's life and his art, a ceremony in honor of a composer who wrote some of the greatest music ever to come out of the United States.

The religious dimension was as big as the universe and as intimate as a family. The love in the cathedral was palpable—Black and white Americans in a cathedral built for whites, believers and nonbelievers united by a religion of humanity and the universal brotherhood of musicians, dancers, singers, and artists. Ellington would have loved it and the gathering of loving people, the singing and playing of those who knew his music best. Ray Nance played "Take the A Train," slow as a dirge; Ella Fitzgerald sang "Solitude"; McHenry Boatwright sang "The Lord's Prayer"; Joe Williams sang and Earl Hines, Mary Lou Williams, Jo Jones, Billy Taylor, and others played; Pastor John Gensel and Stanley Dance talked about him; and Duke was carried out of the Cathedral to the haunting sound of Johnny Hodges, Alice Babs, and the Ellington band playing music from his first *Sacred Concert*.

It was a funeral that at moments reached the level of high theater; it was also an event that could never have taken place anywhere else except to honor so protean a genius in a country whose cultural and aesthetic character he had helped to shape. The sounds and rhythms he made in tobacco barns, convention halls, dance halls, palaces, theaters, night clubs, churches, cathedrals, parks, and concert halls went around the world. The impulses he set in motion changed the sound of the world from Moscow to Buenos Aires.

The service was in essence a union of the sacred and the profane, and what Duke held sacred was music and a transformation of the meaning of the profane and the sacred in religion and in art. It was a satin doll in church, African paganism among the Episcopalians and Lutherans. For Duke there was nothing profane in the whole of life except wars and violence, wars between persons and lack of forgiveness, respect, and kindness. For him, the good and the bad were natural conditions to be dealt with, and he accepted life as it came, as a sacred gift from a benevolent and fair-minded God in whom he believed. What he held most sacred was music and the mission of the artist who must give himself up to his art, and in so doing, to praise God and to worship in the artist's own way. That was his mode of worship. He liked the story of the little juggler of Notre Dame who crept into the cathedral at midnight and performed his juggling before the altar as the greatest gift he had to give. Writing and playing music were his mode of worship, his sacred music as part of the history of religious art.

Everything Ellington touched, saw, heard, and lived went into his music, and the sound of it when he listened gave back to him the affirmation for his life. It was not a self-conscious or cloistered dedication; it was just that he went through the world composing and playing, and that's what he did with his time, night and day. He was almost incapable of walking past a piano and leaving it alone. Since his orchestra was the instrument through which he composed, he couldn't live without it. And in the midst of a total dedication to his art, he stood back and looked at himself with a cool eye and never forgot that he was a piano player with a band that had to do one-night stands. Until the very last days of his life, he was still doing them.

Gordon Parks was once driving with Harry Carney and Duke overnight from Los Angeles to San Francisco, with Duke asleep in the back seat.[5] As they came into San Francisco, the Golden Gate Bridge lay ahead of them and seemed to be floating in the early morning mist. Harry woke up Duke to tell him that here was something marvelous that he might want to write about, since he wrote about almost everything he saw. Duke rubbed his eyes, took a look and mumbled, "Majestic. Majestic. Goddam those white people are smart," and went back to sleep.

He had been laid out in his coffin for two days at Walter Cooke's Funeral Home on Third Avenue, from 8:00 a.m. until 10:00 p.m., just inside the door, fifteen feet from the sidewalk. Fifteen thousand people from uptown and downtown came by, friends and strangers, dancers, musicians, actors, and admirers gathered in little knots on the street to talk. He looked elegant and at ease in his blue pleated shirt and evening clothes. "I never saw him looking better," said one of the musicians. I saw a lot of him during those two days, since I went with his sister Ruth and the family to two funeral services by the Masons and the Shriners held in his room at the funeral home. It was not a large room, and there was an intimacy and an affectionate simplicity about the ritual as the Black brothers in their uniform spoke of brother Edward.

It was a time to think about the meaning of death, Ellington's death and everyone's. The meaning for those in the room that day was that God had given Edward Ellington life and the gifts to go with it and now God had seen fit to call him away. Not a bad explanation, and you could feel the power and comfort in the metaphor. Seventy-five years of a life had been lived to the full by a man who welcomed everything in it, and now that it was over, Edward and everyone else could rejoice in the fact that he was around so long and had done so much with his time.

I discovered as I looked into his face at Cooke's that a whole section of who I was, what I thought, what I felt about being alive at all went back to Ellington. Like the men in the Ellington band, you were never the same after you came close to him. You played and thought differently; he released something that made it possible to do whatever you did better and in ways you hadn't thought of. When Jimmy Hamilton came into the band with his rich classical clarinet tone, Duke didn't try to change Jimmy into something more like Barney Bigard. He simply wrote for Jimmy and gave him a chance to do things he had never done before. With one bar of single notes or one chord, Duke could set off the band, and nobody could create the rhythmic surge that he set up when he was the piano player. He led simply by being present and by playing.

His was a special kind of easy leadership, the kind only possible in one who is fully in touch with his own talent and who goes through the world admiring the talents and qualities of others, secure in the confidence of their admiration of his. When he wrote music, he was giving his musicians through the notes he put down a guide for making the sounds he and they wanted to hear. He gave them the mood and set the structure in which they could operate. He knew what each of the musicians could do and the special quality that each possessed, and he took them farther out in their own direction. He wrote to turn them loose and to make new forms in the total sound of the orchestra. He wrote what he wanted to write for people who wanted to listen. It was intuitive writing, learned through the discipline of having to turn out songs and production numbers for dancers and audiences, reaching out through the manuscript to the intuitions of the players whose ideas would reemerge in the works he later composed. It was as if he were giving a set of directions for the release of enormous energies which his players and listeners could find within themselves.

He worked with the band the way Martha Graham worked with her company. For Martha, right from the beginning, her dancers were the instrument through which she said what she had to say. They danced the way she taught them to and, as she worked in composition, the response of their bodies to the ideas she was developing gave her new forms of expression for those ideas. In both Ellington and Graham, the creative act had been one of controlled improvisation. In Ellington's case, he carried the art of improvisation in composing and playing to such heights that he could compose on his recording dates in those famous sessions when, with a few scraps of manuscript, a few lead sheets and a little help from Billy Strayhorn, he simply told the brass and reeds what he wanted, gave them some notes, and went on from there.

It is the special genius of the greatest and most original of our American artists that they are so intensely personal in creating their own styles—the jazz forms of Ellington, the dance theater of Graham, the musical theater of Rodgers and Hammerstein, the songs of Cole Porter, the sculpture of David Smith, the painting of Jackson Pollock. Ellington made it all as he went along, through scores for films, opera, musical comedy, sacred music, ballet, symphony orchestras, and above all for the Ellington orchestra. For him, these were not so much perilous tests as a series of affirmations of his belief in the power of his own music. He was an original in a time of originators, and he inherited the buoyancy and comradeship of the early jazz players.

∼

His recording sessions were often like family parties to which the musicians, family, and close friends were all invited. Ellington at the piano was in the middle with the brass, the rhythm section, and the reeds grouped around him, then a circle including Billy Strayhorn, Duke's sister Ruth and his nephews Michael and Stephen James, band librarian Tom Whaley, record company and studio staff people, jazz writer Stanley Dance, the Reverend John Gensel, Duke's doctor Arthur Logan, musicians who were in town and had heard about the session, and friends who always knew from Ruth or Duke when he was recording. In a special sense, we were all part of the session. There was an excitement in the studio that Duke generated, in the band and in the rest of us, an expectation that something important was about to happen, although no one knew quite what, including Ellington. Then the music started to flow, and the excitement he had created came through to all of us and flowed back to him. There was something of the same effect when he entered any roomful of people, or walked into the Stage Deli, or sat around at his sister's place, or talked to you in a dressing room with his head in a bandanna and his body in a towel, or stood beside the president in a receiving line at the White House. Something started to happen that wasn't there before. You could feel the beat.

The image of the recording session with Duke at the center and the rest of us grouped around him was a metaphor for the way he lived his life, with the musicians close at hand and his friends in a surrounding circle, or, in real life, in a series of circles. Each of us had his own relation to Ellington and somehow in the crowded life he led he found ways of keeping those relations intact. He knew how to shut himself away from everyone when he wanted to write, but he could write wherever he was and no matter who was around—on trains and planes, in cars, restaurants, hotel rooms and dressing rooms. After his performances, after the people who came to his dressing room had left, after the closer friends had gone home, he often wrote until morning.

It meant that you had to be prepared for some long nights if you were going to see him, and I missed a great deal of time with him simply because I had to be president of a college in the morning. He would suddenly think of you at three or four a.m. and telephone from wherever he was. He called one very early morning. "I've just thought of something. It's a musical about some cat who's president of a women's college. There he is with all these beautiful chicks, and he falls in love with a lady policeman who's come to the college to investigate a burglary. The curtain goes up. One of the beautiful chicks is sitting in the corner on a bare stage holding a glass of water. That's all I've got. How do you like it so far?"

In the spring of 1939, the Ellington band booked a European tour and turned up in London on the way home. By this time I had been living in England for three years, two of them doing a doctorate at the University of London, a third as news editor of a weekly musicians' newspaper, *The Melody Maker*. Since Ellington and the band had a week's time on their hands, I assigned reporters and photographers to cover them and spent most of the week with Duke, Rex Stuart and Harry Carney, and some of the others, showing them around London.[6] Duke was intrigued with the idea of hanging around with a twenty-four-year-old doctor of philosophy who played the clarinet and edited a newspaper, especially after I told him that I probably wouldn't have been any of those things if it hadn't been for him. We became friends for the rest of his life.

In the fall after that English spring, Ellington brought the band through Madison, Wisconsin, to play at the university where by that time I had gone to do my first teaching in philosophy. Billy Strayhorn was traveling with the band then, after Duke had heard some of Billy's lyrics

Rex Stewart, trumpeter in the Ellington band, Taylor, and Harry Carney, baritone saxophonist in the Ellington band, 1939. Courtesy of the Taylor family.

The Day the Duke Died | 7

and music in Pittsburgh and invited him to join up.⁷ Billy still wasn't sure what he was to do except help with the arranging. In fact he spent the rest of his life finding out what he and Duke could do together. The two of them were close as brothers and were a pair of creative artists who learned to work so closely together that often you could not tell where Duke's music stopped and Billy's began. So extraordinary was their collaboration that they were both greater individual artists because of it than either would have been alone.

While the band was playing that first night at the University of Wisconsin, Billy and I listened and talked. He told me about his own music and what he had written for musical comedy, and about what he wanted to do with his life. We compared notes on the deep effect of the Ellington band and Duke the first time we heard them in person. I told Billy about playing second clarinet in the University of Wisconsin's symphony, and about why I had left England to come to Wisconsin, about philosophy and what I was teaching my students. We were two young men starting out in careers which had involved us with Ellington, and we found that we were both in the grip of the Ellington influence. We weren't too sure what that was, except that when you were with him, some very funny things were said. There was absolutely no pretense in the room. You learned the meaning of the words "elegance and genius," and everything seemed to go much better, whatever it was.

Strayhorn then and every day until he died was gracious, delightful, gentle, and incredibly talented. Billy was small and bound in size, about the size of Truman Capote, and I don't believe he was capable of entertaining a harmful or mean-handed thought. He looked at you from behind his horn-rimmed glasses with kindness in his eyes. He never raised his voice. As Duke said, "his patience was incomparable and unlimited." More than anything else, aside from his contribution as a composer and lyricist, it was Billy's natural, generous capacity for friendship and affectionate companionship that made his presence so important an element in everything Ellington and the band did. They called him Swee' Pea because of that, after the character in Popeye. With his shy, gentle smile he was practically unflappable, and he had a lot to do with keeping Duke in balance and the band in a reasonable state of mind. He loved hanging around with musicians. When you wanted to contact him during the late afternoon or evening, he took his calls at a bar where he knew musicians would come by. He was himself a character out of an unwritten musical comedy. When he died in 1967, years and years too soon, we lost a whole section of musical heritage that was still to come.

When the band came back to Madison each year to play at the local theater, Duke, Billy, Rex Stewart, Harry Carney, Johnny Hodges, and whoever else was around after the last performance came out to an old barn which, with the help of my students and friends on the faculty, we had converted into a house with an enormous living room. We played and ate and talked until it was time for the band to catch the early morning train to Chicago. One year after Duke and Rex Stewart and I had been playing "C Jam Blues," a friend from the university psychology department asked Duke what he thought of my clarinet playing. "We've heard Taylor around here for a year or two and he sounds all right, but how would you rate him with the members of your band."

Duke looked down at the fireplace, let three beats go by, and said, "Harold is beyond category. He has such impeccable taste and so many beautiful ideas in his head that he refuses to play them because he doesn't think his playing can capture the true beauty of his ideas. He is at his ultimate best when he is silent."

∼

Then the war came and I didn't see Duke until the spring of 1945 when I first went to Sarah Lawrence to talk to the people there about the presidency of the college. Duke was in town playing at what was then the 400 Club. I had spent two days at the college and was in a fair amount of doubt about being a college president at all. I was by that time deeply involved in what we were doing at the University of Wisconsin. I loved the place and the life there. I loved teaching, I had many close friends, I admired my colleagues, and I was serious about my work as a teacher and scholar. My conception of college presidents was that except for Bob Hutchins, Clarence Dykstra, James Conant,[8] and one or two others, they were all business managers, politicians, anti-intellectuals, public relations experts, fund-raisers—the hired servants of the middle class.

I went down to the 400 Club. Rex [*Stewart*] played "Boy Meets Horn," and Duke came over after the first set. I told him why I was in New York and what was bothering me about the possibility of leaving Wisconsin. Duke said, "Sweety, take the gig if they want to book you. I'm out in Wisconsin once a year. It's a nice place to visit but this is where everything lives and where I am when I'm not away. I hear those cats have a beautiful college. I've got a lot of good friends, but I don't have a college president and I think I need one."

In the years after that, Duke did come up to the college when he could. Rex Stewart often put together a group with musicians like Cozy Cole, J. C. Higginbotham, Vic Dickenson, Buster Bailey, and John Bunch who came up to Sarah Lawrence to play Sunday afternoon concerts for the students and their friends. One night Duke visited and played for the students and, when it was time for the clarinet, I played an A to tune to the piano. Duke hit four A's on the piano in tempo and said, "Hold it, Prez," and then, turning to the audience, still hitting the A, he said, "Ladies and Gentlemen, the Duke Ellington Duo proudly presents the world premiere of Sonata on A, featuring the piano player and the Prez." He then did a brilliant sixty-four bars of chord changes, key changes, and tempo changes while conducting me to hold the A.

～

Duke first came into my life when I was fourteen although I did not enter his until nearly ten years later. I had just begun learning to play the clarinet by listening to records and the radio and by playing in the Sunday school orchestra. I had never heard anything like the Ellington band and Barney Bigard's clarinet, and the first time I heard them I knew that this was the kind of music I wanted to play.

When the band came to Toronto where I grew up, I went to the theater early and sat enthralled, waiting for Ellington. The stage was lit by soft blue lights, and from behind the curtain came the Ellington sounds with a quiet and steady beat which gradually grew in intensity and volume until the curtain parted and there was a stage full of Black musicians in white evening clothes with Sonny Greer high up in his nest of drums and cymbals, his head turning from side to side, his eyes half-closed, with the air of a man possessed by music.

Then Ellington walked on stage in his elegant black evening clothes with a frilled shirt and a collar that rolled an inch above his coat. The effect of the whole thing was staggering. I felt that I was in the presence of history and that characters I had read about and heard about had come to life before my eyes. The music they played, now that I was hearing it in person without the tinny sounds of the 1920s' radio and records, was strange, wild, and intense. The men in the band brought with them intimations of a sophisticated Black world of night people where things went on that the rest of the world did not know about. Their very blackness held a mysterious quality. They didn't try to be entertaining with all the chuckling and eye-rolling that people were used to in the 1920s. Hodges was sinister and a little intimidating. Harry Carney rolled out his beautiful big tones in the manner of a concert cellist. Ellington was charming, witty, at ease, and in full command of the band and the audience. I waited at the stage door an hour before he came out. He was gracious and smiling, he asked what I played, and when I said clarinet, he said, "Keep blowing, son. Someday it'll start to play pretty."

There were very few jazz musicians in Toronto when I was a boy and, like other hardline Methodists in Canada, my family thought of jazz and dance halls as horrifying parts of a sinful world. In fact, there were few parts of the world that they didn't find sinful, and to protect me against it they didn't allow my sister or me to go to movies or to play card games or even parcheesi since it was played with dice. We had a family regimen of going to church three times on Sunday and once a week to prayer meeting. It was all right to play hymns in the Sunday school orchestra and to learn the Weber Clarinet Concerto and the exercises, but there was to be no jazz.

From the day I heard the band and met Ellington, all that changed. There was something about the way Duke did what he wanted to do with such grace and certainty—playing music that no one else could write, using stage lighting, wah-wah mutes, band uniforms, and soloists who came to the front of the band to play, two clarinets and a muted trombone for "Mood Indigo," making the band on stage into a piece of theater—all this gave me a sense of purpose. It was a sense that even as a fourteen-year-old who couldn't play the clarinet very well and had never played in a jazz band, if I kept blowing it every day the clarinet would start to play pretty.

After a while it did, and I discovered that it was possible not to go to church if I simply announced to my parents that I was not going except to play in the Sunday school orchestra, and that if I thought of myself the way Ellington did, I could become a musician and hang around with other musicians. That meant that I lived in a different world from the others. It was the difference between the square world which did as it was told and the inner company of artists who played a special kind of music with its own romantic heroes, who stayed up all night, left school, drank whiskey and gin, smoked reefers, hung around with beautiful and available women, died young, and were more like poets than regular people, with a special vocabulary and a nonchalant way of talking and thinking. I joined the underground while keeping my place in the square world of school and the Canadian family. For the first time in my life, I knew what it meant to be an artist. My deepest regret was that I had not been born Black.

I found four others who wanted to join the underground, and we organized a band. My mother and father hated it but let us rehearse in the living room, and little by little we began to be invited to play at high school dances and parties given by friends. We had a great advantage in the fact that we didn't charge very much, usually whatever our sponsors could pay. We bought the standard orchestrations of popular tunes, and at first I played the trumpet parts on clarinet until we found a trumpet player, at which point I branched out and borrowed the money from my father to buy an alto saxophone.

Then we found a pianist with perfect pitch and an acute musical memory who could listen to a tune once on the radio and dictate the melody line and the chords. I would then write out the parts for the trumpet and alto sax. The guitarist who doubled on violin already had the chords and the lead sheet, and the drummer didn't need anything. Because of his marvelous ear and memory, the pianist could imitate anyone from Eddy Duchin to Earl Hines just by listening to their records.

It was a simple step from there to learn how to listen and to copy out the parts from Ellington, Fletcher Henderson, or Chick Webb, and from there to start writing simple arrangements for the band and to develop a style of our own. I had taken to hitchhiking down to New York for a week during school vacation to hear whoever was playing. I found that I could rent a room for $5.00 a week and live on porridge, oranges, bananas, and milk and have enough money left over to pay the cover charge or the general admission.

I was learning to be a musician by being one. To compose meant either writing down notes the way you write down a poem and then playing the notes on an instrument, or reading and playing what someone else had written while learning to understand the structure and sound of the music of other composers. There was no great mystery in the creative act. Once I knew what I wanted to hear, I wrote it out. While a nuisance to have to write out parts for ten to twenty other people, there was no other way of letting them know what I had in mind. It was like sending a telegram asking someone to meet you at a certain place and time. After I got used to the vocabulary of notes, keys, and chords, I could imagine the sounds in my head without having to play them on an instrument. I simply sat down and wrote out a score.

But most of all I learned by listening. I could tell the authentic music, the natural tone, the inspired burst of improvisation by letting myself be influenced and taught by the masters of the instruments. It was not so much that our local musicians in Canada tried to imitate American jazz players directly. It was that the Americans set the standards for style and performance which we believed in and did our best to meet. They had cast a spell, and we were gladly under it. To feel the music coursing through your whole body, reaching a serene state in which you have control of your instrument and what you are playing while at the same time feeling yourself lifted and moved by something in the instrument and the music itself. Like our American counterparts we had close ties to each other and were quick to recognize each other's talents and to help each other the way the older generation of pianists helped Ellington learn how to play by ear when he was growing up in Washington. In Toronto we were in some sense pioneers. There had been nobody there before us.

Bill Clifton was our young pianist who had more talent than most and would be picked up and carried off to the Paul Whiteman Orchestra and Benny Goodman band. He was handsome, tall, sat very straight at the piano, and was one of the most severe critics and demanding performers I had ever met. I was impressed by the fact that even when he was most broke he refused to play with some of the orchestras around Toronto because he couldn't stand their banal style or he thought the drummer had no beat. Bill applied his own standards to the Whiteman and Goodman bands and at one point had a classic feud with Goodman over the beat he was keeping in the rhythm section. He felt that both Lionel Hampton and Gene Krupa were rushing the beat when they got too enthusiastic. Goodman thought that Bill was slowing down. The perfectionist element in Bill's character made him hard to live with. He also found it hard to live with himself.[9]

What I had learned from Bill when we were beginning to play seriously in Toronto was that no matter how informal, spontaneous, and free jazz sounded, the spontaneity and the freedom came from having full command of the instrument and full knowledge of the materials of jazz. If I was going to be able to improvise, I needed to listen to the masters of improvisation and to practice constantly. It was not unlike

William James's set of rules for making a lecture in philosophy—you read everything there is to read on the subject, discipline yourself by asking what it is you want to say, and write it out in notes. Then, after having been properly immersed and prepared, you leave your notes behind, walk into the lecture hall, and talk freely about what you know.

I was also learning about improvisation and the way I could be influenced and taught by listening to records and broadcasts. I set up a schedule for myself of two hours a day for improvising on the blues and the standard jazz tunes. In class at school I found myself playing tunes in my head and improvising imaginary solos. Some nights in bed I was rendered sleepless for hours by the silent improvisations I was playing and the imagined backgrounds the band was playing behind me.

∼

From the start I made no separation between higher and lower forms of music in playing a Brahms clarinet quintet with four string players or the clarinet part in "Royal Garden Blues" with a jazz band. It was all music. The composers were different, the origins of their ideas were different, so were the oral traditions out of which they came, but they all had the same problem—the problem of writing down notes that would let the musicians know what they wanted to hear them play. For jazz composers and players there was merely a difference in the degree of rhythmic intensity, in the tone produced on the instrument, in the style of phrasing, and in the degree of freedom to give to collective or solo improvisation.

The classical composers, except for an occasional cadenza, held you firmly in hand, gave you room in performance for modest differences in tempo and phrasing, and the tradition of your instrument told you how the notes should sound. The jazz composers gave you fewer notes and a lot of room to improvise. Again, the tradition of your instrument told you how the notes should sound. But even here there was much more room for personal style and mutual influence. Pee Wee Russell's clarinet was plaintive and tinged with melancholy in the ballads he played, and it was unmistakably Russell. Barney Bigard had his own sound and style. So did Jimmy Hamilton, Sidney Bechet's soprano, Johnny Hodges's alto, Cootie Williams's trumpet. You could choose to be yourself with your own kind of music as long as you had something to say.

Taylor at Sarah Lawrence with Maxine Sullivan, a leading jazz vocalist of the 1930s, and Art Lund, singer with the Benny Goodman and Harry James bands, early 1950s. Gary Gladstone, courtesy of Sarah Lawrence College.

That idea of individual character could be carried over very easily into life in general. Once I reached a sense of confidence that I could work things out in my own way, I could choose to be myself with no need to be like anyone else or even to be what I was brought up to be. I had absolved myself from the need for approval. The freedom and joy I found in the life of a musician opened up an entire area of new experience, and I was never the same the rest of my life. I knew that whatever else happened to me, I could always make my way as a musician, and I would always find people wherever I went who loved Beethoven and Ellington. I had made a sudden entry into a new world of friends who were out there waiting for me everywhere. I also knew that I had found a whole new self and that I really was becoming the kind of person I wanted to be.

Chapter 2

A Student's Journey

Harold Alexander Taylor was born on September 28, 1914, in the Danforth district of Toronto and grew up in a conventional home setting with his parents, Charles W. Taylor and Elizabeth H. Wilson Taylor, and elder sister Gladys Taylor (Neilson). Charles Taylor had immigrated as a child with his family to Toronto from England (Birmingham) and, for this reason, Harold viewed himself as a second-generation Englishman as well as a first-generation Canadian. He describes his upbringing in a "moderately poor section of Toronto";[1] however, his father would become an administrator for government and commercial entities (an office administrator at a Ford assembly plant in Toronto) and later superintendent of an office building in downtown Toronto. Active in the Methodist Church, Charles met Elizabeth when both were members of a Toronto-wide Methodist church choir, the Alexander Choir. Elizabeth grew up in a rural community, Brampton, outside of Toronto and was a homemaker throughout her life. Charles became a lay preacher in the United Church of Canada during the merging of the Methodist and Presbyterian denominations and, with only a basic elementary education, he participated in the Danforth Literary and Debating Club of Toronto where he would serve as president.

Taylor attended Kitchener Primary School, completing the eight-year program after four years (graduating at age eleven), and then enrolled at Riverdale Collegiate School. With thoughts of becoming a writer, he started smoking a pipe at age sixteen,[2] an activity he enjoyed throughout his life until the seemingly inevitable diagnosis of throat cancer in the 1980s. He continued his studies at Victoria College, the Methodist college of the University of Toronto, completing his undergraduate degree in 1935 and a master's degree in

1936. While Taylor's account of his college years is full of enthusiasm, he also admitted being intimidated by some of his future Rhodes Scholars classmates as well as others, including, notably, Northrop Frye, two years his senior, who became a distinguished literary critic and theorist.[3]

Taylor describes his youth through the completion of his master's degree, discussing briefly his break from the Methodist Church, and continuing to reflect upon his intellectual awakening through music. He comes to view reading as a form of action and realized "that the way to learn something is to do it, that all learning is a series of acts of creation, and that to know something is to grasp it and feel it with your whole body."

The reason I became a musician, like the reason I have ever done anything else that turned out to be important, was an accident. My uncle was moving from an old apartment to a new one, rediscovered a clarinet among his belongings, gave it to me, and I therefore played it. If my uncle hadn't moved, I wouldn't have played. From that accidental beginning, a stream of consequences flowed. I learned to love playing and the joys of practicing. Aside from the elements of sheer delight, I learned how to organize an orchestra and write for it and to deal with annoyances and tedious details of all kinds—trumpet players who called up the day of the engagement to say they couldn't come, bass players who claimed not to have a way of getting there, booking agents who failed to turn up the money. That kind of thing taught me to keep hold of my temper while making lists of other trumpet players and booking agents. If you can run an orchestra, you can run almost anything.

But more than anything else, to become a musician in the full sense of the word and to learn to do what true musicians do was to enter an entirely new world with a new set of people in it. To enter the world of music was to enter the entire world of the arts and to realize that once I had reached the point at which I could absorb myself in the intention of the composer and the sounds and rhythms of the musicians around me, I had come to understand the nature of all art. Seated among the musicians playing the Beethoven Third, I could open myself to the intention of the composer, certainly, but also to the painter, the poet, playwright, or architect or any of the others who inhabit the territory of artists. I could then begin to see and feel the unity of all the arts and the intuitive forms of knowledge that lie within them. I could feel the common bond that holds artists together in a community whose values transcend time and space and location in history. When you reach the kind of musical self-confidence that only a command of the instrument can bring, you can then understand the intention of the composer and allow yourself to be carried along by the sounds and rhythms of the musicians around you who also understand the intention of the composer. You join a congenial and informed group. Above all you could then recognize the primacy of the experience of art in living a life.

It is from that boyhood experience with music and what it did to my life *then* that I have drawn the ideas for education with which I have been working ever since. Many things became much simpler and more profound once I accepted the fact that the way to learn something is to do it, that all learning is a series of acts of creation, and that to know something is to grasp it and feel it with your whole body. I found out a few years later when I first read John Dewey that he had made an entire theory of education from my simple principle of the clarinet. It was already clear to me from the experience with Duke Ellington's music that once I began to function as an artist, various magical and fascinating things began to happen. Ever since then I have wanted to make such things happen everywhere I could, starting with children in the schools.

∽

I had decided at the age of twelve that I would be a writer, preferably a poet, but a writer. By the time I was sixteen I was ready for college, having bought a pipe and joined the musicians union. I had reached this point in my life by a series of happy accidents, including the fact that I nearly died when I was four years old. My parents had decided that my sister and I needed to have our tonsils and adenoids taken out. Since hospitals were too expensive for my father's income, a doctor came to the house with his operating table and a trayful of instruments, and he set them up in the kitchen. It had been decided that we should not be told about what was going to happen on the grounds that it might frighten us. At seven o'clock one morning, I was routed out of bed and taken to the kitchen table where I was absolutely terror-struck by the sight of the doctor in his white coat and mask with his shiny instruments on the table.

They finally got me to lie down on the table, still crying and screaming, and the last thing I remembered was some sort of frightening hum and the face of the doctor with the mirror on his head like a moon sailing through the sky. I had nightmares for years afterward in which I would wake up terrified by a moon descending on me to the sound of a low hum.

Whether it was the trauma of the operation and its total assault on my body and mind or another medical reason, I developed double pneumonia and while they were worrying about that, the doctor discovered something wrong with my heart, possibly caused by the strain put on it by the pneumonia. There was serious doubt that I would survive, and my parents called frantically around the city to find a heart specialist who knew what to do with the problem of a dying child's heart and lungs. They found one, an expert who had seen cases like this before, and he diagnosed a leaking valve in my heart, a condition that turns up in some children and under proper care heals itself as the child grows older.

Under the specialist's care I began a slow recovery, first with six months around the house with half each day in bed. After that I was allowed outside in a wheelchair with a lot more time in bed. The upshot of the illness was that I couldn't go to school until I was seven nor play with other children or do anything much that children usually did, and I saw a very great deal of my mother. She was good about it, especially since her instructions from the doctor were not to let me get upset and to keep me very quiet, and she had to cope with me night and day for nearly two and a half years.

She was not a person to whom affection came easily and, having been raised as a farm girl in a strict family, she had very clear and severe ideas about discipline. In the situation with me, it was a miracle that she didn't go out of her mind since the kind of discipline it was her custom to apply was countermanded by the doctor's order not to let me get upset. Few boys have ever had such complete mothering.

In our mutual bondage we became fond of each other, and she tried her best to do what I wanted. This turned out to be a passion for being read to, which then developed into a passion for learning to read. Between us we managed it, by getting through the alphabet and having my mother explain what the words meant. By the time I was allowed to go to school, I was reading magazines, newspapers, and books, and the passion for reading was set for life. My mother took great pride in my accomplishment and my survival, and although the years of the illness had made her more possessive and more concerned about everything I did, I was a lucky and happy child. My father was gentle and kind and devoted in his own way. My sister and I were good friends, although I didn't see her much once I started to go to school.

∼

The next good luck had to do with going to school. Perhaps because I had been held back so long and was so excited about the idea of school with the other children, perhaps because of all the reading I had already done, and certainly because of the quality of the teachers in my classes, I did well in school once I got there. I was eager to learn anything they were prepared to teach, and the school responded by letting me go as fast as I was able, which meant skipping every other grade and finishing the first eight years of the regular program in four.

This in turn meant that from that point on I was always younger than the others in my class or in anything else I did, and I was counted on to go on being as bright as people had been led to believe I was. With a mother and a father who believed that, too, and a sister who was a friendly companion, I developed an easy confidence in what I could do since everyone around seemed to be on my side. When the mathematics teacher put the homework on the board, I wrote the answers instead of taking down the problems. I did the same with Latin and French translations, and I loved working in every subject except chemistry in which the memorizing was a bore and the experiments seemed always to be a fake since they all had to come out to an arranged conclusion.

I had also learned what it was like to be an athlete and to have a chance to run for my school—to dress for the part, to put on silk running trunks, a sprinter's shirt with a number on my back, and a pair of track shoes that could take me twice as fast as I ever ran before. Then there was the football team with its ritual of practice every day and the permission to walk out of class early on Fridays to get ready to play in the game. I was captain and left halfback of the junior football team in my senior year in high school, and we put on the field one of the least effective teams in the history of football in the Toronto schools. Defeats by scores like 42 to 6 were not uncommon. We dropped the ball a lot and didn't seem to have enough plays and, in my final high school year, didn't win a single game.

I think that this was probably good for me in its own way. It meant that we all had a good time and, although we tried our best to win, the fact that we weren't expected to made it easier to enjoy the game. Most of all I enjoyed just being on the team with the others, wearing the uniform, feeling the rhythm and the drama of the unfolding plays, knowing what each of us was to do when we heard the signals in the huddle, and feeling the excitement of coming out of the huddle with the knowledge that my number had been called and I would have another

Taylor as halfback behind center, circa 1929. Courtesy of the Taylor family.

chance to break loose with the ball. For me the game had the same sense of excitement and the same kind of improvisation within a basic structure as playing in a jazz band. There was a set of tunes and chords, an arrangement I had in my head, and with a group of friendly allies behind me and around to give support, I had my turn at a solo where I could show what I could do.

I had the same feeling about basketball, in which our junior team did a little better. There was the same necessity of a rhythm to be set up, with a part for each of us to play, and a final burst of improvisation as the shooter drove for the basket or paused to shoot from outside or passed to another player. I liked the discipline of practice every day and the preparation for the drama of the game we were to play on Friday in the same way that I enjoyed practicing the clarinet or doing the homework and reading for next day's class. It was a preparation for a next stage, a discipline gladly self-imposed, not merely for self-improvement in the conventional sense, but to learn to do well whatever I was doing, to apply to myself the standards of those who were the master of the art of the athlete, the scholar, or the musician. If I didn't do too well at any given point, there was no need to worry. I would have another chance to correct what went wrong, to try again. I had to come to terms with myself and recognize that whatever it was I wanted myself to be and what I wanted to be able to do, it wasn't always possible to rise to that expectation.

As a result, I grew up without the stress or anxiety that I had to compete with those who could do things better than I could. If I was lucky enough to play in an orchestra or on a team with those who were better than I was, this was a happy good fortune since I could take delight in their performance and could learn from what they did. They would carry

Taylor in 1930. Courtesy of the Taylor family.

me along with them and give me new ways of thinking about myself. This was true of the best writers as well as the athletes and artists. The great ones were those who carried you along with them into new territory and told you things you would never have thought of on your own.

~

When I presented myself as a sixteen-year-old freshman to the registrar at Victoria College in the University of Toronto, in the long line of freshman who came to enroll, the registrar said, "Well, Taylor, what do you want to be?"

I wasn't quite ready for the question. I was coming to college because it was the next thing a Canadian boy in my situation would do after he graduated from high school. I didn't think I should say that, or should say that I wanted to play in the Ellington band. I didn't know much about what colleges did, but I had a general idea that it would be a good place to continue doing things I already enjoyed and that I could count on reading literature and learning to be a writer.

I replied, "I want to be a writer."

The registrar said, "In that case, take the honors work in philosophy and literature."

I said, "Yes sir."

That was the whole conversation. The registrar hadn't learned much about me, nor had I learned anything about the college. But it turned out to be another favorable accident. I had never divided my life into parts—schoolwork, athletics, music, home. Everything was part of everything else, and the center of it all was the school. That was where my friends were and where most of my growing up was done. I was so busy with what was going on there that I wasn't home very much.

The college and the abrupt advice of the registrar gave me an intellectual base and set me on the way to study the very things that came to matter most to me for the rest of my life. To be in the honors course in philosophy and literature meant that in four years we read the major Western philosophers and writers, from the pre-Socratics and *Beowulf* to Bertrand Russell and James Joyce, with background courses in British and European history and year-long excursions into biology, French, anthropology, and psychology. There were only ten or twelve students in the program, and except for a few large lecture courses in history and literature, all our classes were small. In retrospect, I can see that it was a narrow set of studies, dealing with a systematic survey of Western ideas and Western culture, devoid of any reference to the major issues of the 1930s and the disintegration of the very civilization whose history and character we were called upon to understand. It was a literary education, carried on in a social and political vacuum, at several stages removed from the reality of contemporary life.

All beliefs were somehow of equal value in a sequence of thinkers and writers who followed each other in the syllabus and whose ideas were to be read, explained, and written about but never confronted. What was not mentioned was that in Hitler's Germany, Franco's Spain, and Stalin's Russia the application of political ideas and social strategies were raising the most fundamental philosophical questions in which the answers were matters of life and death to tens of millions of human beings. As students of philosophy we studied issues of peace and war, the individual and society, good and evil, and political systems by reading about the Peloponnesian wars, Kant's categorical imperative, Hume's theory of causation, and Hobbes's social contract. But at the time, it seemed to me that I was being taken into the biggest kind of thinking of which the human mind was capable. A great deal of it I didn't understand, even though I found ways of writing and talking which continued my reputation as a student.

My professors had themselves been educated in the British tradition of the late nineteenth century and treated us very well, called us by our last names, encouraged discussion among us in class, and did whatever they could to help us along. Without intending to, they also provided various surprises and adventures as we went through our list of thinkers. Descartes, for example. It had never occurred to me to doubt my own existence, and I was astonished to find that this was not only possible but was the subject of the most intense debate leading to Descartes's radicalism in concluding that the mere act of thinking proved that the subject doing the thinking existed and that everything started from there. Or Hume's proof that you could never prove that one thing caused another but could only form a habit of thought that if one thing continually preceded another, it led you to the expectation that the same thing that happened before would happen again. And especially Henri Bergson, whose idea of creative evolution and a universe in a constant flux of change struck me with the forcefulness of an absolute truth.

Above everything else, the college gave us a healthy and congenial place to grow up and a friendly atmosphere to learn what a group of kindhearted faculty members thought we should know. We were almost entirely second-generation British with names like McDonald, Nichols, O'Brien. We were white, Protestant, fairly well behaved, some of us poorer than others but nobody terribly well off. If the college lacked intellectual vitality, I was too young and uninformed to notice it or even to expect it. We were taught to take ideas and good writing seriously, and we did.

I liked the idea of studying philosophy, and I liked the idea of myself as a writer, intellectual, musician, athlete. The college was a place in which I could be those things; there were football players, tennis players, writers, intellectuals, and musicians all around. I could join the tennis or the football team, organize my own orchestra, write for the student magazine and newspaper, and actually be the person I had imagined as a possibility. I could try myself out with no punishment for failure.

I also had the advantage of having a fairly full life outside the college as well as inside, with the independent income of a professional musician, playing sometimes with my own group, other times with orchestras at college dances and local clubs. I discovered that I couldn't be as righteous about the purity of the music I played. Not many people who hired orchestras were interested in serious jazz, and they didn't take kindly to the idea of hiring a group of romantics who wouldn't play requested numbers and refused to use music stands or music. I learned that you either played what they wanted to hear or you didn't play at all.

I can remember the agony of the decision in agreeing to play two nights a week at the Balmy Beach Canoe Club with an orchestra led by Jack Kent Cooke who would later own many professional sports teams as well as New York City's Chrysler Building.[4] Cooke knew what the public wanted, and he decided that what they wanted was music that sounded like Guy Lombardo's. In the circles in which I moved, playing that kind of music was the equivalent of taking up crocheting. I told myself that it was a way of financing a college education and had nothing to do with music. I'm sorry to report that Cooke's band with its whiny, nasal saxophones was much more successful than mine.

Life inside the college, aside from the athletics and the music, was almost entirely going to class for lectures and reading, writing, and talking about what we had read or written. There was so much obligatory reading that there was not time for any other kind, and I was dutiful and conscientious in reading what I was told to read, whether or not I understood it or got anything from it. A great deal of the time I had to force my way through the text, going much too slowly, with the words observed and noted but without any effect on my thinking. I hadn't learned to take notes properly since I did not know what were the most important things to take note of. Other students impressed me and frightened me a little with their knowledge of philosophy. When given writings by T. H. Green, they seemed to understand what was being said.[5] I found the text impenetrable. Green's words simply passed before my eyes, whole paragraphs went by without comprehension even when I went back over them.

It was not until my junior year that anything approaching an intellectual awakening took place. It started with my picking up Virginia Woolf's *To the Lighthouse* one afternoon in something called the Browsing Room at the college, a room separate from the library with easy chairs and shelves of books not on the regular reading lists. We hadn't reached Woolf in our survey of modern English writers, but I knew her name, having heard it used by one of the more formidable students. I read straight through *To the Lighthouse* that afternoon and for the next two weeks dropped everything else to read everything by Virginia Woolf in the university library. This was a different kind of reading from any I had ever done and more of it than I had ever done at a single stretch. I knew then that I would have to go to England. It was not only my first experience of reading an author I couldn't leave alone. It was an awakening to the fact that true reading was an action and that it did not matter so much what I read or by whom. What mattered was my capacity to respond fully to what was being said.

I learned for the first time that I could interrupt the regular flow of an orderly curriculum and even skip classes if there were something very serious I felt I had to do, like reading the whole of Virginia Woolf in successive days. So deeply engrained was the habit of dutiful attendance that it was only in the last few years I have stopped having nervous dreams in which I suddenly find at the end of a term that I have been enrolled in a class whose examination is almost due and which I have completely forgotten and haven't attended. In later years the only difference in the scenario of the dream has been that I've been scheduled to teach the class rather than to take it. I also discovered through the experience with Virginia Woolf that a large part of the way I was presenting myself to myself was false. The conversion to Ellington was real and visible. I was a musician. I played music and played it well enough to know that I belonged to a tradition of musicians and that after a while when I had paid my dues I would be accepted fully into the tradition.

But in the case of my statement at twelve that I was going to be a writer and my sixteen-year-old's answer to the registrar, I was identifying myself with a cast of characters which included Robert Louis Stevenson, Walter Scott, and G. A. Henty. I was drawn toward the idea of being a writer not because I wrote unusually well or had read an unusual amount but because I wanted to be a certain kind of person. My short stories and poems, on rereading, I found to be a boy's exercises, and I congratulated myself on not having shown them around.

Writers were cultural heroes. They had a place in the world. They traveled, observed people and events, wrote about what the people, real or imagined, were doing, what they said to each other. To say that I was going to be a writer meant that that was the way I would like to be identified. When I recognized in Virginia Woolf the enormity of her talents and the size of her accomplishments, I came face to face with the size and shape of my own talent. I knew that if I were going to be a writer, I would have to write about what I knew, and I didn't know enough yet to write about it. Perhaps I never would.

∽

By the time my senior year had come around I decided that four years of college, studying and living in Toronto, which then had the general characteristics of a cultural desert, had exhausted the possibilities of any experience that would be either useful or interesting. I would take my clarinet and typewriter, go to England, travel from there to Europe, make my way as a musician and writer, and see how it all came out. I would gather experience.

In the spring of that senior year I was walking through the main college building one day when a fellow senior stopped me to ask if I had been nominated for the Moss Scholarship. This was a university-wide award given each year to the best all-around student in the graduating class, with the students and faculty from each of the colleges electing their own candidates. The award carried with it free tuition to go on to the MA degree and a stipend for living expenses.

When I said that as far as I knew I hadn't been nominated, he went off to put in my name. A day later he called to say that it was too late; they had already printed the ballots. A week later I received a call from the college to say that I had been elected. They had decided to reprint the ballots. The next step was to appear before an awards committee of university faculty members who interviewed the finalists and who wanted to know what research I would carry out if I received the award. I was as unprepared for this question as I had been at the beginning with the registrar, but by this time I had learned to improvise. I chose the two writers who meant most to me in my courses and said that I would like to do a study of the relation of Bergson's philosophy to Virginia Woolf's novels, hoping to God there was some relation. The committee must have thought there was, or at least liked the idea of my trying to find out.

I have sometimes wondered what would have happened if they hadn't reprinted the ballots. I certainly wouldn't have gone on to do an MA, and if I hadn't done that I wouldn't have completed a doctorate in England, and if I hadn't done that I would never have taught philosophy in Wisconsin, and I would never have come to New York.

The year with Bergson and Woolf was in fact a turning point. It made it possible to go on with my music and at the same time to work in a concentrated way with one set of ideas in philosophy and literature and to go deeply into the work of two writers whom I admired and sought to understand what they were really saying. I learned what it meant to be a scholar and to have ideas of my own. I found that I had an orderly mind and was conscientious about looking things up. That was one of the reasons I had done so well as a student, since that was the kind of mind the educators were looking for and rewarded with their approval.

But then I found the disadvantage in having that kind of mind. It contradicted in too many ways the kind of person I wanted to be and what I thought I was. It wasn't that I objected to being orderly. My teachers had given me a sense of fair-mindedness about other peoples' ideas, and I liked being able to look at things systematically. It was one part of coming to understand, and if I were to have an intellectual conscience, I had to take as much as possible into account, and that meant having a certain sense of order in how I assembled the ideas which were truly my own.

There were too many ideas in the world of which I was ignorant—in Marx, Freud, Kierkegaard, Dostoyevsky, Baudelaire, Picasso and the surrealists, Hemingway and the émigré American writers in Paris—all the writers and artists who were left out of my education and whom I hadn't found by myself. When I began to hear about them, it was too overwhelming. I could see that my neat little body of knowledge that I had thought to be so encompassing was in fact a small slice of parochial lore handed over to me by second-generation Britishers who weren't even in touch with their own culture. They had told us about T. S. Eliot but not a word about Spender, MacNiece, Isherwood, and Auden at the time when these were the poets who had most to say to their own generation.

Nor had I ever come to terms intellectually with my boyhood break with the Methodists. That had been a break with the family pattern of moral and social codes and the authority of parents to control a boy's life. It had given me the satisfaction of a successful rebellion and to that extent had emotional roots, but it had nothing to do with religion or the search for believable certainties. That was another subject that never came up. The people at church seemed to me to be stiff-necked bores, the minister a long-winded dullard, the church services a form of imprisonment, and only the Sunday school picnics had any content of religious pleasure.

When I refused to go to church, I was refusing to accept orders, and part of the orders had to do with believing in the God of the Methodists, the divinity of Jesus, and the stories in the Bible. It didn't occur to me to make a conscious rejection of Protestant theology. The theology was one part of going to church, and I became an atheist simply by not going. I had no metaphysical or religious concerns, no struggles of conscience about loss of faith. I had never had that kind of faith to lose.

～

When I first came to read Bergson, I was drawn toward the quality of his writing and the size of his ideas. Here was a writer who didn't argue about the existence of God or the conditions of immortality. He worked from a base in the biological sciences and provided a general scheme for explaining nothing less than the universe. The mind was not a separate entity; thoughts were not disembodied essences. Thinking and knowing were the outcome of natural causes, and the mind had evolved along with other phenomena of evolution into modes of consciousness helpful in adapting the human organism to its environment. I had noticed that Virginia Woolf had come upon some of the same ideas, not, apparently, from having read Bergson, but because her sensibility as an artist took her in the same direction. There was something in the air, a movement in thought, and the artist and the philosopher unconsciously joined together in making a general set of assumptions which underlay the development of their ideas.

I read all of Virginia Woolf's novels and essays and most of Bergson, along with a cross-section of comment on their work by others, and proved to my own satisfaction what Whitehead had already shown in his *Adventures in Ideas*—that in any given age there was a climate of opinion, created by the writers, philosophers, and scientists working independently of each other but united in the general assumptions they accepted. My study of Bergson and Woolf was a small case study of that cultural fact. It was much more than that in its effect on me. It gave me a sense of urgency in going on with the study of philosophy and literature now that I had come to grips with a pair of writers whose ideas were almost completely persuasive. I could see connections among ideas that I had never seen before especially in the relation between the creative acts of the artists and the forms of knowledge they produced. In the simple ways in which I had made connections between the act of writing music and the art of playing it, I was groping toward some form of aesthetic theory which could remove the mysticism most people invested in the act of creation. To me it was all very practical.

Although I did not know enough to realize it at the time, I was being taught by superb scholars who were unusually kind and especially generous in giving me time in tutorial sessions to ask questions and talk back and forth as scholars together. There in his office with time to spare for teaching me was G. S. Brett, author of one of the first comprehensive histories of psychology, written when the history of philosophy was the basis on which contemporary psychologies were formed. Across the hall was Fulton Anderson, authority on Plato and Greek thought, seeming to be diffident about students but careful to give them his own sort of quizzical attention. In a nearby building was Herbert Davis, editor of the Oxford University Press edition of the works of Jonathan Swift, who taught us a course in prose satire which served as a weekly example of what a seminar in literature at its best could be. Just as I had learned how to be a musician by becoming one, I had now learned to be a scholar because Brett, Anderson, and Davis had taken me into the middle of their own intellectual lives.[6]

But all through that accidental year which turned up in my life only because I had walked through a college building at the same time as a college friend, I was still answering the registrar's question, What

Taylor's master's degree graduation photograph, 1936. Courtesy of the Taylor family.

was I going to be? I had Bergson, Woolf, Auden, Ellington, a clarinet, and an MA. What does a person do with this equipment? By this time I knew that there were two complete sides of me and that whenever I thought about them, they were in conflict. There was the Ellington side, the side that wanted to live as a free spirit, go out into the world, play music, write, stay away from responsibilities and institutions, making a life piece by piece the way Bergson had. Then there was the other side, the student of ideas, the young scholar in the university, the one with a slim body of knowledge he longed to expand. For quite a few reasons, the year of study in philosophy had been a success. I learned what it was to be seriously involved with ideas, to face the fact that they were not objects to be sorted out and filed away. They were states of mind and preparations for actions.

Taylor with his parents, 1939. Courtesy of the Taylor family.

When I was sixteen years of age and had just graduated from high school, my mother and father told me that the family did not have enough money to send me to college but had cashed an insurance policy to pay for my first year if I could make enough money to handle the rest. It didn't occur to me at the time to be grateful, or to find anything unusual in their willingness to sacrifice themselves for my sake. As I look back, I feel humble in the face of their faith in education and in me, especially since in the latter faith they hadn't much to go on except that I liked books and that this was unusual in the circles in which I moved. I am also deeply grateful for the fact that they did not try to tell me what I should take in college, what profession I should follow. They left that to the college and to me. As a result I studied the most practical of subjects, philosophy, history, and literature. Through them I came to know and appreciate the study of science and society and had a chance to find out what I could do and what I couldn't do.

—Harold Taylor, "Why Go to College?," 1951

Chapter 3

Coming Down from Cambridge

I share with Immanuel Kant only one philosophical attribute. We were both awakened by David Hume. What followed after the awakening is another matter, a matter connected with the quality, range, and depth of a philosophical mind which turned the course of Western philosophy in a new direction. For my part, I am content to say humbly that I have continued to learn from great philosophical minds other than Kant, to accept the influence of radical empiricism, and to enjoy learning from the philosophers of organism, principally from Bergson, from James, from Whitehead, and from Dewey.

—Harold Taylor, "Thinkers Who Influenced Me," 1952

Unlike other chapters in this collection, "Coming Down from Cambridge" includes a section where Taylor inserted a metanarrative, indicating his intent to introduce a "state of mind" perspective for a memoir that he had planned to title "A State of Mind." Taylor writes, "At a distance of many years and many experiences I find it intriguing to see what was happening then to a young man who, by all accounts, seems to be me at an earlier age." While brief and, I assume, not fully developed to the length he had intended, he proceeds to link the section to Scottish philosopher David Hume who, he states, "first startled me with a view of the self which then seemed radical but which now seems conventional." I suspect there would have been other moments in subsequent chapters where he would have included such psychologically oriented asides.

Throughout his life, Taylor reconciled his mixed feelings toward becoming, first, an analytic philosopher and, then, a moral philosopher. "Coming Down from Cambridge"—leaving Ludwig Wittgenstein's circle for more traditional normative philosophy—describes Taylor's intent to engage with the world, to address social issues through action, and, as he notes, to put his ideas about human nature into practice in schools. He would ultimately accept a position in the philosophy department at University of Wisconsin and begin what seemed as a traditional yet promising career as an academic and philosopher. His early writings on Hume's Theory of Imagination are cited in the professional literature decades after their publication.[1] Yet, his reputation as a philosopher suffered when he left Madison to accept the presidency at Sarah Lawrence. He never returned to an academic post as a professor of philosophy.

"Coming Down from Cambridge," reconstructed from fragments, offers an insightful and entertaining juxtaposition of life as a doctoral student and jazz musician. Taylor may have expanded this essay into two separate chapters since so much more could have been written about the jazz scene in London. I rearranged what have now become the closing paragraphs of the chapter and, with great angst, removed Taylor's philosophical analysis and detailed interpretations of Hume and Wittgenstein.

I left Canada when I was twenty-one. I still had the registrar's problem, What was I going to be? I felt that I had been preparing myself for something long enough, and I had to decide what that something was. A writer? That was the original answer, and it still seemed like a good idea. The only question now was, What kind of writer? In philosophy? A novel? Stories? Or a musician? Then, where would I go? To New York, where some of my friends had gone? To London, where there were other Canadians? When I thought about it hard enough, the answer became fairly easy. I would simply go ahead doing what I had been doing since I was thirteen, go on studying, keep on playing music, and see what happens.

Letters of recommendation from my professors went off to Cambridge in England and, not long after, I followed, working my way on a cattle boat from Montreal to Glasgow with three hundred dollars and my instruments. On board the ship I had personal charge of fifty cows and six horses for nearly twelve days at sea and was seasick the moment we were out of sight of land. Our three-thousand-ton ship lurched and rolled at even the sight of any wave over three feet, and at one point I was so weak from the seasickness that I fell three decks down the open hold and had to be carried back to my bunk. Only the hay at the bottom of the hold saved me.

I had hoped for a scholarship at St John's College in Cambridge but hadn't received word from the authorities before I left home. When

I got there and talked to the man with the hyphenated name who would have been my tutor at St John's, I found that there were few scholarships for incoming students who wanted to take the PhD degree and that in any case the money had been given out. My three hundred dollars would last about six weeks. When I asked the students at the college about places I might play jazz, they told me that there were none.

I also took a closer look at the way the curriculum in graduate studies was organized and what would be expected of me if I could somehow borrow the money to stay. It was a most enlightened arrangement. The candidate worked on his research for two years with the help of his tutor and others interested in his field, attended occasional lectures he and his tutor thought worth attending, and conferred with anyone else in the university who would be useful and agreed to help. At the end of two years he would be judged on the quality of his research and, if approved, would receive the degree. The university did not put much store by the doctorate, saw very little need for taking it, and found it hard to understand why anyone would want to. The MA degree was awarded to anyone who sent in twenty pounds and came to dinner two or three times in a year.

When I talked further with people at the college, I found what I should have already known—that the almost complete emphasis in Cambridge philosophy at that point was on linguistic analysis and that the sort of study that interested me in the relation between philosophy and literature was not considered work in philosophy. With Ludwig Wittgenstein on the premises and in the saddle, philosophy had been redefined as a disease that had no cure, and he had most of the students frightened of doing anything else but the analysis of propositions and sentences. It was said that Wittgenstein's general attitude toward students was that if they brought up a problem on which he had already worked, there was no point in trying to take it further. And if it was one he hadn't brought up, it wasn't worth dealing with.

When I looked at my enthusiasm for Bergson and the development of some of his ideas, I realized that they would probably chop him to pieces before my eyes. He was exactly the kind of philosopher who annoyed the analytical-minded most, since his writing was full of metaphors and images, and his romantic view of the creative element in nature and in humans, along with his delight in intuitive forms of knowing, would make them question everything but his enthusiasm and his sanity.

Added to this, the students all seemed so much more mature and knowledgeable than I. They seemed to have read everything, knew about wines and new playwrights on the continent, and they talked so brilliantly and had so many inside jokes that I felt like a boy at his first grown-up party. They were pleasant enough to me and asked friendly questions, some of them were intrigued by my relation to jazz. But on the whole, they seemed to me to be characters out of Forster's *Howard's End*, and I didn't feel up to the strain of either trying not to be like them or insisting on being myself. I very quickly learned the meaning of the word "colonial."

I packed my bags and my instruments again and went off to London.

I knew very soon that this was the right thing to have done. It was a way of breaking out of my past into a completely new world. Philosophy was not something to be done in a special situation in rooms on the banks of a river in a beautiful ancient town. It was a way of opening up my mind to the intellectual impulses and flow of ideas which can originate in the cosmopolitan cities of the world. London in the 1930s in the years before the war was very close to the center of everything that was happening everywhere else. To read the papers and the magazines, to talk with painters, writers, and radicals in Bloomsbury where I found a room in Russell Square, to meet Germans and Frenchmen on their way to fight in the International Brigade, to listen to young Nigerians and Indians talk about the actual plans they were making to throw the British out of their countries, to follow day by day the progress of Hitler on his way to conquering Europe, to be involved in political debates at the London School of Economics with angry young men from every part of the world—all this gave a new context and a new meaning to what it meant to be a student of philosophy. I felt that in some way I was part of a worldwide movement of intellectuals.

There was also a sense of intellectual and political security, no less real because it was based on an illusion. Great Britain in the 1930s was still a major power, and it was comforting to a young man who had read so much about British institutions and their history to see them in operation at close hand. The mere sight of the House of Commons, Westminster Abbey, the British Museum where I worked every day, the Tate Gallery, Albert Hall, Virginia Woolf's house, and Buckingham Palace gave me the feeling that everything was too stable to be seriously threatened by the growth of Hitler's power. It was not until Munich and the occupation of Czechoslovakia that I realized the vitality and strength had gone out of the institutions.

In the meantime I had met my teachers and had set to work to be a student again. It was a most informal and rewarding arrangement. I had simply found my way to University College of the University of London on Gower Street, gone to the office of the registrar, presented my credentials, and asked if I could enroll as a candidate for a doctorate in philosophy. I was referred to Professor John MacMurray, then holding the position of Grote Professor of Mind and Logic at University College.[2] He was a slim, bearded, and kindly man who looked a little like the pictures I had seen of D. H. Lawrence, with a pleasant Scottish accent and a serious interest in what I had to say. He had written *Reason and Emotion*, a well-regarded work by philosophers who were not linguistic analysts, and was held in esteem among his colleagues in Great Britain and Europe.

We talked about my work at the University of Toronto and what I had been doing with Bergson and Woolf.

"Ah, Bergson," MacMurray said. "What a delightful thinker and what a joy to read. But you mustn't take him too seriously."

"But I've already taken him seriously, that's one of the reasons I am here."

"Do you think that all ideas are simply ways of adapting to an environment? What do you do about mathematical reasoning? What is it adapting to?"

We were off for an hour's discussion of the nature of reason, something that had never happened to me before, and right in the middle of it I realized that MacMurray had already started teaching me and that he was going to take me on as his student. It was like playing a duet with a superb musician who had performed it all his life and whose tone and tempo were exactly right and who knew every note in the score. He was willing to grant to Bergson that in an ultimate sense, the basis of all knowledge lay in intuition. That is, no matter what your view of the reality of the world outside your mind, you could not prove that your view was a true one. You arranged your thoughts in words, sentences, and mathematical symbols in ways that satisfied your wish for certainty in what you believed. You relied on others whose ideas you trusted, the great scientists, for example, for help in reaching ultimate belief. In the end your certainty that your beliefs were correct depended on a *feeling* of certainty, an intuition, and not on a logical proof.

But MacMurray wanted more than that. He wanted to find an objective reason, of the kind Kant had found, reason as a pure form, unavailable to ordinary proof from the evidence of experience in the senses. He was not prepared to desert his interest in social philosophy and psychological explanations for why we believed what we believed, and he found the Cambridge philosophers brilliant but sterile. I gathered from his remarks that they found him woolly-headed and an obscurantist. If you applied linguistic analysis to his books, you would be left with nothing but a string of preference—sentences and unprovable value-judgments and, in a sense, he had been read out of the philosophy fraternity. He was working down in London on pseudo-problems at an inferior university while the real action was going on in Cambridge and Oxford.

When I told him why I had left Cambridge after two weeks, he smiled and said, in effect, welcome to the club. "Why do you suppose those young men who made you ill at ease are analyzing sentences? Is it because they are passionate about symbolic logic and analytic philosophy? No. They are doing what they are told, and they are doing philosophy the way G. E. Moore, Bertrand Russell, and Wittgenstein have defined it. They have cut the heart out of speculative thought. They have taken on a kind of snobbery about what they do. They take no risks. They make no interesting conclusions or hypotheses. They live on the work of others and the only truth they find is in tautology—a tree is a tree. You can say yes to that. Or you can start with a mathematical axiom, and once you accept it as axiomatic you can then go on with your proof. But you are still saying a tree is a tree, because the axiom itself is unprovable. It is just something you start with and once you start you can go on with endless deductions."

MacMurray asked me if I had ever heard of Susan Stebbing.[3] I told him that her name didn't come up in our fast run-through of all the contemporary philosophers in one semester back in Toronto. He said that Stebbing had one of the finest minds in British philosophy. She was a friend of Bertrand Russell and a skilled practitioner in the analytic school. She had written a review of Wittgenstein's *Tractatus for Mind* in which she made some serious criticisms, some of them on technical points. Wittgenstein's response was to dismiss her from serious consideration as a philosopher and to forbid his students in Cambridge or any of his colleagues from allowing her to have a copy of his famous Blue Book, the unpublished notes on philosophical problems that he used with his classes.

MacMurray said that he thought I should start with some work on the nature of reason. Was there any connection between the despair of the poets and writers, the gloomy ideas in Eliot's *Wasteland*, and the implicit social nihilism of the analytic school? Was the refusal of philosophers to come to grips with philosophical issues in contemporary politics the result of intellectual factors or the result of economic and social forces so powerful that the intellectuals simply gave up and vacated the field? Was there any significance in the fact that the major literary figure of the Western world was an Irish genius whose masterpiece was a work in which the language was so involuted and complex that its meanings were available only to a small group of initiates who could follow the extravagant puns, inside jokes, and literary references?

Obviously I had never thought of any of those questions. I didn't know enough even to have raised them. MacMurray asked if I had ever read Karl Mannheim's *Ideology and Utopia*. Again I had to say no. MacMurray said that he thought that the first thing I should do was to read Mannheim and then go over and have a talk with him. He was on the faculty of the London School of Economics, and MacMurray would give me a note to ask for an appointment. He would also give me a note to meet with Susan Stebbing who was on the faculty of Bedford College, the women's college of the University of London. It was possible that she might agree to act as one of my tutors, and that it would be good to have a member of the analytic school as a counterpart to his own tutoring. Then there was Russell who often lectured at the London School. I should go to his lectures, no matter what the subject, and perhaps have a talk with him. My God, what a beginning.

~

Ideology and Utopia was a long, hard book to read at that stage in my education, and I was nervous about going to see Mannheim in so unsophisticated a state about the whole idea of the sociology of knowledge. It was just another thing I did not know in a generalized ignorance which seemed to spread everywhere I looked. In this case it was due to the small amount of attention we had given in Toronto to the work of Hegel and Marx.

After wrestling with the long sentences and the unfamiliar vocabulary, I began to see that here was another ally to go along with Hume and Bergson. What Mannheim was saying in essence was that ideas were social and political instruments which *could* change the world and did. Ideas were not abstract entities arranged in systems by thinkers who were outside their own society. They might live a separate life as scholars from the rest of the society, but their ideas came out of a social, economic, and political context and their conceptions of the ideal society and the relation of the individual to it were projections of an existing society into alternative futures.

These were Hume's "habits of mind," except that Mannheim was much more sophisticated about the intricacy of the relations between social context and mental constructs. If every idea could be traced to its origin and explained by its place in a social setting, then it could be argued that knowledge was created by a social process and the individual knowledge-maker was embedded in a nest of unconscious assumptions of his own era.

I hadn't needed to be nervous. Mannheim had read MacMurray's note in which he said that he and I were starting work on the nature of reason and that perhaps Mannheim would have some suggestions to make about how to go about it. He certainly did, and the suggestions flew from behind his desk like the sparks from a pinwheel. He settled on the late seventeenth- and early eighteenth-century European thought, and on Voltaire in particular. It was a period, he said, when no matter what they all wrote, the writers, poets, and philosophers, from Dryden and Locke to Shaftsbury and Leibniz, were all talking about the same kind of universe. It showed in the architecture, the gardens, the political and social arrangements, the social classes in their orderly hierarchy, and the idea of God as a master mathematician in a universe running on mathematical principles. Voltaire's satire on the best of all possible worlds, studied as an event in social history, would make a fascinating piece of research on the sociology of philosophy. The period was sufficiently distant from the twentieth century to allow a degree of objectivity, and there was a wealth of material in Voltaire's letters and published works, contemporary essays, poems, biographies, and in later works of scholarship. Mannheim became more and more excited by the possibility in the study as he went on talking about it. The only trouble was that he made it so thoroughgoing a project with such a wide variety of subjects to be dealt with that it seemed to me that it would take me three or four years to carry it out since I would be starting from scratch rather than from the advanced position with which Mannheim began.

My next visit was to Susan Stebbing at Bedford College in Regents Park. She was as sympathetic and interested as Mannheim had been and asked me some questions about my education in Canada. She was involved in a school her sister had started in Hampstead, one which ran on progressive lines. When I told her about my consternation in finding that I knew so little about anything after my five years of study in philosophy, she smiled and said, "You can only know as much as you have learned, and then add to it what you can."

I asked about the difference between a progressive school and any other kind. She said that it was a question of thinking first of all of the child and the child's development, not about the system of subjects the child must master. The child was a natural learner with a natural gift for inquiry, and the school was a place to set the child's learning in motion by projects in science and the arts, by having the child *do* science and the arts rather than simply being told about them. She discussed the two best known progressive schools in England, Summerhill and Dartington. She thought that Summerhill was too wild, disorderly, and messy and depended too much on the father figure of A. S. Neill, the headmaster. Dartington, on a former estate in the southern part of Devon and started by Dorothy and Leonard Elmhirst as an educational experiment in the late 1920s, was a much better school. It did its best to help with the education of the children and parents in the Devon village and farm communities, although Stebbing thought that there were too many unmanageable children of radical intellectuals in residence to make a properly balanced student body. Bertrand Russell had also shown some interest in education and had started a school of his own in the 1920s.[4] Russell didn't have the patience, nor did the children and their parents have much patience with him.

This was another surprise for me—the idea of philosophers putting their ideas about human nature into practice in schools, a college professor who taught children as well as young adults. It seemed even more surprising that a distinguished member of the analytic school of philosophy had so great an interest in child psychology. When I raised the question with Stebbing, she said that she had always been interested in the spread of philosophical thinking in many directions. Even though her own work had to do with questions in logic and linguistic usage, which all serious philosophy had to deal with, she was concerned about the separation of philosophical thinking from the rest of British culture. She had written a nontechnical book in logic called *Thinking to Some Purpose*, published in 1939 in the Penguin paperback series as one means of bridging the gap.

When we turned to the question of what to do about my choice of a topic for my research, Stebbing said that she liked Mannheim's idea about Voltaire but agreed with me that I wasn't ready to tackle anything as complicated as that. She said that the eighteenth century was her favorite period in the history of philosophy. Everything was laid out so clearly. You could see the influences of the writers and philosophers on each other and the way their political and social ideas were linked to a common set of assumptions about a rational universe. Why not do a study of the concept of reason in eighteenth-century philosophy and literature, starting with John Locke and going on with Dryden and Pope and the essayists with the main emphasis on David Hume as the key figure, especially since I was already intrigued by Hume. She said that she would be happy to help me in any way she could and to act as a second tutor with MacMurray as the first.

I went back to MacMurray with an account of the talks with Mannheim and Stebbing and of Stebbing's proposal. MacMurray said that if I really wanted to look at the relation between philosophy and literature, there wasn't a better period to choose and to settle on the definition of what the eighteenth century meant by reason, rationality, science, and philosophy would give me a focal point for an interesting and useful piece of research. If Stebbing wanted to take it on, that made the idea even better, and MacMurray would enjoy working with me and with her. Even though I would have to tell Mannheim that I had decided not to do the Voltaire project, he would understand and I could count on him for advice and suggestions.

Everything had been settled within a week of my coming down from Cambridge. By that time I knew enough about the British universities and the state of British philosophy to know how lucky I was that three such distinguished and sympathetic scholars were willing to take an interest in teaching me and that I had a research project that we all wanted me to do. MacMurray said that he thought it would be better for me to work at the British Museum rather than at the University College library, since the museum had everything and was right around the corner from my flat in Russell Square. I was to start with a thorough reading of Locke's *Essay concerning the Human Understanding* and come to see him for an hour once a week through the year to talk

Russell Square colleagues (l-r): Les Mackay, Bob McCrea, Taylor, Bern Hill, 1937. Courtesy of the Taylor family.

about what I was finding out. He would leave it to me to make my own appointments with Susan Stebbing.

Let me stop here and explain something about the state of mind I am reconstructing with what I can remember of my own past. I feel a sense of continuity with the person I was then and the person I am now. In one way this has nothing to do with the study of philosophy and psychology and any conclusions I might draw from what I have learned through such study. Everyone has the sense of linkage to a self in the past that can be remembered, although the terms of the linkage do not often become self-consciously known. That kind of knowledge involves burrowing into oneself to find what is there now and how it connects with what was there before. Few people have the time and the inclination to undergo the effort at introspection, and they are busy with other things and can take the continuity of selfhood for granted. At a distance of many years and many experiences I find it intriguing to see what was happening then to a young man who, by all accounts, seems to be me at an earlier age. I feel him there, I recognize him, and I have an interest in explaining him to myself. In doing so I can see that the theory of knowledge which can help to explain that self, to me or to anyone else, was already in the process of formation.

∽

Both MacMurray and Stebbing were as surprised as Duke Ellington to come upon a doctoral student in philosophy who was a full-fledged jazz musician supporting himself by playing in nightclubs and writing for *The Melody Maker*. In England of the pre-Beatle period, jazz musicians and those who played popular music of any kind were considered members of the lower classes who, I discovered, were signed on as members of the crew when they played on shipboard and were told to use the servants' entrance and elevators when they played at hotels, clubs, or private homes. University students were just that—university students. Some of those who were poor but clever got scholarships. The others who were poor didn't, and they didn't work their way. They just didn't go.

John MacMurray discovered my other life one day in the second term of our first year together when I asked him for permission to be absent from the university for two weeks to play with the orchestra on the *Queen Mary*. At a tea given for Canadian scholars studying in London (we always went to any event where food was served), I had met a friendly shipping executive who, on learning that I played the clarinet, asked if I would like to have an audition for a position on one of the Canard liners. I thanked him and an audition was arranged. The booking agency was a one-man staff, a young man who sat at the reception desk and greeted the visitors. He took me inside to a rickety old piano, handed me the sheet music for "Rosemarie" which we then played together, followed by "Three Little Words" which we were to play by ear.

"Do you do any busking," asked my receptionist-maestro.

"I might be able to if I knew what it was," I replied.

"You know, faking it, playing what isn't written."

He did an umpy-dumpy accompaniment [*i.e., boring and repetitive*], as Duke would say, on the lower end of the piano, and I did two choruses. He said he would call me if there was anything they could do.

Three days later he did call and asked if I could substitute for an ailing tenor saxophone player in the orchestra on the *Queen Mary* for one trip. I didn't tell him that I did not own such an instrument nor that it was unlikely that I would be able to be absent from the university for two weeks. I simply said yes and was told when to be in Southampton.

Professor MacMurray was most understanding and arranged his teaching schedule so that I would miss only one tutorial session. He asked me to be ready to talk about John Locke's theory of perception when I returned from the voyage. I borrowed a tenor saxophone from a music store and went off to sea with a cabin of my own and steward to look after me. There were around two dozen musicians of various kinds on board, some of them playing for luncheon, tea, dinner, dancing in the evening, some in the tourist section, others in cabin class or first class, with a lot of doubling of instruments—trumpet players who played viola. They kept pretty busy with all that music at all those eating times, and once we set sail few of the musicians saw each other except in the groups in which they were playing.

The one person in our group I came to know well was the bass player, who had played soccer for Scotland in some of the famous matches against England. In addition to a boisterous wit which he used to make funny remarks about my being a colonial and a refugee from the Royal Canadian Mounted Police and Guy Lombardo, he could throw a ping pong ball over his shoulder and, without looking, kick it with the back of his heel in an arching curve calculated to land on the head of a designated passing dancer.

My absent colleague, the tenor saxophonist, had a crowded schedule. He played the violin all day, at lunch, tea, and dinner, then played his tenor in the first-class ballroom at ten in the evening. Since I had the good fortune not to play violin, I went to work at ten and played until midnight. During the day I swam in the pool, worked out in the gym, and studied John Locke. If the mood seized me, I could join the jazz quartet that played from midnight until two in the lounge on the top rear deck of the ship. After that we could sit around with the passengers or go down to the wireless room with the radio operators, listen to the international broadcasts, and enjoy the telephone conversations of the passengers.

The leader of our orchestra in first class was a balding, plump, flush-faced, middle-aged violinist named Bunny who played every tune at the same brisk tempo. His way of starting the band was to face us, begin bouncing up and down in tempo on tip-toe with his violin under his arm and his bowing hand spread out as if he were holding a teacup, and at the point he was ready for us to start, would say Ping . . . Pong . . . on the first and third beats while conducting us with his bouncing body and his bowing hand. He always played the first chorus himself, and once that was over he went on conducting us while facing the dancers. He played one standard jazz number a night, usually "Honeysuckle Rose." One night in a fit of enthusiasm he gave me two choruses instead of just one.

MacMurray and I had a good talk about John Locke when I got back to London and suggested that since Mrs. MacMurray played the piano, it might be pleasant for us to arrange for my tutorials to be held at the MacMurray home so that we could have some music after the tutorial sessions. For the rest of the two years of our work together, a good deal of the tutoring took place with a musical aftermath, in a few of which I taught American popular songs to John, who sang in a warm Scottish tenor, and I coached Mrs. MacMurray in the accompaniment. I tried for a while to make her into a stride pianist but she was too fond of Chopin and Debussy to spare the time for the practicing.

Taylor on board the *Lancastria*, 1937. Courtesy of the Taylor family.

MacMurray was therefore not surprised and quite understanding when, a month before the term ended, I had another request to make about going to sea. This time it was to take the post of orchestra leader for a cruising liner, the *Lancastria*,[5] which listed as her ports of call nearly every place a young man's fancy would have recommended, starting with Casablanca and the Canary Islands and going on to Venice, Naples, Dubrovnik, Brioni, back to London, then to the North Atlantic and the Baltic, with a new set of ports to visit every three weeks and a new set of passengers to take along with us. MacMurray thought it was a good idea, although he didn't think it would be wise to include it as part of the formal record of University of London's preparation for the doctorate degree. He made only two conditions. I should come to him for a two-hour tutorial in London each time the *Lancastria* returned from her three-weeks cruise and that I absorb myself thoroughly in Hume's *Enquiry concerning Human Understanding* which was the main text that we were to work on during the summer and fall terms. I was to make a similar arrangement for a regular tutorial with Professor Stebbing.

Life on board ship resembled that of a big hotel in a modern city except that the entire population moved out every five days and another 1,500 residents moved in. The musicians were of average professional ability and could play fairly well the limited repertoire demanded of them. Some of them had played on the ships for five to ten years and had lost all connection with the musicians' community of England or, for that matter, with the rest of the world outside the hull of the *Queen Mary* or *Lancastria*.

The days went by one after another with a pleasant enough routine; nothing was ever particularly urgent except for some swift chases in the four and one-half days at sea of lady passengers by musicians from one or another of the orchestras. Even that pursuit was relatively infrequent. In those days few single ladies traveled on ships by themselves.

It was as if all of us, officers, crew, and musicians were suspended in space and time and out of touch with the reality of the world's life. In the case of the musicians, most of them seemed to have given up any ambition to improve their talents as performers, and they simply stayed at sea because the living conditions and regular pay were better than they would be if they were on land. Others among them preferred to stay at sea, out of harm's way from wives whom they disliked and would have had to live with if they left the ship.

The Cunard Lines and their booking agency for musicians had a most peculiar way of arranging things at sea. They didn't select an orchestra and leader who had played together or had even met each other before the ship sailed. They must have done it all by means of a card file in the booking office. I was told to report to the ship in Southampton the day the *Lancastria* was to sail. Once I arrived on board I went to the captain's office, announced who I was, and asked where I could find my orchestra. The captain's aide didn't know but sent me on to the purser who gave me the cabin numbers of the musicians, three of them. That was it. Three.

I found a trumpet player who doubled on violin, a drummer, and an umpy-dumpy pianist who, although very nice, couldn't sight-read even the simplest piano parts, couldn't play by ear, and was incapable of improvising or embellishing in any way the piano music that lay before him. There were other indications of disasters to come. There was no place to rehearse except in the ship's dining room where we were to play for lunch, tea, and dinner and whose acoustics and location were such that whatever we played could be heard practically all over the ship. I went back to the purser to ask about where the music and music stands were located and was directed to a small room where furniture was stored and where I discovered a box of assorted orchestral parts for string trios and dance bands—nothing written for our combination and very few orchestrations of tunes necessary to include in teatime, lunch, or dinner music for a British audience on the high seas.

I wasn't prepared for the enormous amount of interest the British shipboard traveler seemed to take in having tinkling music, a sort of live Muzak, in the background for all meals at sea. It would have annoyed me to have to sit through such meals, forced to listen to the kind of thing we were capable of playing, and it annoyed me to have to play it and to take musical responsibility for what I heard my newfound orchestra members doing. I had a longing to distribute cards with the familiar request, "Don't shoot the piano player. He's doing the best he can." Later on during the first trip, as the passengers settled down, I discovered that most of them were so used to hearing music badly played in seaside restaurants on shore that they didn't mind our music. It was what they had come to expect, and we were a little better than most.

But on the first afternoon after sailing, I suddenly found myself confronted by a Major Hughes, retired British army officer newly converted to the role of cruise director aboard the *Lancastria*. Major Hughes gave orders that we were to furnish the music for the ship's first gala dinner. I explained to the major that I had just met the other members of the orchestra, that we had not sorted out the music to see what we could possibly play, and that we had no place to rehearse out of earshot of the people we would be playing for later on at dinner. It would therefore not be possible to celebrate our first night at sea with a musical treat at dinner.

Major Hughes further reddened an already ruddy complexion and assured me that he was in charge of social events on the ship and that when he gave an order, it was an order and not a request to be discussed by an orchestra leader or anybody else. I replied that I didn't take orders from strangers and that the day when retired army officers could come aboard ship and order orchestra leaders around had passed, along with the supremacy of the British Empire. I suggested that since I had signed on as a member of the crew, Hughes should go get the captain and have me put in chains.

The major saw the captain. The captain sent for me. I explained the problem. The captain agreed that it would be better not to have our musical debut made in the form of a first run-through by strangers before a live audience, and he then invited me to sit at his table since I would not be playing and would therefore be available for a dinner engagement the first night of the voyage. I accepted.

The next day I called my orchestra together and explained to them my plan. We would have only violin and piano at teatime, since there was enough violin and piano music available for the two of them to work on. There was no need for drums at lunch or tea, and only occasional need for the clarinet at any of the eating times. Since we had so few orchestrations of the tunes we needed for the evening dances, I would write out the melody lines and chords for the standard tunes—in that year "The Lambeth Walk," for example—and for the traditional jazz numbers. The pianist and the trumpet player could learn them, and we would have terribly quiet and nonobtrusive rehearsals each morning in the dining room.

We survived. I drew up a list of titles for which I wanted the music, and we sent it off to London. I worked with the pianist to enlarge his musical vocabulary and free him from his umpy-dumpness, and I maintained a steady beat of hostility toward Major Hughes. Knowing that he would do everything in his power to have Taylor and his quartet fired from the ship after our first voyage, I conferred with my friend the captain about the contribution the orchestra had made to the welfare of the passengers. I told the captain that the major would be doing his best to get rid of us and that there was a lively group of passengers led by an Australian who hated the major and that this group would write a report about how the quartet had won the hearts of the entire passenger list and was a jewel in the crown of the *Lancastria*.

Major Hughes did turn in a request to have us replaced and suffered the indignity of having it refused on the grounds that he was wrong about the orchestra. He had a few miserable things he could do to inflict his will on our lives. While the ship was in port, he ordered us to stay on the ship and play for all those mealtimes and for dancing at night, even though there was no one on board but us. To defeat that caper, we made an arrangement with one of the deck hands to let us know when the major had left the ship, which he did almost as soon as we docked in a new port, and we left too, to return a little before midnight and resume our playing as if we had been playing all the time.

During the day, aside from the rehearsals and the copying out of parts for the trumpeter and pianist, I spent my time reading Hume, often

Taylor with John MacMurray at Sarah Lawrence College, 1958. Gary Gladstone. Courtesy of Sarah Lawrence College.

sitting on the seaward side of the lifeboats, out of sight of everyone on board. I believe I did more reading and more thoughtful analysis than I would have in the British Museum had I stayed with my regular routine in London.

∽

When I recall what John MacMurray said and did at our first meeting in 1936, when I remember his face and see again the streets of Bloomsbury, the courtyard and wide steps of University College, and remember Jeremy Bentham in a glass case in the front hall dressed the way he was when he was alive and well in the early days of the college, I am reconstructing both of us in the context of that time in London and that time in my life. I am also reconstructing the history of the ideas which went to make up my intellectual development, and I can understand what I now think by what I began to think then.

As I write I find myself continually tempted to say "and then there was another happy accident," that I was ill when a child, that I met Ellington, that I went to schools with good teachers, that my mother and father and sister were warm and supportive, that because my uncle turned up a clarinet I started to play, that I won a scholarship I hadn't tried for, that the registrar told me to study philosophy, that I stumbled upon Virginia Woolf and Henri Bergson, that I left Cambridge and went down to London where John MacMurray miraculously appeared. As I look ahead at what I intend to write, I can see another set of accidents turning up. And I know that I will have to be careful not to make everything that happened, from going to Wisconsin and then to Sarah Lawrence to starting up a world college, into the story of another accident.

But when I consider my life carefully, I have to say that the most important things happened without my having had much to do with making them come about. Except for a fairly vague and romantic image of myself as a writer and musician, I had no ambition or goal I was pursuing. I did the things I enjoyed doing most and as well as I could, and the rest seemed to take care of itself. I don't necessarily recommend this to others as a way of going through life, but it does have certain advantages in achieving a peaceful state of mind.

∽

Harold Taylor would leave London in September 1939 for a research and teaching position at University of Wisconsin just days after the Nazis' invasion of Poland and England's entry into World War II. Taylor admitted, "[I] felt guilty about leaving at the time I did. I would have joined that happy little band of fighter pilots. I was the right age, an athlete, and all the rest of it. That was our way of saying, 'We are the romantics. We are now anti-fascist. We're going to show you what our generation can do.' I had that sense of loyalty to the people I left behind. Had I stayed, I think I'd have probably been killed within six months to a year."[6]

Chapter 4

The Wisconsin Years

A Serious Concern for the Relation of Thought to Action

When I went to Wisconsin and Sarah Lawrence, I didn't have a well-constructed point of view about either teaching in Wisconsin or about educational philosophy and practice at Sarah Lawrence. Over the six years at Wisconsin and first five or six years at Sarah Lawrence, most of the things that I believed in I learned through having to work them out in the hard boiled job of being president and having to decide what to do.

—Harold Taylor, interview with Michael Rossman, 1974

While the Sarah Lawrence presidency defined Taylor's professional life, the years at University of Wisconsin, in what was a chance faculty appointment, determined the direction of his academic work and proved more significant than indicated in his originally planned memoir. Taylor had mentioned that upon receiving the doctorate at University of London in 1938 his future was still unclear. From the time of his graduation through the summer of 1939, he continued to work as a jazz musician and full-time jazz news editor. He decided to seek a faculty position in the United States, believing that he could become a writer if he was employed at a college.[1] With enthusiasm and naivete—"I'd make up my mind whether or not I wanted to live the life of a university philosopher"[2]—he sent off letters, seemingly more as inquiries than formal applications, to six American universities selected from a directory at the British Museum.

Taylor was offered a one-year instructorship at University of Wisconsin beginning autumn 1939, permitting his hiring without a formal on-site interview, and subsequently a postdoctorate research fellowship for his second year. He would then receive an assistant professorship which he held until his departure from Madison to the Sarah Lawrence presidency in spring 1945 (with his Wisconsin position then temporarily filled by Alain Locke).[3] Arriving in Madison with no sense of what to expect and with no preparation for the college classroom, he was disarmed by the warmth of intellectual companionship and the casual, informal, and generous demeanor of his colleagues who were "not interested in where you came from or your credentials—only what you could do."[4] Taylor threw himself into university life in many different ways—as scholar, faculty colleague, classroom teacher, tennis coach, assistant dean of men, faculty advisor to the student newspaper, Armed Services faculty representative, and concert programmer[5]—but he always saw his activities as an extension of being a working philosopher, committed to public service and social and educational activism.

Taylor and Muriel Taylor at their Wisconsin home, 1941. Courtesy of the Taylor family.

At University of Wisconsin we were activists, fresh from the warm-hearted liberalism of Wisconsin where the progressives had had their own political party and the philosophy department in Madison was running with pragmatists and other people known to our right-wing critics as evangelical atheists. In those years the university was alive with ideas, where it was said that anyone who had been fired from elsewhere for dissident or unpopular views could find a welcome, where the university would teach anything to anyone anywhere, where Alexander Meiklejohn invented his famous Experimental College, and where C. Wright Mills was rattling his cage as a [*Department of Sociology*] graduate student in our philosophy courses.

The life in Wisconsin was one which I had always thought might be somewhere. I was made so welcomed immediately on arrival by being invited to join in the discussions about educational policy and by my seeing in reality, day after day by living in Madison, that there was a direct relationship between the work of the university and the work of governing the total society. That was an idea which I had supported, without knowing anything about its social and intellectual origins, when I was in England. I felt that not only should intellectuals take part in the political and social life in their own time, take responsibility for events and how they happen, but that the universities and colleges were the major force in developing strategies for peace and for the welfare of the human race. I'd never known any other university and any place like this one. Here was the place that was doing it. I immediately felt at home in the intellectual and social atmosphere.

I was a faithful reader of Sartre, Malraux, and Camus, and their concern for contemporary politics and social change shone not only through their work but in the way in which they put their ideas into action. So when I was teaching philosophy, this was a place where the intellectual university people were taken seriously and were invited to talk with the state legislators about education for Wisconsin. There was no exclusion of anybody's ideas, and Wisconsin in the golden age of its history was known around the world for the quality of its social thought and the quality of its scientific research. The president of the university and the governor of the state were good friends, and they thought of the university as having its campus all over the state. Two weeks after I arrived, my colleagues asked me to join the teachers' union and, as a member, to attend a hearing on legislation at the State Capitol which had to do with the future of higher education in the state. I thought, "My God, this is just exactly what a university should be."

The liberal atmosphere of teaching and learning which existed on the campus was one in which young people, whether students or teachers, could find stimulation and congenial intellectual company. My colleagues in philosophy, led by Max Otto,[6] had formed one of the most vigorous and creative groups of teachers of philosophy of any university in the country. Professor Otto's leadership was one which focused our attention on two things: the development in our students of philosophical insight and the development in ourselves of a serious concern for the relation of thought to action, of philosophy to education, of ideals to reality. We represented a variety of perspectives as we worked together, but whatever phase of the work we undertook, we were given an opportunity to express that point of view in our teaching and to enrich our own research by relating it to the teaching itself. For me, this was a liberating and rewarding experience which I was fortunate to have had.

I began lecturing to large groups of relatively unselected students. In those years, having had no guidance in the art of teaching and having had a great deal of instruction in the art of being a philosophy graduate student, which consisted of reading texts very fast, preferably commentaries on the original texts and not the originals, and being able to hand back very fast what one has read in the commentaries on the philosophers, I was in an absolutely pristine state. I had to examine in myself what it was that I knew, as a young philosophy instructor who was professionally prepared to do whatever it was that young philosophy instructors were professionally prepared to do, which is to talk to other philosophers. I had to decide what it was that I knew that could possibly be useful to these students who couldn't understand me. And I had to decide how, in my terms, I could become understandable to them.

I grew fascinated by the problems of how to get students to think, to become involved with ideas, when most didn't even know what intellectual involvement meant. We were interested in students and were interested in philosophical questions from the point of view of their relation to people's lives and to society rather than the academic philosophy usually taught in college, which accounted for the fact that there were so many students at Wisconsin interested in studying philosophy. They were looking for paths to some kind of truth and some kind of personal and intellectual stability. It was possible to arouse their interest in philosophy by dealing with them and their problems as young people in America. Philosophy became the study of issues and problems rather than just repetition of the history of philosophy.

I learned back in those early years to look at students not as opponents, not as people whom I could instruct in the things that I had been taught, but as individuals with whom it was my responsibility to work in order to raise the level of their sensibility, to deepen the depths of their awareness, to further their knowledge of a number of questions about which they had never thought before. In order for them to come to grips seriously with their own concerns and with their own lives, it was necessary that they should do the thinking. This meant that the entire educational pattern of the lecture system, the academic credit system, the examination system, and the grading system should be thrown out so that we could start all over again.

We tried new ways of teaching the students and discovered a fair number of simple devices which came naturally to some of the teachers in the philosophy department through which it was possible to reverse the usual bad effects of a system which in my judgment seemed designed to bore students and to make their knowledge trivial. Having come from the British system which operated without the continuing series of tests and without grades carried out to two decimal points, I was appalled by the American system and have remained appalled by it ever since.

Five of us in the department set out to reform completely the methods and content of the beginning philosophy courses, with some positive results which were to me astonishing. After that I got involved with the horrors of the academic advising and the obsolete deaning system and, before I knew it, I wanted to reform the whole university. Suddenly, my life changed in the autumn of 1943. I was converted overnight from a philosopher to a psychologist by signing up for a secret project with radar, and we were working out new ways of tracking enemy targets.[7] When I returned to Wisconsin from the war in 1945, I resumed my teaching.

But then I was invited to become president of Sarah Lawrence, and I accepted on the grounds that the college had within it an entire program of continuing experimentation and that there was nothing which one could not try, nothing which might not possibly be invented. For fourteen years I had a chance daily to work with the implications of a philosophy and program of education which had its roots in the Emerson-James-Dewey-Whitehead tradition and could draw on its resources and practical applications from a brilliant faculty, a lively student body, and the whole environment of New York City, the United Nations, and the suburbs, including lower-, middle-, and upper-income communities.

What I learned at Wisconsin was not only that it was possible to relate directly the work of university intellectuals to the growing problems of the society, but that I could help build an atmosphere in which students carried over into their lives the knowledge they learned in college. The university had a really quite serious influence on me—that and the fact that I realized that so much could be done informally. I appreciated the way in which members of the philosophy department greeted me and allowed me to do all the different things that I wanted to do. There was a congenial atmosphere in which I found colleagues who were as interested in some of these issues as I was. I enjoyed teaching much, and the writing I did in philosophy grew out of the courses I taught and the ideas I talked about with students. I learned more philosophy while teaching the Wisconsin students than I had during my formal education.

Whatever merit there was in the educational ideas that I explored further, they were based upon the learning experiences of those days with my colleagues in philosophy and the privilege of teaching in an institution where new ideas were encouraged and liberalism was an indigenous philosophy which permeated the social and intellectual atmosphere.[8]

~

Taylor's professional writing and research while at University of Wisconsin attended to issues of aesthetics, Hume's treatment of imagination, and the nature of philosophy in society. Yet, his experiences in the classroom caused him to discover progressive ideals and to recognize a different approach to education that, as he would later define, was "one of process and development, whether in individual human growth or in the case of whole societies."[9] He came upon this perspective not only from his experiences at University of Wisconsin but, also, from the birth of his first child while in Madison. Taylor would describe the importance of parenting and its influence on his views of instruction—namely, teaching represented an act of caring for others, yielding to a child's demands while also providing structure, love, and support. Without fatherhood, he felt he would not have understood education as a way of caring for students.[10]

Unlike many progressive educators of the 1930s and 1940s who preached Deweyan gospel, Taylor sought not to institute (or instigate) progressive education programs. He actually lived progressive education and approached projects more as an activist and adventurer than disciple or evangelist. Progressivism never consisted of specified pedagogical practices to be implemented but, more, as an openness toward experimentation. His many instructional,

Taylor with his daughters (l-r) Jennifer and Mary at Brushwood, 1951. Courtesy of the Taylor family.

social, political, and cultural experiences at University of Wisconsin arose from his curiosity as he joined with students and faculty to explore the process and development of ideas and beliefs.

Living the "Wisconsin Idea"[11] where research should be applicable to societal issues, Taylor began moving away from traditional philosophical theory and began searching for activities that expressed "ideals and means of reaching them which, in forming the core of new human institutions, will help to change the actual operating principles of society."[12] He became impatient with others in the field of philosophy who were not engaged in social action and, in a 1942 article, "What Good Is Philosophy Today?," acknowledged that too many academic philosophers "become involved in obscure professional problems which are unintelligible to the non-philosopher."[13] Accepting a larger administrative role at Wisconsin and, ultimately, leadership of an Eastern, liberal arts college represented this view that higher education offered an appropriate setting for a philosopher to engage with the world. Explaining his decision to accept the Sarah Lawrence presidency to Max Otto, he wrote that the new role afforded "a great opportunity to apply the ideals and philosophy which we *jointly share to the operation of an experimental college."*[14] *Taylor would feel his first sense of "a real vocation" being a teacher and philosopher at University of Wisconsin, and, in later years, would often use as an opening statement in his speeches (well into the 1960s) that he came before the audience as "an unreconstructed progressive [from] the golden age of Wisconsin and its State University, when the intellectuals were called upon to plunge into the problems of their society."*[15]

Chapter 5

Sarah Lawrence Remembrances
A Community in the Making

> I feel like a juggler who has set flying in the air about forty-seven different articles including Indian clubs, frying pans, golf balls, and assorted vegetables. Everything is fine as long as the assortment is on its way up, but when they all begin coming down and have to be caught and flung into the air again, the situation for the juggler becomes more involved.
>
> —Harold Taylor, correspondence to Lenore Sagalyn Cohen, 1946

Sarah Lawrence College provides the cultural and institutional context for this entire collection; yet, Harold Taylor chose not to include a chapter describing specifically his experiences as president. This decision is more than unfortunate in that he was witness to many significant events during his time at the college and was aware of various accusations if not gossip that would inevitably be attached to his administration. His thoughts would have added much to the history of Sarah Lawrence, and his reminiscences would certainly have been entertaining. I have arrayed an assortment of material, a collage of Taylor's remarks about the college, drawn from interviews, published works, correspondence, and presentations. My contextual comments have been interspersed.

"Sarah Lawrence Remembrances" presents Taylor's role as an active participant in guiding the philosophy, curriculum, and instruction of the institution and stresses the importance of experimentation with educational methods. Taylor came to the college expecting to serve as an educational leader but ultimately

found himself a fund-raiser. Reduced, in his estimation, to an administrative clerk in charge of finance and personnel, this unanticipated role along with administrative and personal tensions at the college would ultimately precipitate his resignation. This chapter does not present a sanitized portrayal of Taylor as college president; rather, "Sarah Lawrence Remembrances" reveals some issues that he confronted throughout his administration, sometimes successfully and sometimes not, and seeks to display his demeanor as an academic and president.

In today's higher education entrepreneurial climate of school rankings and standardized instruction, with an emphasis upon career training, Taylor's and Sarah Lawrence's educational beliefs and practices from the past seem foreign. However, this account is presented not for the purposes of reverie, comparison, or implementation. Democratic education communities of the 1940s and 1950s were, in many ways, refreshingly different from today's college and university programs, and readers may consider what insights from the past could be reconceived for today's college students and faculty members. I hope this chapter will encourage higher educators to examine the professional literature of progressive education at the postsecondary level. Sarah Lawrence College, upon Harold Taylor's arrival, represented a spirit of programmatic experimentation and, during his presidency, displayed how a college could address pressing social issues while adhering to a fundamental Deweyan belief of education (and democracy) as "a community in the making."

Becoming President of Sarah Lawrence College

> In terms of what I cared about in life over a whole range of ideas and values, what was being expressed by Sarah Lawrence represented what I believed. As I described my early life and the time in London and the rest, you could see that that's the direction I was moving in. But what the college did was to make it possible for me to combine all these interests and whatever energies and talents I had in making Sarah Lawrence into what Sarah Lawrence needed to become.
>
> —Harold Taylor, interview with Carole Nichols, 1985

People ask me how on earth did I ever turn up as president of Sarah Lawrence, having been a teacher of philosophy at the University of Wisconsin. One day at an invitation to lunch with Merle Curti, the Pulitzer

Prize winner for American history back in the forties and fifties, he said he just had received a letter from Sarah Lawrence College and wanted to apologize. "They're looking for a president," he said, "I mentioned your name." I said, "Well, that was a ridiculous thing to do. I don't like college presidents. I never met one I approved of, and it's not the line of work that I'm interested in." Merle said, "Well, I knew you'd feel like that, but I had to say somebody." Helen Lynd, a faculty member of philosophy at Sarah Lawrence, had friends out at Wisconsin, including the chairmen of the political science and psychology departments and the president of the university, and she wrote to them, too. As it happened, they were all friends of mine who knew my work well. I had to know the president simply to get his car away from him [*to drive the Pro Arte Quartet to performances*]. They all wrote back, "There's one person out here—Taylor—but he's too young and he wouldn't leave and he doesn't like administration. But here he is." So the Sarah Lawrence College search committee of faculty members and trustees wanted to investigate further the person who was unanimously voted as the one they should have, and they sent Helen Lynd out to talk to me. I apologized for her having come all that long way, and I said, "No, I do not like that kind of work. I will not be a college president. I would love to talk to you about the college and about what we're doing in Wisconsin. But I'm not going to have my name stand."

Helen didn't put up with any obstacles in the course of either her thought or her political actions. She spent a couple of days around the university finding out what made me want to stay. She discovered that I was deeply involved with what I was doing, but that she felt I was wrong in thinking so negatively about being a president. So she asked for another interview, which I graciously granted, and she said, "Well, I checked about you. While you say you don't like people who make speeches and you don't like making them, you were speaking at the White Water High School last week to the graduating class, and you apparently did that on your own and enjoyed it. You're coaching the tennis team, but we have tennis courts at Sarah Lawrence." Step by step she answered every objection that I made. Then she asked if I would come and look at the college in any case and give them my advice as to what new things they should be doing. I went out to the college [*arriving April 12, 1945*] and was swept away with enthusiasm for what Sarah Lawrence faculty members were doing.

I took a half-hour walk with Joe Campbell. If Joe wants to persuade you about something, he does it! By the end of one walk down by the wisteria trees, I was beginning to change my mind. Joe said he wouldn't teach anywhere else but Sarah Lawrence. I met faculty members, alumnae, and the trustees, and I asked the questions I wanted to know: why there were only two Black students in the whole college among the three hundred students there. I asked why the tuition was so high since that kept people from coming. It was explained to me that Sarah Lawrence had mortgages rather than financing, a kind of negative endowment. It didn't make me any happier about being the new president. So we talked about that, and I said, "Well, my image of what I want to do with my life is that I'm a scholar and a teacher, and I don't want to take the time to do all the administrative things." So the answer to that was that I could make my own schedule. If I wanted to have two days or three weeks or whatever, it was up to me to make the time, and I could read and write to my heart's content. For example, it was suggested that I just take one day a week where I couldn't be found. They would give me a room in the library where I would have a typewriter and the service of the librarian and then it would be—"the president's thinking!" Everybody would have to tip-toe around the campus so as not to disturb the president. Well, we found each other's company quite delightful, and I changed my mind about considering being president. We all signed up and I had my Thursdays for thinking.[1]

Inauguration and Early Days at the College

> At a special meeting of the Board of Trustees of Sarah Lawrence College held in New York last Wednesday evening, the Board voted unanimously to invite you to accept the presidency of the college. After considering over 200 candidates, the Committee on a New President came to the conclusion that you more than any of the others combine those qualities of scholarship, integrity, personality, and understanding of the future possibilities of our college that will be needed in the years ahead.
>
> —Burton P. Fowler, chair of the Sarah Lawrence College board of trustees, May 11, 1945

Harold Taylor's selection as president of Sarah Lawrence was announced to faculty and students on May 21, 1945, with much clamor from the national press since, at age thirty, he was considered the youngest college president in the country at that time. A New York Times reporter would later write of the unanimous vote "to give the presidency to a 30-year-old professor of philosophy who had never done anything spectacular, who had no particular reputation, and who had never wanted to be a college president. They chose him because he had a deep conviction about progressive education and great confidence in its possibilities and future and because he looked upon the college and its organization as a cooperative enterprise in which he would participate with the rest of the community."[2] Support at the college was strong and, while much was made of his youth, Taylor's characteristic enthusiasm and charm had also captivated the campus prior to his arrival as president.

Yet, while applauded and warmly received during the interview process, Taylor most likely would have been somewhat startled by correspondence he received after the announcement of his hiring. Beatrice Doerschuk, the director of education (i.e., the provost) of Sarah Lawrence, wrote on behalf of the search committee informing him "that it is wiser not to have an inauguration" on the grounds that since he was so new to the college, he would not be representing the beliefs of the faculty. Doerschuk maintained, "Because we want to stand with you when you speak as president of the college, we believe it is better not to make a general public statement of your position now, but sounder to wait until you and the college have had a chance to know each other."[3] Taylor responded in an undated letter suggesting otherwise, characteristic of what would become his straightforward administrative style as president. In his letter to Doerschuk, he identifies many of the educational values that would define his beliefs and would guide his work for the rest of his career.

Dear Beatrice,

Thank you for your frank comments on the question of the inauguration. I shall be equally frank.

The practical considerations involving travel, limited accommodation, limited number of persons attending, and the lack of an assembly hall are good reasons for eliminating the inauguration, or at least, one kind of inauguration. When I think of being excused from the nervous strain, personal expense, and responsibility which an affair of that kind would entail, I have a wonderful sense of release.

However, it seems to me that question has to be decided by asking what benefits would accrue to the college by a celebration marking the formal beginning of a new period in the history of the institution. These benefits might be (a) increased interest on the part of other educators in the work we are doing; (b) a revival of interest in, and commitment to, the college by its graduates; (c) attention of educational foundations, social agencies, and individuals who may wish to help the college, drawn to our existence and ideas; (d) publicity in the press, which may help in accomplishing the three ends listed above.

If these benefits are important, and I think they are, the next question is, What would be the most effective way of obtaining them? One way is the conventional, let's-all-stifle-in-our-robes-and-have-a-procession kind. It has certain advantages. But we could do something which would be more appropriate as an inauguration for a president of our place. We could hold a one- or two-day series of meetings of liberal educators, select topics for discussion in the field of teaching literature, science, the arts, and social studies. We might have papers, something from John Dewey (poor man, it would be a shame to ask him but I'm sure he would help), V. T. Thayer, Sidney Hook, and others whom we could find by mutual effort. The papers could be published in an informal volume, invitations could be sent to alumnae in the area as well as any other people whom we thought might be interested, and the occasion might be one of general rejoicing and get us all ready to tackle a difficult period ahead with a feeling of union with others in a common enterprise.

My part in such an affair would be to read an essay on some aspect of the philosophy of education, to discuss it with those who came, and to be host to all good people who were wise enough to come. These could include not only administrative officers, presidents, and the like, but also thinkers and teachers. Probably a list of fifty people who think creatively in education would exhaust the available number, and we would not need to face any problems connected with ODT [*Office of Defense Transportation*], troop movements, or accommodations.

The institutions from which we invited our people could be asked to pay the expenses of their representatives, as is customary with inauguration proceedings. Since such a program will take a good deal of planning, a date in the spring of 1946 might be most appropriate, perhaps at the end of the spring term, so that we could do commencement and then go right on inviting some parents to attend discussions of the role of the parent in education.

This brings me to a point made in the fourth and fifth paragraphs of your letter, to which you refer as the main issue. To have an inauguration of the kind suggested above would mean that any public statement made by the new president would come after he and the college had had a chance to know each other. But I would very much dislike to see it start a new tradition of appointing a president whom it could not trust to speak at a public inauguration without first being groomed for a year or two. It is surely a very curious reason for not inaugurating a president. What you refer to as my educational past has a good many things in it which are so firmly embedded that I doubt very much whether ten, twenty, or thirty years will make much difference to their future. Some of these are the social responsibility of the intellectual, the non-existence of absolutes, the necessity of the use of scientific method to discover truth, the value of aesthetic experience, the sociobiological character of man, the importance and dignity of the individual personality, the theory of education as growth, and so on. I suspect that I'm stuck with these for good, and that they are the things I shall talk and write about in their bearing upon education.

I expect you will be with me in what I say to the public, unless I have made a horrible mistake about this whole venture. But I do not want to feel that there *must* be a one-to-one correspondence between what I say about the college and what the faculty thinks, although there probably will be, due to the fact that questions of policy will be decided by constant joint discussion. When I speak, I shall speak as a philosopher who is trying to get clear on certain problems and issues. Since I know we share the same general convictions about what the issues and problems are and how to solve them, I know that everything I do will show the marks of discussion and consultation with all of you, and that it will be a very rare occasion when you will not be with me in what I say, since in a very real sense it will be you who are speaking. But I refuse to be un-inaugurated because my educational past has not been identical with yours. It may be that that may turn out to be a virtue.

All this, of course, is not what you meant. You meant that you and others among the faculty have been working with these educational problems for fifteen years or more, that you have knowledge of the road you have taken, a sense of the direction of the institution at present, and some ideas about its direction in the future. Therefore, in view of the fact that an inaugural address might be expected to contain some of this information, you think that I should live with the ideas and get the feel of the college before making any predictions, or before volunteering any information about where we are now. This seems to be a narrow conception of what should be done by an inaugural address. I hadn't thought of talking about the institution itself but, rather, about some of the characteristics of American life and thinking which express themselves in various ways in our educational system, with a few indications of the value of a naturalistic or progressive point of view in achieving ends of the importance for American life. The inaugural addresses of people like Mommsen at Berlin or Van Hise at Wisconsin tried to contribute to the body of original thinking on matters connected with education; Mommsen discussed the nature and scope of history and philosophy and Van Hise the vision of the state university as the democratic counterpart of the English aristocratic private school system.[4] I felt that it might be possible to say something sensible about "general questions of educational philosophy" by discussing some of the problems of philosophy which have a bearing on education.

On the other hand, I would very much like to know what you all think, since the above arguments simply represent my state of mind at this point. It may be that the trustees will have some ideas on the subject which they will wish to express.

With very best regards, Harold Taylor[5]

Ultimately, a conventional "let's-all-stifle-in-our-robes-and-have-a-procession kind" of inauguration was held on October 21, 1945, with over one thousand students, parents, and educators in attendance. While Doerschuk and others may have been concerned that Taylor would misrepresent the beliefs of the Sarah Lawrence community, he presented himself as "a philosopher who is trying to get clear on certain problems and issues," and his address attended to more universal themes—the significance of the university as a place for experimentation, the search for new knowledge, and the importance of social agency and social action for the academic and the student. His speech underscored if not served to further a sense of responsible engagement in the social sphere for the college, its faculty, and its students and responsive social action that would become a way of life for Taylor long after his departure from Sarah Lawrence.

Harold Taylor, the new president of Sarah Lawrence, 1945. Hone Photographers, courtesy of the Taylor family.

> Taylor wrote to his University of Wisconsin mentor, Max Otto, the next day describing the inauguration:
>
> The afternoon was bright and sunny, with the autumn leaves sailing around and the lovely mellow lights which the afternoons have this time of year. The thing that touched me most about the occasion was the point at which the chorus suddenly burst into song in their fresh young voices and, after singing a short Bach chorale [from St Matthew Passion], sang about how everybody had something to sing about. The words they sang were written by Genevieve Taggard who teaches here, and the music [Holiday Song] was written by William Schuman who was here until last year. . . . The whole day was a moving experience to me. I think I realized for the first time the depth of my responsibility, not only to this community but to all the people who are trying to do the right things.[6]

Introductory Talks to Students and Faculty

> Whatever else can be said about this college, it is never dull, it is never quiescent, it is never static. It contains a body of beliefs about human values, and it demonstrates a variety of ways in which moral and intellectual virtues can be achieved. Its ideas are provocative, creative, and important.
>
> —Harold Taylor, "Sarah Lawrence Reconsidered," 1958

There was much press about hiring the "boy wonder" at Sarah Lawrence, with articles appearing in national news magazines and local papers—Time, Life, *the* New York Times, Daily Herald, *and the* PM *newspaper. Much was made of Taylor's youth and appearance.* Life *magazine would write, "His extreme handsomeness . . . even put movie stars to shame" and, representative of the misogyny of the time, "Sarah Lawrence picked him as successor to spinster Constance Warren, its president since 1930. Taylor is only 30 years old and therefore one of the youngest college presidents in the country. He is easily one of the best looking."[7]* Time *magazine reported, "As informal and curious as the liveliest of his students and only a scant dozen years older than most of them, handsome, curly-headed President Taylor fits easily into Sarah Lawrence's small seminars and faculty evenings where students and tutors relax and argue in easy chairs or sprawled on floors."[8]*

Such a reception from the press would haunt Taylor during his time at Sarah Lawrence and beyond and, while he developed a reputation in academic circles for addressing difficult administrative issues and questioning many of the generally accepted practices in higher education, his youth and "golden boy" reputation was said by some to undermine his stature among his former peers in the field of philosophy. What follows are Taylor's thoughts, written as private correspondence to University of Wisconsin friends, at the beginning of his presidency as he describes with excitement and fear his first meetings with Sarah Lawrence students and faculty.

This past week has been one of the more rugged ones in my short life. On Monday we had the Convocation marking the opening of college, and our boy had to say something which could sound sensible to the students and the high-powered faculty. I never had to hit against this kind of pitching. Photographers were there from *Life* and from *PM*. Right in the middle of my talk, just when I had begun to discuss world-shaking ideas, the *PM* man shot off a flash lightbulb two feet from my nose. This seemed funny to the students and for the next five minutes, since the *PM* man went right on shooting, it was a straight fight between photography and philosophy for the audience. In the scuffle I lost the only two good ideas I had in the whole goddamned speech. I must ask you to pick up *Life* gingerly next week and to bear with me when you see the college and myself plastered all over its pages. We are all frightened here about what they might do to us in their inimitable way.[9]

~

I am becoming more and more alarmed about what sort of person I must be, if the only impression the writers assigned to cover me get is one of a frivolous character who is turned loose in a girls' school. They all seem to be trying to pin that kind of label to our boy Harold and there doesn't seem to be anything I can do to stop it, although I have tried deep frowns, dull talk, and a dignified posture to discourage them from thinking me in the slightest degree alive. I have now given up trying to do anything about it and intend just to do dignified things which cannot be reported in any other way than stuffy. I am living at about three times the tempo that I ever have before and find the most difficult thing to do is to make speeches which are not just mumbling over educational cliches. There doesn't seem to be much chance to develop into too bad of a president since I have found a group of people here who are quite eager to point out the ways in which I might go wrong, by caustic comments, to prevent me from doing anything too bad.[10]

~

The college is a place where people really know about education, and I have learned a good deal already. There are philosophers by the dozens among the faculty although they teach courses in English, science, and painting. The students themselves are creative and publish a first-rate literary magazine, of which I will send you a copy when it is published. When we have committee meetings to decide about curriculum, or about who should come here to lecture or about almost anything, what happens is that we have good discussions about all the things which you and I used to like to talk about. It is a community of wise and learned people who believe in liberal social action. I hope to be able to think better and to write better after having associated with them.[11]

The Context and Practices of Sarah Lawrence College

> Sarah Lawrence was less a theoretical than a practical approach to progressive ideas. When I arrived, it was a going concern basically with the present pattern of small classes, conferences, work in contemporary arts, work in science, what would be the most important thing for the student—what attracted me to the college was the excitement of seeing a whole institution trying new ideas.
>
> —Harold Taylor, "Conversation with Harold Taylor," 1958

Sarah Lawrence College had existed for nineteen years before Taylor's arrival and was finding its way as an experimental school. President Constance Warren's 1940 book, A New Design for Women's Education, *describes her beliefs and activities at Sarah Lawrence through a collection of thoughtful anecdotes of general practices.[12] Taylor would contextualize Sarah Lawrence's program into a larger theoretical realm of progressivism while bringing national attention to the college.[13] Yet, he acknowledged the difference between the* public image of his role and his actual role. "The public assume that the young boy wonder had done all of this work because the college hadn't been written about. I would be falsely given credit for starting the college."[14] He was criticized by faculty for taking credit for "inventing" the Sarah Lawrence program; however, from this material, he talks of being educated by the job and by faculty and students. In fact, perhaps the most distinctive aspects of the Sarah Lawrence program, all underway before Taylor's arrival, were the donning system, field work, and the first-year exploratory courses.[15] As president of an experimental college, Taylor defined his role publicly not as designer but as a guide and an advocate and spokesperson for progressive education at the postsecondary level. The following excerpts portray Taylor's enthusiasm for the experimental aspects of Sarah Lawrence and his willingness to be educated by the position and his colleagues rather than insisting that the faculty bend to his will.[16]

Sarah Lawrence College's educational philosophy was formed by a series of historical accidents. Mr. William Lawrence didn't like Vassar College, and when Mr. MacCracken, the president of Vassar,[17] asked him for money, he said, "I wouldn't give you anything. I sent my daughters to you, and they turned out to be man-hating women who keep giving me arguments." But then Mr. MacCracken suggested they start a new college for women who wouldn't talk back to him, I guess, at dinner. Mr. Lawrence put up $750,000 in stocks and bonds and his estate to start the college, but there was no process of study with the board of trustees in order to decide what kind of college it would be. Mr. Lawrence had offered his estate in Bronxville to the people who were starting Bennington. He had heard William Kilpatrick and some of the others talk about what they wanted to do,[18] and I imagine that it was the enthusiasm of the Bennington people for that kind of experimental college which made Mr. Lawrence excited about doing one of his own at Bronxville.

There was a curious twist to the results of Mr. Lawrence's thoughts about founding the college. It wasn't a feminist point of view he was taking. It was the view that there was an education appropriate for women because they were girls and because occupationally, vocationally, and in their personal lives, they wouldn't be active in business or in social agencies or in the other places occupied by men. Therefore, Mr. Lawrence felt there should be an education which dealt with what they were going to be doing in their lives, and not a masculine curriculum.

Mr. Lawrence stumbled into a radical view of education in that if you wanted to have somebody who is self-fulfilled and who is an interesting person and not a wife and mother of the ordinary kind, then the regular curriculum of a college wasn't appropriate. His image was of a college where young women would go, study the things that interested them the most, and not worry about taking academic credits or degrees. Originally, there were no degrees given and only after Sarah Lawrence had been going for a few years was the two-year diploma awarded. As I say, he stumbled on a radical view. Once you begin recruiting faculty members, women or men, who subscribe to that conception of education [based on the interests of students], then you're off and running as a progressive college.

In most colleges, there was very little emphasis on seeing the student as an adult and for giving students enough freedom. Sarah Lawrence students were treated as adults, making them self-governing, taking their choice of classes seriously, and planning their courses around their interests and capabilities. In the beginning, the college was not based on a theory of political democracy as much as on the fact that if you think about students more and subject matter less, you give students more responsibility to make a new system. If students are to be taken as individuals with their differences respected, then you plan a program that treats them as individuals with different aims and capabilities. MacCracken knew the regular system, and he had a sense of what could happen if it were changed.

When I arrived at Sarah Lawrence in September 1945, Constance Warren had been in office for fifteen years, and there were three or four colleges that came along in the late thirties which were progressive, including Bennington, Goddard (which put a heavy emphasis on field work), Antioch, and one or two other places, in particular Black Mountain, where the philosophy of education was one of badly organized anarchy. Some of the best work in the arts in America came out of Black Mountain, and it was an experiment which was considered to be just a little wilder than ours.

Also, there was a right-wing perspective in the Great Books program at St. John's College.[19] So there was a national controversy about educational theory with lots of publications and lots of conferences. The country's higher educators were seriously divided between those considered on the left wing of the progressive movement and those on the right wing who figured that St. John's was the answer with Alexander Meiklejohn, their chief spokesman, Scott Buchanan, Stringfellow Barr, and a group of educators at St. John's College.[20] They had an influence on the University of Chicago and Robert Hutchins's program which was all-required courses for the first two years, and then students could go on to graduate school if they passed the BA degree tests. That was a radical shift for most college programs, but it was a way of applying all the courses that were considered valuable by the University of Chicago faculty, rather than allowing the freedom of choice that we favored and which worked so well in the more open-ended, generous attitude toward education. To put the division sharply, University of Chicago faculty and St. John's fellows thought of the mind as a rational unit which needed to be sharpened and trained and put to work on abstractions. When students went through the major philosophical concepts in discussion with their teachers, the philosophers of the Great Books would train the mind to function both in society and in the student's life.

It was in that milieu of educational controversy, with the left wing doing the Black Mountain approach and Sarah Lawrence being not quite fully conceived as a formal progressive institution. We were more like Bennington College, having been formed to release the restrictions on the curriculum, to bring the creative arts to a central position in the lives of the students, and to conceive of a college as a center for creative thinking and creative action as well as for the arts in general. The sciences were taught as a form of art, if I may be allowed that ambiguity. That is to say that when one worked in chemistry, it was not to become a chemist in the formal sense of the chemistry courses at the big universities, but it was to understand science at a deeper level and to understand structures in the universe. We were trying to develop a total curriculum that represented a performance art. Students performed the curriculum rather than observing it. Students were counted on to make their personal contribution to the class rather than receiving lectures and receiving the insights at second hand. Students had to provide their own thoughts and were responsible for helping other people in the class to achieve some degree of clarity about what the insights were.

The aim at Sarah Lawrence was one that tried to develop certain qualities which go beyond the techniques of living. The college was trying to give to each student a sense of purpose and an experience with serious intellectual activity. If we were going to do that, we needed to help her to choose what kind of life she wanted to live, how to find the things which could mean most to her, situations which came from serious intellectual activity—which is why we did not have required courses or think of education as subject matter. We were interested most of all in the students and their total life. College courses were not chopped into subjects. Students worked in only three courses during the college year. There were very few lectures, most classes were taught by seminar methods, each student usually had a research project of her own, and, instead of examinations, reports were made by teachers on the individual student's work.

Since there were no formal departments or academic rank from instructor to full professor, the faculty were teachers in their own right and members of a community of equals, each of whom were responsible for their own students and for creating their own courses, and the college ran as a radical democracy for both the faculty and students (the students were also self-governing) with the president as a kind of chair of the whole rather than a separate administrative officer. Since there were no examinations or grades or test scores, students learned to judge the quality of their own work with the help of their teachers and fellow students. Since there were no required courses, the curriculum for each student was built by a series of conscious choices made by the student with intelligent and informed advice from teachers who acted in the role of tutors and mentors. Since the arts of theater, dance, music, painting, sculpture, design, and the graphic arts were central to the over-all curriculum, formal studies in the arts and humanities could be combined with the actual practice of the art form itself.

Our classes met only once a week, and this was an occasion for sharing ideas, not for being presented with information or lecture material by the teacher. In between the weekly classes, the student was digging up the information she needed for the class meeting, doing assignments, and getting ready to meet. Class time was wasteful if it was just an occasion for telling things to students; they could get the information better by themselves. Then when the class met, they could share ideas, ask questions, discuss and discover what it was in the material that was most important. But they discovered it for themselves. They weren't told what is important beforehand. The concern for the individual student expressed itself in the fact that each student had a don who dealt in a friendly way with all the problems the student brought and the fact that there was one teacher for every six students. The classes were organized in groups of not more than fifteen. Each student's program was carefully selected through mutual consultation between the don and the student, and joint committees of faculty members and students were elected to work together on community policies.

~

A great many people have mistaken our educational philosophy here for that practiced at Stephens College and similar places, where the needs of women were narrowly conceived as those related to the function of housewife and mother. [But] whenever you conceive the curriculum to be a program of college life fitted to the needs of the individual student, you depart from the academic curriculum and introduce any number of subjects, activities, experiments, and programs which are designed to ask what the young people themselves believe that they need and to discover what guidance we can give them in helping them become clear as to the kind of education most appropriate to their lives. In other words, if we begin with the student and move outward into the curriculum, we develop a program of education which includes a preparation for family and community life as well as for a career. Where the Sarah Lawrence program departs from other ideas about education is in its relating of courses and teaching to contemporary life and to those parts of the liberal arts and sciences which can yield the most understanding of contemporary society.

When there is a sense of educational purpose on the part of faculty, the curriculum and the organization of the college will be the outcome of the creative intelligence of the teachers and students as applied to the development of their own community. Too often, members of college faculties take no part in the formation of educational policy. They regard the discussion of educational questions as the function of deans and their own role as that of teaching subjects. This is partly due to the training they have had in the graduate school programs, where scholarship is so often divorced from learning and teaching. But it is also due to the fact that the conventional college is organized as a hierarchy, and that the senior members of the faculty, departmental chairs, and the administrative officers hold the power and set the rules by which the rest of the faculty must play if they are to rise in the system. This often produces a form of cynicism which leads those who have ideas for the improvement of the curriculum to mumble them in private to their students but to take no responsibility for helping to change the college program in an educationally valuable direction. The most significant thing about Sarah Lawrence was its advanced educational experiments, its social idealism, and its concern for the individual student. As far as the educational philosophy and practices were concerned, these were designed to develop in each student a fund of knowledge and an inquiring attitude of mind.

The social idealism involved the college in putting responsibility for personal behavior upon each student, both in classroom work and in college life. Accordingly, there were no housemothers, deans, or disciplinarian figures on the campus. Each house was responsible to an elected house president who sat with the Student Council. The students themselves were a functional part of the planning for the college, through their own committees working with the faculty to decide college issues. The college selected its student body purely on the basis of the ability of the individual student, without any regard to race, color, or religion. Since there was no faculty rank among the professors, a faculty-elected Appointments Committee worked with the president to determine salaries. College policies were settled by a joint committee consisting of students, faculty, the director of education [*the provost*], and the president.

The character of the college has been created, not from a strict educational doctrine as such, but by the free intermingling of a diversity of ideas and people, by the fusion of many ideas into a common aim. The common aim was to develop an institution where the liberal arts and sciences would flourish at the highest level of excellence, and where each student may have the fullest opportunity to use her talents and to enlarge her view of the possibilities of human life. This was why our curriculum and our educational program has taken the form it now has, and why the philosophy of experimentation was basic to the life of the institution.

Sarah Lawrence is known as an experimental college and in particular ways is a progressive college. It has been praised, criticized, defended, understood, misunderstood, deplored, loved, respected, damned, and admired. I think that the variety in the responses to the college by the general public is due to the variety of things which go on at Sarah Lawrence, each of them touching at some point the interests and concerns of those who hear about the educational program.[21]

Taylor with Frank Lloyd Wright, commencement, May 1958. Courtesy of Susan Greenburg Wood.

I can remember the day Frank Lloyd Wright came to town and not only wandered among the audience during the pre-commencement assembling until he had to be taken by the arm and put into his place in the academic procession, but disappeared off the terrace as soon as he got to his seat. When asked by the president [*Taylor*] what should be said to the audience about his absence from the commencement proceedings, he replied that they should be notified that he was neither ill nor did he have to go to the bathroom, that he found other speakers boring and would be back when his turn came in the program. The president notified the audience to this effect, and sure enough, Mr. Wright made his appearance at his assigned time, having spent the interlude wandering around the ground floor of Westlands, where, lucky us, the piano was locked, and then complimented the college on its green trees and expressed delight that he had the opportunity to talk to so many young prospective home-builders before they had had a chance to hire an architect.

—Harold Taylor, "A Garland for Mrs. Stone," 1973

Discovering a Role as President

> No idea or set of ideas belongs to the president, even though he may sometimes be the first to make suggestions. Ideas belong to those who have the responsibility for carrying them out and those who make the commitment and spend the energy in doing so.
>
> —Harold Taylor, "The Task of College Administration," 1950

While often compared to Robert M. Hutchins as another thirty-year-old "boy wonder" who had become a higher education president, Taylor was different in ways other than ideology. Hutchins accepted the presidency of University of Chicago in 1929 after having served as the dean of the Law School at Yale University. Taylor accepted the presidency of Sarah Lawrence after having served as an assistant professor at University of Wisconsin for merely four years (being off campus for sixteen months during that time for military service). While much was made of his youth, with Taylor turning thirty-one in less than a month after taking office, he may well have been one of the few, if not the only, assistant professors in the country to have been selected for the presidency of a nationally known college or university. As he readily admits, he learned to be a president while being a president.

Taylor wrote about the college and popularized its ongoing experimentation while working with and assisting the faculty as they explored and developed new projects and programs. During a 1974 oral history session, Taylor discussed his approach to the presidency and described how he became known as "that's the one from Sarah Lawrence."

I had developed a style of teaching and organizing education for myself with the help of my colleagues in the philosophy department that gradually formed some views about what was wrong with the University of Wisconsin and what should be done instead. I thought my way through to the importance of having a completely open elective system, but I hadn't looked at any of the details. I was just moving in the general direction of a much more open and informal progressive philosophy. Sarah Lawrence put into words and into reality a lot of the general ideas that I had before I arrived but had no idea how to work them out. What do you do when you don't have exams? I never thought my way through that. So as I lived in the college and went to committee meetings and occasionally taught classes when teachers were away or when they would invite me in to take over a class on a given day, I became familiar with all of the aspects of a college program. While I believed before that painting, theater, sculpture, music, and the creative arts should be a central part of the curriculum, I had never been in an institution where that was the case. So I went to classes.

I learned technical solutions to the problems of a progressive system. We had a reporting system in which each faculty member and don reported twice a year. They would write a sketch of the progress of the student up to that point—not so much evaluative but more like coaching the student. It was a perfectly adequate and important substitute for an exam. A typical class would meet once a week from an hour and a half to two hours and then each student would have a conference with the faculty member for the course some other time during the week. Students would also have conferences on a fairly regular basis with their individual dons who would be responsible for how they were doing in a total sense.

At Sarah Lawrence, I was taught by the position. I was open to what comes next, but very seldom did I have a closed idea about what should happen or how things should be done (although I always had strong convictions about how I wanted to do it). So, for example, my first year I decided I would have regular meetings with the student council. Before that my predecessor had appropriate relations with the student council but only met with the students when invited and when there was an issue on their agenda. I decided I would meet with the editor of the student newspaper, the president of the student council, and a few other students regularly once a week.

I didn't sit down and say that now that I am a president I must do this or that. I just thought it was a natural thing to do if I was going to stay in touch with the general mood, ideas, and convictions of the student body. I can still remember the first meeting I had with the student council, just a year after World War II ended, on the question of whether maids should be brought back to take care of the living rooms and whether waitresses be brought back to wait on students in the dining room. I had assumed that when I first visited the college, there was a Quaker work camp arrangement. It never occurred to me that they would have paid waitresses. During the war, since there was such a labor shortage, everyone in the college donated two to three weeks of their time to wait on tables. I assumed that was part of the philosophy of the college. So the students asked me to talk to them, and they had voted that the waitresses and maids be brought back. I said, "My God, what type of college is this. Where are you going to get $75,000—that's how much it would cost—to do this. The college is already broke and the tuition is the highest in the country. How would you like me to be going around raising money for Sarah Lawrence and my big pitch would be that the students want to get the waitresses back into the dining room." Well, we really were going back and forth. Two or three students were tough anti-administration people. It didn't matter that I was just a new boy coming in with all the fuss made over me.

They said, "Well, if it is the highest tuition in the country, then we should get some service." I said, "I'll tell you, I'm not going to lift a finger to get this money. If you want to conduct a fund-raising program, you have a perfect right to do so. But just don't count me as part of it. Tell your parents and anyone in the alumnae that you want $75,000 for the budget so that you can be served by waitresses and have your rooms cleaned by maids." They just had never heard anyone talk like that. They assumed a student democracy was a student council making its own legislation, but they didn't recognize that they were part of a community larger than the narrow limits of their own thinking. So, I left and said let me know how it comes out. About two weeks later when I met with the president of the student council, she said that they had reversed the vote and decided to continue the work program.

From that point on I realized that students had no conception of how the college worked or what the social philosophy of that kind of community meant. I think had I not jumped into the middle when I first started, I might have had the sour, internally quarreling, the "who do they think they are" type of attitude that develops instead of being part of a whole community and being willing to wait on tables because it's part of the ethos.

With my egalitarian convictions, there I was in what was a college where the daughters and the occasional son of the rich were enrolled. But after that first year, I realize that the finances of the college were a key point in making it possible for us to create an institution that I could be proud of. I loved the faculty and students were marvelous, and there was nothing wrong just because students happen to have wealthy parents. But I decided that one of the first jobs that needed to be done was to enlarge the variety of the student body—that meant getting scholarship money for the deliberate recruitment of Black students and students from lower income brackets. And it meant doing a lot of other things that had not been done with enough vigor. It also meant having an implicit social philosophy for which the student council and the student body in general had some sense of responsibility to society itself. Of course, I could do a lot of things back then because I was new and these were all programs that had never been done before. There wasn't any opposition because there was no set pattern about how the president should behave, and I always took it through the faculty and student council. Obviously, I wasn't trying to control anybody. I just had these ideas and wanted to try them out, and I was unpretentious about the way I presented them.

When I started talking educational philosophy, making speeches, and doing lectures, I was really drawing conceptually on what I had learned. I must have made ten to fifteen speeches in education my first year. I had to draw generalizations of the wider significance of what we were doing at Sarah Lawrence. If I were to come as the president of Sarah Lawrence to the PTA in Yonkers or a national conference of associate principals of schools in New York, then I had to do more than just tell them what we did in terms of the mechanics of how the college worked. I found myself more and more talking about national issues and educational change in general using what I knew to be true about the way I considered education to be done from the experience at Sarah Lawrence. I was being invited because I was seen to be a leading progressive among the college presidents. I really hadn't written enough to be viewed as a leader, but I was in all the news magazines, *Look* and *Life*, and on the radio a lot. For one thing, there weren't very many presidents around who produced any kind of copy. If they were asked questions, they would give simple answers. I can recall for example there was a survey of the opinions of college presidents on whether faculty members should be allowed to teach if they were in the Communist Party. I was the only one who said, "Why of course, a person's political affiliation should not determine his status as a scholar." That caused the fur to fly around, but the others all said no. I found myself in all sorts of public controversies, so I became known as "that's the one from Sarah Lawrence" because my point of view was then associated with the college's.[22]

President Taylor with pipe, ca. 1956. Gary Gladstone, courtesy of Sarah Lawrence College.

The Changing Role of the President

The college president of the second half of this century . . . is called upon to administer an organization which contains, among other things, a real estate development, a public relations program, a fund-raising and financial apparatus, and a population ranging from 500 to 40,000 in size lodged in a chain of small hotels. He is more like the mayor of a small town than an intellectual leader, more like the executive of a business corporation than an educator. He talks about money, while bankers, politicians and industrialists have the privilege of talking about education.

—Harold Taylor, "College President—
Not Just a Fund-Raiser!," 1959

Taylor's presidency occurred during an era of the professionalization of colleges and universities as roles and expectations for higher education administrators became more formal and standardized. Yet, throughout his time at Sarah Lawrence, he lived a life as an academic and public intellectual while his role shifted from educational leader to full-time administrator and fund-raiser. He saw himself, however, as a working academic first and as an administrator second. Perhaps since he had never planned to become a college president nor did he seek out the Sarah Lawrence position, he viewed his post more as a faculty member helping both students and colleagues rather than as an administrator managing a college. Similar to the presidential careers of Robert M. Hutchins at University of Chicago and James Conant at Harvard University (whom on most occasions he viewed as adversaries), Taylor's intellectual breadth caused him to reexamine the purpose of a college and liberal education and to speak to students, faculty, and the general public.²³ And, as with Hutchins and Conant, Taylor objected to, if not sought to redefine, the emerging bureaucratic expectation of the college presidency.

Taylor described his personal conflicts with the expectations of the presidency during a conversation with John Dewey.

[John Dewey] wanted to know was I happy as a president and did I miss teaching philosophy? He would ask these questions as a friend, an older friend, about the younger one, and would give me a kind of fatherly warning about being president. He said, in one conversation, "I think you will know the time to leave the presidency because you will have learned all you could learn, and you will have given them all that you can give them. For goodness sake, don't stay too long because what you are learning is crucial to your development as a philosopher and educator. You are learning the operational side of ideas, and there is no other way you can learn that except by being in an experimental school."

It was this parallel he was drawing when he said, "I learned what I meant to do in education through the Chicago experimental school [*the University of Chicago Laboratory School founded by Dewey in 1896*], and this has been a lasting influence on everything I have thought since. The fact that I was always a teacher kept me close to the problems of education. You must always think of yourself as a teacher, because, obviously, this is where your gifts are, but after a while you've got to stop being a president, otherwise, you will not ever be a teacher, and you will not be a philosopher because you will be too busy with the administration."

As it turned out, that one insight meant that I could look at myself differently, partly because a man whom I dearly loved and respected, above all of the persons I have known, believed in me. He gave me a sense of mission (not in the self-righteous sense) and a feeling of confidence. The support from him freed me from a lot of the possible anxieties. The fact that he believed in what I was doing and had this kind of advice to give me about what I might do meant that from that day to this I felt that the "laying on of the hands" was an honest wish on his part. I would go on in this direction and try to do some of the things in the second half of the century to which Dewey had devoted his life in the first half.[24]

Chapter 6

Assault on a Small College

At his meeting with [American] Legion representatives on November 2, 1951, Dr. Taylor made the statement: "If a member of the faculty came to me today and said I joined the Communist Party last night, I wouldn't know what to say to her." Given an opportunity to retract the statement, Dr. Taylor said: "Well, I might have added, Oh!". . . . Lest anyone get the idea that we are accusing Dr. Taylor of being a Communist, we wish to make it plain that we are doing no such thing. Still we believe that Dr. Taylor by his own statements proves that he has a lamentable tolerance for those who have shown their liking for red causes. Indeed, he seems to take a perverse pride in siding and abetting people who have allied themselves with those who are conspiring to destroy us.

—FBI File: Harold Taylor, 1956

The history of Sarah Lawrence will always include accounts of its fight for academic freedom and attacks by the American Legion and the US Senate Subcommittee to Investigate the Administration of the Internal Security Act (commonly abbreviated as the Senate Internal Security Subcommittee—SISS). Taylor refers to one of his essays, a manuscript titled "Assault on a Small College," during his 1985 oral history.[1] Unfortunately, a copy was not among his professional papers at the time of his death and is now assumed to be lost, this being especially tragic since, among the various themes to be included in his memoir, the planned academic freedom chapter could well have been the most insightful (if not the most controversial) and certainly of great importance for the history of the college. Fortunately, the Sarah Lawrence College

Archives has prepared a comprehensive documentary web exhibition from this era, *Sarah Lawrence Under Fire: The Attacks on Academic Freedom during the McCarthy Era*, portraying its institutional lore.[2]

Even if Taylor's original draft was extant, the story of Sarah Lawrence, SISS, and the American Legion would need further explanation. Different accounts exist, and the narrative would include much more than Taylor's recollections of the 1953 resignation—or firing—of Sarah Lawrence faculty member Paul Aron. Sarah Lawrence came under scrutiny and was accused of "harboring communists" as early as 1949 by the US House Un-American Activities Committee (HUAC), shortly after Taylor's appearance on the ABC Radio program *Town Meeting of the Air* at New York City's Town Hall, as he admits in this chapter. College faculty were accused of membership in the Communist Party and hunted by HUAC and SISS (also known at this time as the Jenner Committee for the then-serving chair). In the late 1940s, education organizations encouraged universities to dismiss Communist Party faculty members on the grounds that they were unfit to teach. Many professors who testified at HUAC and SISS meetings lost their university posts due to pleading the Fifth Amendment.

Taylor argued for the right of all college faculty to hold membership in any political party as long as their political views did not undermine the integrity of their research or their role as teachers and, by the early 1950s, he and Sarah Lawrence would be attacked by the Hearst press, the American Legion Magazine, ex–FBI agent Theodore Kirkpatrick's anti-communist newsletter *Counterattack*, and "red scare" pamphleteer Allen Zoll and his National Council for American Education, among others.[3] Taylor's views would become the foundation for Sarah Lawrence's academic freedom statement, where faculty appointments were determined not by political affiliations but as defined by professors' candor, honesty, and scholarly integrity in the classroom and their ability to deal candidly and honesty with controversial issues. Taylor was also proclaiming, in response to the American Legion's accusations, that there were no known members of the Communist Party or communist sympathizers on the Sarah Lawrence faculty.

The personal and professional dynamics on the Sarah Lawrence campus must have been interesting during this time. While eleven faculty were originally suspected of being communists by the Jenner Committee and nine were interviewed in public and private hearings, other faculty members were known to be staunch anti-communists. Also, while students would have supported and defended their college from these various attacks, their political leanings varied. A survey of political attitudes of students (administered in spring 1952 *and spring 1953) concluded that there was "surely no uniformity of political attitudes among the students on the campus" with 23 percent of the student body supporting the Republican Party and 50 percent of the students planning to vote for the 1952 Republican Party presidential nominee.*[4]

Board of Trustee member Harrison Tweed and Taylor planned a defense against charges by the Westchester County (NY) American Legion and SISS, upholding First Amendment rights, and Taylor was applauded for his efforts as noted in oral history interviews with Esther Raushenbush, Helen Lynd, and Alastair Reid, and in the press.[5] *His handling of the "Aron case," however, becomes quite complicated, with criticism from Raushenbush, Lynd, and others. Further explanations by Taylor in his now lost chapter would have been a welcomed addition for future researchers who wish to explore this controversial time in the history of Sarah Lawrence and the field of higher education.*

This chapter has been reconstructed from Taylor's 1985 Sarah Lawrence College oral history interview, the 1974 Rossman interviews, accompanying correspondence and internal documents by Taylor, and text from two scraps of the "Assault on a Small College" draft.[6]

> Because of the attacks on colleges for "harboring subversives" and "teaching communism," the educational philosophy of colleges and universities has in many instances become more cautious and less independently democratic.
>
> —Harold Taylor, On Education and Freedom, 1954

Before coming to Sarah Lawrence I had not given much thought to what colleges should or should not do publicly about current political and social issues, although I was very clear about the educational value of introducing issues into the main stream of community life on a college campus. I felt that Sarah Lawrence had a special responsibility in the political education of its students and that the best way to carry that out was to have the students become involved with the issues. Most college presidents and their boards of trustees at that time held the belief that colleges and universities had no business meddling in public affairs or public policy questions. Most of them still hold that belief. The general view was that faculty members and scholars may take action and make statements on their own, but the college or university as a corporate entity does not hold views on matters of public policy. It conducts research, it teaches, and it stays out of politics and social policy. The trouble with that view is that it is impractical and unreal, as the colleges discovered in the 1960s and as we had assumed at Sarah Lawrence in the 1940s and 1950s. If you don't deal with political and social issues, they come to you and have to be dealt with anyway. Even if I had wanted to, there was no way that I, the board of trustees, or the faculty could escape responsibility for developing college policies on issues raised by the society as a whole.

∽

It was in those pre-1950 years that the first real danger of McCarthyism began to stir after Mr. Truman signed the executive order listing the organizations said to be subversive.[7] A sizable number of the Sarah Lawrence faculty had belonged to many of the organizations. Not only were the US congressional committees beginning their investigations, but state legislatures were starting up their own. Of national importance were the 1948 committee hearings [*of the state of Washington's Joint Legislative Fact-Finding Committee on Un-American Activities*] for three faculty at University of Washington who, refusing to answer questions about their activities, were dismissed from the university after an interminable amount of accusations and faculty turmoil.

Early in 1949, the *Town Meeting of the Air*, a major public events radio program of that time, chose the subject *Should Communists Be Allowed to Teach in Our Colleges?* and invited Raymond Allen, president of the University of Washington, T. V. Smith, a popular philosophy teacher formerly at the University of Chicago, Roger Baldwin [*director of the American Civil Liberties Union*], and myself to debate the topic [*broadcast on March 1 from Town Hall in New York City*]. Roger and I were to support the affirmative; Allen and Smith the negative.

I knew what I thought about the issue, and I believed that what President Allen had done in dismissing the faculty members was dead wrong. But I didn't know what I was getting into. I think that every professor and student in the country with the slightest interest in political freedom, every right-wing critic of colleges, every anti-communist liberal or pro-communist radical was listening that night. Even before the broadcast I had hundreds of letters from everywhere in the country, some of them from faculty members at the University of Washington who spelled out what they would like to have me say. Each speaker was to make a four-minute opening statement, followed by short rebuttals from each, then questions from the floor.

This was the first time I had been involved in a public debate on a serious and controversial issue before a national audience, and I went into training for it as if it were Wimbledon or the Army-Navy game. I spent nearly two weeks working on my four-minute statement, stayed out of the president's office, worked in the library on everything from the United States Constitution to the history of the American Association of University Professors and the Sacco-Vanzetti case.[8] I thought up questions which our opponents might ask along with ringing replies developed from reading factual accounts of academic freedom cases and the content of all that mail I had been getting from scholars and students in the state of Washington and around the country. Roger Baldwin and I exchanged manuscripts for our opening statements, talked for two hours, speculated on Raymond Allen's and T. V. Smith's opening remarks, and learned that the two of them were being coached by Sidney Hook, which made it easier to figure out what they would be saying.

From what I read in the University of Washington material, it was clear that Allen, aside from his personal convictions, had fired his faculty members under political pressures produced by a vicious small-time Un-American activities sort of committee operating in the Washington state legislature under the chairmanship of a freshman legislator named Albert Canwell.[9] It also seemed likely to me that it was an open and shut case for Allen. If he hadn't fired the faculty members, the board of regents would have fired him. It wasn't just the communists that the Canwell Committee was chasing. They were tracking down liberalism and liberals. By 1955, six years later, Raymond Allen's successor in the presidency had banned Robert Oppenheimer from lecturing on the University of Washington campus.[10]

On the night of the debate, Town Hall was packed to the roof with a crowd in the lobby trying to get in. The audience was volatile and responsive. They applauded nearly everything that was said on either side and shouted their agreements and disagreements as we went along. The central point in my argument was that if you are going to judge faculty members on their qualities as scholars and teachers, you have to look at their scholarship and their teaching, not at their political affiliations. To do the latter, you have to set up FBI checks and police state tactics of political investigation.

In the case of the men Allen had dismissed, there was no evidence that either of them had ever misled their students or had engaged in dishonest scholarship during the twenty years they had been teaching at the University of Washington. They were highly regarded by their colleagues for the integrity of their teaching and for their work as members of the university community. Allen and Smith argued that all members of the Communist Party were under intellectual orders to think and act as they were told and to take the party line on all political, social, and philosophical questions. They were therefore not free and by definition were unfit to teach in an American college. Roger Baldwin asked what Allen and Smith would do about Joliot-Curie [*an eminent French atomic scientist and avowed member of the Communist Party*]. Would he be turned down as a teacher of atomic science because he belonged to the Communist Party? How could a man as notoriously independent as he be accused of taking his intellectual orders from the party?

What it came down to was the question of whether members of the Communist Party who were also members of college faculties actually did their own thinking, in the context of a Marxist ideology, or whether they took the party line whenever it was enunciated and taught to their students or anyone else they could get their hands on. Is there such a creature as a communist or a Communist Party that does not take intellectual orders from the party hierarchy and the Soviet Union? There certainly have been a lot of such creatures in Europe, especially in France and Italy, although the American Party had not been widely known for the quality of its intellectual activities in general.

Roger Baldwin and I told our American audience in 1949 that according to the political philosophy of a liberal democracy, teachers or anyone else were judged by the quality of their acts, not by their classification among the political parties. We felt then, as we feel now, that you are just as likely to be subverted by a Republican or a Democrat as by any other political affiliate and that political affiliation is not the point. I stated that "our teachers serve democracy best when they protect our young people from subversion by making them think for themselves, and when they guarantee to America that the daily encounter with truth is free and open. To refuse the encounter because of public fear is to betray the search and yield to a failure of nerve."[11] It was an intense evening and we had the impression that we won. What I didn't realize at the time was that the mere defense of the idea that there could be a Communist Party member or a Marxist who was honest and acceptable as a scholar and teacher made the defender of the idea a target for all the political hacks who were busy in Congress and in their dirty little list-making organizations with what they called rooting out communist subversion. In their canon, any college president who talked about the rights of communists immediately became an apologist for communism, a hidden "Red," to be dismissed from his presidency if he failed to dismiss whoever the list-makers chose to attack.

∼

When I think back over the fourteen years of my presidency, it was a continuing series of attacks and replies. In the theory of education we always had the attacks about the weaving and the basket-making and all, dismissing our kind of education as being decadent in some way. Then we had political attacks because we were an open college politically, and then the Town Hall meeting. Well, I had no notion that this broadcast would arouse the antagonism of practically every conservative or moderate liberal in the country, because the argument made by our opponents was the one made all through the 1950s against colleges. That is to say, that if I didn't formally ban Communist Party instructors from teaching in the college, then I was supporting the Communist Party. I had to be against them. They had no rights for tenure or anything else, and I should devote myself as president to turning out the communists. Any opponent of mine could use the saying, "Here he is, sheltering subversives again." The American Legion Post in Westchester [Westchester County, NY] was looking for something to do to increase its membership.[12] There weren't any issues around much. So they held a meeting and presented a resolution that said Sarah Lawrence was advocating communism and all sorts of terrible things.

The *American Legion Magazine* published an article about the reds in the colleges and included [Sarah Lawrence College faculty] Helen Lynd, Joseph Barnes, and Bert Loewenberg. We replied to the Legion that these were first-rate people in our faculty and that we had no intention of investigating them or doing anything about them. Then there was a series of right-wing pamphlets produced by various ideologically corrupt political enemies, and they accused those three people of subverting the American people and particularly the students at Sarah Lawrence. I made the mistake of inviting Westchester County American Legion members over to discuss our policies. They came over and we explained how we ran Sarah Lawrence [on November 2, 1951].

The chair of the Legion's Americanism Committee and his cohort expressed appreciation for the chance to talk. He explained that it had come to the attention of the American Legion members around

Westchester that several people whose names had been associated with organizations listed by the attorney general as subversive were on our faculty, that this had disturbed them, as citizens, and that they felt it was their duty to do something about it. One Legionnaire added that he had heard me speak and that he thought my point very well taken about the fact that if one teacher had radical views, this would not mean an undue influence for this point of view. Students in one classroom from one teacher could not be expected to have their whole lives changed, when everything else in the school and outside it was having opposite effects. He said he thought this very sensible, but that two or three of the people with whom he sat were horrified at the thought that anyone should allow freedom of this kind. He went on to say that the American Legion Post was divided on the question of what to do about Sarah Lawrence, that about half of them wanted to blast us in every way they could and the other half, which included the members of the Americanism Committee, wanted to find out our "side of the story" before they did anything else. There was no hint of any threat in this, and he seemed genuinely interested in finding out what I would have to say to their questions. He had six to eight pages of typewritten notes which, he later revealed, consisted of lists of affiliations and activities of Helen Lynd, Joseph Barnes, Bert Loewenberg, and myself.

The committee chair asked what would I do if I found out that a member of my faculty had joined the Communist Party? I replied that it would depend on who made the announcement, and that I would not know what to say at this point as to my reply if a member of the faculty came to the office and said, "Last night I joined the Communist Party." I would have to judge this individual case in terms of whether or not I believed in his integrity, but I repeated that this was putting up an unreal problem. I asked the visitors if they would like to meet Helen Lynd and they said they had no objection. As Helen came in the door, I said, "I hope you have your horns with you," turned to the Legionnaires and said, "I would like to introduce the subversive character you are interested in." (I admit this was corny, but it was one way of getting things started.) One Legionnaire took the remark more seriously than it was intended and wanted to make sure that Mrs. Lynd was not being accused by them as being subversive. I allowed as how this was a joke and then we all laughed nervously.

I said that as far as I was concerned I could not possibly control the actions of the faculty or the student body outside the college and that there was no way I knew how to prevent a student from taking any kind of political actions which she felt in her conscience she must take. We had some discussion on this point, and the Legionnaires all agreed that students could not be allowed to take political action of this kind and should be punished if they did. They also agreed that faculty members should not join organizations which might be considered subversive and, when there were social issues on which people could take sides, faculty members, in fairness to the youth they were teaching, should not take an unpopular side because this would reflect on their qualifications to teach. Here again we had some discussion as to what was the correct policy for a college. I then said that I could see where we disagreed basically, that is, that the Legionnaires wanted control of faculty and students on all political action and that I felt that such control would stultify thought and initiative on the part of the faculty and students. I pointed out that the policy I supported was in effect at most of the colleges and universities in the country. Another Legionnaire then said that he felt that young men and women were not mature enough to be given dangerous ideas until they had already had the intellectual discipline to know the truth. I basically disagreed, that the teachers and students in America were worthy of the trust we had to put in them to become thinkers and able to decide issues for themselves.

I mentioned the fact that I had spoken at a Town Hall meeting on the issue of whether or not members of the Communist Party should be allowed to teach, and the three men nodded their heads violently and said, "Yes, we know." A Legionnaire said he had listened to the broadcast and found it very interesting. At that point, I produced a transcript and pointed out that I began by saying that I am against the Communist Party and that my defense of the right of communists to teach was based on the fact that I felt all teachers should be judged by their personal qualities and not by their affiliations. I said that this was a very difficult point of view to present without seeming to be trying to help the communists, but that if I did not protect the rights of every American citizen against unfair treatment, other citizens who had nothing to do with communism would then be accused, and that it was almost impossible to clear one's name from charges of communism once they had been made. Individual rights, whether for communists or anyone else, had to be protected in order to protect everybody's rights. The Legionnaires said that they disagreed, that all communists should be hunted out of wherever they were working and that you could not allow such people to be dealing with our children. I said they would not be dealing with our children if we judged teachers by the qualities of character and the effort they showed in their work in the schools and colleges.

I again made the point that as far as the disagreement between the Legionnaires' point of view and mine was concerned, it was basically a disagreement on the amount of freedom which individuals in America should be allowed to have—that they wanted much less and I wanted much more. The committee chair said that the important thing for him was that I would not hire a known member of the Communist Party if one presented himself to me. As we were going out the door, I said that if at any time they wanted to talk to some of our students to see in person whether or not they were being subverted, I would be happy to arrange it, and that perhaps a group of our students could come to a Legion meeting to talk about their ideas on politics. One Legionnaire said that this would settle the whole thing, and another said, "Oh, no, it wouldn't, they would just say the things they were told to say." I said, "You people don't know the Sarah Lawrence girls."

Two days later there was a big headline in the local press as well as the New York press, "Taylor Admits Red Connections." The meeting was one of the stupidest things I could have done, but I was inexperienced being president and had no notion that anybody would be that silly. They translated what we had said, that "we believed that our faculty members should be able to join any organization that's legal." This was the "Red Connection" which I was said to be encouraging. We just clammed up at that point and agreed that's all we would do and wouldn't answer charges of any kind.

~

The situation had one amusing part to it. As I was walking out the door at Westlands one Saturday morning, a charming young lady came up and threw her arms around me and gave me a big kiss and said, "Good morning." I said, "Good morning," and she took another look at me and turned around and ran upstairs. She thought I was her date from Yale. She didn't know him very well or me either, as a matter of fact. That student [*Constance (Connie) Walter*] was the daughter of Francis Walter, a member of the House Un-American Activities Committee. When the American Legion had attacked us and we were in the throes of a newspaper fight and various political threats, Francis Walter came up to the campus [*on February 13, 1952*] to see Connie and, while he was there, he asked to see me. I hadn't known at that time that her father was a politician.[13] I believed he was another parent named Walter, until he identified himself as who he was in Washington. He said, "There are a lot of people who want to have you investigated—you as president, and your college, and this faculty. A lot of them are up here in Westchester, but there are a lot around Washington. I have a file from the FBI about what you've been doing, and I'd just like to talk to you about it." I said, "Well, do you think I should get a lawyer now or later?" He said, "I know that this college isn't subversive. I've read your speeches, and I know you're not subversive. And as long as my daughter is here, nobody is going to lay a finger on you." I had a funny feeling that if Connie left, we'd be in trouble. He said, "I'll tell you what I'll do. I'll ask the Westchester Legion to come to Washington to a hearing of the Un-American Activities Committee. I'll have them lay out the charges, and then I'll invite you to come without a subpoena to reply to the charges. We can clear this all up because you're getting bad national publicity. People are saying that you graduate communists every year, and there was one student here who went to work for TASS after she graduated from Sarah Lawrence.[14] So this would be a way of clearing up all that."

I could hardly believe my ears. A friendly witness before the Un-American Activities Committee can turn into a victim very quickly. Whether or not Walter had this in mind, what the counsel of the committee was doing in those days was to get friendly witnesses, have them accused, and then start asking incriminating questions. The publicity was worse than if you didn't go at all. So I said, "Mr. Congressman, I appreciate your concern for my welfare, but I'd rather you didn't help me. If I were to walk down the street in my hometown with a policeman holding my arm just under the elbow, my friends would know that he was a friend of mine from boyhood. But everybody else would think I was arrested. So, if you don't mind, the best thing you can do is abolish the Un-American Activities Committee." He smiled and said, "Oh, all right," and left. He did keep the Un-American Activities Committee off our back but not the Jenner Committee.

[*Victor S. Navasky, in his memoir,* Naming Names, *mentioned that Taylor, whom he described as Sarah Lawrence College's unorthodox president, once said to Constance Walter, "We can't choose our parents, and you lost the toss."*[15]]

In 1953, I had a call from Robert Morris, the counsel for William Jenner's US Senate Internal Security Subcommittee which was conducting an investigation of colleges to find communists. He wanted me to distribute eleven subpoenas to members of the Sarah Lawrence faculty to come to hearings where they would be questioned. [*Faculty included Paul Aron, Irving Goldman, and Charles Trinkaus who were to testify in both private and public hearings. Adele Brebner, Madeleine Grant, Horace Gregory, Bert Loewenberg, Helen Lynd, Kathryn Mansell, Lois Murphy, and Marc Slonim were called for private hearings only. These teachers who were to meet with the Jenner Committee represented approximately 15 percent of Sarah Lawrence's faculty; however, Grant and Mansell were no longer employed by the college at this time.*] They had their private hearings down on Centre Street at the [*New York City*] Municipal Court Building [*on March 20, 1953*]. I took a table at a nearby restaurant so that when they all came out from the hearings, they came over to the table and told their story so each could hear what the other said.

Morris called me later and asked if I would have lunch with him. I said, "Sure." In the middle of our conversation he said that he was ready to drop all the hearings about the rest of them if I would fire Paul Aron. He said, "You've got a bad one there." I said, "Well, that isn't the way we run the college. We don't fire people because the Jenner Committee and Robert Morris tell us to. There's nothing in the record to justify firing. We surveyed Paul Aron's teaching record and his faculty membership, and there's nothing that indicates he's anything less than a first-rate scholar and teacher." And I said, "Also, I don't like that whole idea of your swapping the rest for Aron. What you're saying is you'll stop the inquiry (which, therefore, couldn't have been very important or why would you have stopped it?) if I will let you have Aron."

He said, "Oh, no. That isn't true. It's just that I wanted to give you the opportunity to protect your college because most college presidents don't have the staff to investigate the way we do." I said, "Well, I think the best thing to do is for us to conclude this luncheon. You're operating in a completely different frame of reference than mine. I believe in free scholarship and you don't." He said, "Well, that is the difference." I went out and called Tweed on the phone and said, "I don't know what's going to happen next. I think I just turned down an offer to call off the whole thing if I would fire Aron."

I called an all-student meeting and explained about each of the faculty and gave a blanket approval of the entire eleven, including Aron. The procedure for dealing with an individual case at Sarah Lawrence was that the faculty member who was called to a government committee would be aided with a lawyer or money to support the hiring of a lawyer. It was a matter between faculty members' government and themselves. Whatever they wanted to do—plead the Fifth Amendment saying, "I refuse to answer on the ground it might incriminate me," or plead the First Amendment and talk about themselves and refuse to give the names of anybody else. Or refuse to answer at all but, if they refused, they could be convicted of Contempt of Congress which was the threat that the Jenner Committee always had.

If faculty members who were called wanted to talk to me about how they were going to respond, then they were free to do it. But I didn't ask. It was college policy as well as my policy not to ask. Paul Aron came to see me and said, "I've never been in the party, but I'm pleading the Fifth Amendment because I have associates who were communists. It would be very easy if I have to talk about myself to be trapped into saying I went to a Communist Party meeting, when all I did was to go to a meeting where these friends of mine were present. But I've never been in the party." That's the way he explained it to me and to the Faculty Academic Freedom Committee—that he had never been in the party but was pleading the Fifth Amendment.

In the week and a half preceding his closed hearing and the four days between the closed hearing and the public one, I did everything to persuade him that he would do serious and perhaps irreparable damage to himself, with incidental damage to the college, by taking the position he did, especially when equipped with a lawyer who has been going through life scared to death and whose idea of the way to help a client was to put him into the same frame of mind. We had Telford Taylor, Arthur Garfield Hays, Lloyd Garrison, and Harrison Tweed all on the coaching squad and even that was not enough.[16]

After his hearing, Aron had said he wasn't in the party. But he took the Fifth Amendment. He said he'd been instructed by his lawyer. I don't know if he had his lawyer with him; he might have. So, they put him on for a public hearing [on *March 24, 1953*]. If you evoke the Fifth Amendment in the private hearing, they figure they have a hot publicity item for a public hearing. Well, of course, they've got the record on you anyway. The FBI had a complete list of all the Communist Party members, and the party was riddled with informers. So, it was a fraud to hold the hearings. They didn't need to.

It looked really bad when viewed just in terms of not answering a question as serious as: Did you ever recruit Sarah Lawrence students into the party? If you say, "I refuse to answer on the grounds it might incriminate me," it looks very much on the surface as if you had. So, no matter what you do, you incriminate yourself. Paul had explained that he could account for not being in the party right up until the day before the hearing, but he couldn't prove that he hadn't been at certain meetings and the rest. So, Robert Morris, as counsel, took him back a few weeks and said, "Were you in the party on such and such a date?" Then he asked about whether Paul was in the party two weeks before the hearing, and after a few more questions, brought him up to the night before the hearing. Paul said no, he wasn't in the party. Well, that looked very much as if, having used the Fifth Amendment to protect himself from having to answer questions about his party membership, he resigned from the party the night before the hearing so that he would be able to say under oath that he wasn't in the party as of the day of the hearing. What with all the Fifth Amendment self-incriminating pleas and then the denial, it was a bad-looking transcript to anyone involved in the case. Listening to or reading that testimony, it would be almost impossible not to think that the witness had been in the party all along and had resigned the day before the executive session hearing of the committee.

In the case of Irving Goldman, we had a person who said simply that he joined the party because he thought that this was his best way of doing something about the Nazis, the Depression, and the danger of war. He said, "I left it in 1942 because I felt that the things I believed in could best be achieved by the major political parties." As for the people at Columbia University and Brooklyn College who were in the party with him, Irving said that there was no indication that the work they were doing at the time was damaging to the United States, and since he had no knowledge of what they have been doing since then, he did not feel that he should say anything which might damage their reputations. In any case if they were conspiring, Goldman said, "I would not know; the FBI would."

At his March 20 private hearing and his April 1 public testimony, Irving Goldman was said to have introduced the "calculated contempt" defense, permitting him to maintain his moral convictions about not incriminating others without using the Fifth Amendment.[17] *He spoke to the committee of his personal* activities, refusing to testify about others on moral grounds. Sarah Lawrence's board of trustees supported Goldman since his decision upheld standards of fairness and was not meant to defy the committee. The Jenner Committee did not cite him for contempt. In contrast, Aron's March 24th testimony was ridiculed in a Washington Post article under the title "Witness Says He Woke Up Not a Red."[18] Charles Trinkaus, the third Sarah Lawrence faculty member appearing before the Jenner Committee in a public hearing, stated that he was not a member of the Communist Party at his June 4th session but, when asked if he had ever been a member, invoked the Fifth Amendment. His hearing was adjourned to June 18th and then postponed indefinitely.

On April 2, Taylor sent a twelve-page, single-spaced memo to the board of trustees describing his two weeks of "serious and continued study" concerning Paul Aron's appearance before the Jenner Committee. He concluded, "By reason of these facts, taking in full the recommendation made to me by the Faculty Advisory Committee on Appointments, and by reason of my own knowledge of Mr. Aron's work as a teacher, I do not believe that his contract should be cancelled." Taylor recommended to the board of trustees that Aron be retained as a faculty member.[19] This all changed, as described in the forthcoming passages, and Aron would subsequently resign on April 8, 1953. The next day, Taylor called an all-college meeting announcing Aron's resignation and wrote to the board of trustees explaining the turn of events.

> By complete accident, I discovered that Aron had been in the party all along because Charles Trinkaus, who had been subpoenaed while he was away, was checking out his public hearing with his lawyer. As is the case sometimes, a lawyer will put his witness through the questions that he's likely to get when he hits the stand. One of the questions was: Were there any other members of the faculty at Sarah Lawrence who were in the party when you were? Since Charles was talking to the lawyer about his own case, he answered the questions openly. He said, "Yes, there were," and identified Paul Aron, but not for quotation because that would be squealing on his colleague.
>
> So the lawyer said, "Don't you realize what this will mean. Taylor's been backing all of you to the hilt. If, then, it's discovered that Paul lied to him about party membership, it will blow the whole case wide open. You owe it to Taylor and the college to make sure that he knows that Paul Aron's been lying. They're all ready to make a public statement saying Aron had never been in the party, in which case Robert Morris will probably call him back to the witness stand and prove that he had been lying." So Charles agreed to have his lawyer tell me that

Aron had been in the party all along. If it hadn't been for the fact that Charles was out of town when he was first called with the others and was therefore going over his case with that particular lawyer, we'd have lumbered right into a trap.

Aron may have been following party orders and that he had been told what to do and had been assigned a lawyer who was also following orders. Or it may have been that he was just plain scared and did not think the college would support him if he had told us the truth when Goldman and the others did. The day we found out the truth, I called him up to the president's office to meet with the Advisory Committee, the dean, and Trinkaus's lawyer. I said, "Why did you do this? How could you do a thing like this to all of us who trusted you?"

Aron replied, "I thought you and Tweed both knew." I blew up and said, "Get right out of here and leave the campus. We'll send your books after you." I think I would have hit him if he hadn't gone. I can remember that Marc Slonim, who was at the meeting, stood up and motioned Aron to the door. Aron then cleared out his desk and left me a letter of resignation he had written out and signed when he was first called to the executive session of the Jenner Committee. We packed up his books and delivered them to his house the next day.

What angered me was the betrayal of honorable colleagues who had stuck by him when he was in trouble. If we hadn't found out about him through the Trinkaus episode, I'd have probably felt obliged to resign. Once the press and the media had picked up the story again, the board and I would be publicly identified as a bunch of soft-headed dupes who had been protecting a dishonest communist, and all the charges about Sarah Lawrence being a haven for hidden subversives would have been cited by the Legion and the right-wing columnists as being true. It would also have shaken the confidence of a fair number of our supporters who had been cheering us on by the sidelines.

The irony in the situation is that as far as our college policy was concerned, we would have gone through exactly the same procedure to establish Aron's qualifications as a member of the faculty if he had either said nothing at all about his political affiliations or had told us the truth from the beginning. There was no doubt about Paul Aron's work as a teacher. It was first-rate. He had been widely respected by his students and had not given any indication of political distortion or indoctrination. However, as things now stood, it was very difficult to make clear to everybody that Mr. Aron was allowed to resign because of his dishonesty and not because of his political affiliations.

An all-college meeting was held [*on April 9*]. Before, I had praised the whole bunch that had been called and said we believed in them; they were our teachers. [*However, on April 9th*] I made the following remarks: In a meeting yesterday with Mrs. Raushenbush and the Faculty Advisory Committee on Appointments which I invited Mr. Aron to attend, it became clear that the information which Mr. Aron had volunteered to the Faculty and Trustee Committees was not true. Following the discussion, Mr. Aron submitted his resignation to me, and this morning at a joint meeting of the Faculty Appointments and the Faculty Academic Freedom Committees, the dean and the faculty committees agreed to accept the resignation and to forward it to the board of trustees. It was not the new facts discussed at this meeting but the previous misrepresentation of facts which were unsolicited and given to the college voluntarily which compelled the college to accept Mr. Aron's resignation. Our college policy, that teachers must meet the test of candor, honesty, and scholarly integrity, was applied in this instance and was the operating principle on which the resignation was accepted.

At an April 14, 1953, faculty meeting, when Taylor was absent, a "Report of Advisory Committee on Appointments Concerning Mr. Aron's Resignation" was presented with faculty noting the "very dramatic reversal after the previous meeting" and, after Raushenbush mentioned that Aron's resignation was freely offered, faculty seemed to suggest that actual circumstances contradicted that statement.[20]

∽

I found the Jenner Committee's conduct deplorable, its methods dishonest and devoid of any sign of integrity or interest in strengthening free institutions. From a close analysis of the work of that committee, I would say that Jenner himself was only interested in publicity which would advance his career and that the reports based on the public hearings (I assume they were written by Robert Morris) show the opposite intention from that of helping free institutions. I read the complete record of all the hearings of 1953 and was shocked by the absence of fairness in the treatment by the committee of the witnesses they called. The only persons who were treated with any degree of respect or fairness were those who had indicated beforehand a willingness to cooperate with congressional committees and who wished to provide material which the committee could use in their publicity.

It is true that every college has a responsibility for the political activities and point of view of its students, just as it has a responsibility for the moral values of the total college. But the most that a college can do is to provide its students with honest information and, by example, demonstrations of honest thinking; give them experience with democratic political activity, with a variety of political and social philosophies, and thus furnish the means and encouragement to think for themselves. Students who promote political organizations should not be prohibited from doing so. Nor can a college of liberal arts forbid students to think what they believe or to hold pro-communist political views. The most it can do is to make certain that the student who does so understands fully the intellectual and social consequences involved. Some of our students came to us with dogmas about politics. In the case of those who developed political interests and affiliations after coming to college, we did everything in our power to develop flexibility where rigidity exists, to develop a rational approach where irrationalism existed, and to develop independence of judgment. Once you start people thinking, you have no guarantee at what point or with what idea they will stop.

Harrison Tweed who served as chair of the board was as steady as a rock in the middle of all the fuss we had with the American Legion and the Jenner Committee and gave fatherly advice in a brotherly way, taking into account the fact that I was young and inexperienced. I remember once in an argument about something I had done he said, "Goddammit, you always go too far." I said nothing in reply and after a slight pause, he said, "I suppose if a few men like you didn't go too far, nobody would go anywhere."

Chapter 7

On Being Written About
Mary McCarthy and Randall Jarrell

> Have you read Randall Jarrell's *Pictures from an Institution*? While Randall and Mary [McCarthy] were teaching here, Randall was storing up pictures of his own to use in caricature of Mary. This made a very interesting series of mirrors, all of them distorted. I am now pretty cautious about putting any more creative writers on the faculty unless their neuroses are fairly well tested.
>
> —Harold Taylor, correspondence to Carl Bogholt, 1955

Few college presidents can say that they inspired characters in two works of fiction by leading American literary figures. And, no doubt, Harold Taylor certainly wished that this distinction could not have been attributed to him after seeing how he was depicted in Mary McCarthy's The Groves of Academe, published in 1952, and Randall Jarrell's Pictures from an Institution, published in 1954.[1] President Maynard Hoar of Jocelyn College in The Groves of Academe *and President Dwight Robbins of Benton College in* Pictures from an Institution *far from exemplify distinguished, thoughtful higher education leaders and, unfortunately, both came to represent Taylor during the mid-1950s.*

Randall Jarrell felt any reference to a young, curly-haired college president of a progressive college on the East Coast would have elicited thoughts of Harold Taylor; however, McCarthy and Jarrell added to their descriptions of the philosophical gadfly and academic evangelist Hoar and the spineless, vacuous, boy wonder/idiot-savant-of-success Robbins. Taylor became connected quite directly to these characters among McCarthy and Jarrell readers and the general academic community, even though Jarrell would later write that there was little relationship between Taylor and Robbins. Unfortunately, his explanation was perhaps even more insulting to Taylor than the original portrayal in Pictures from an Institution.[2] Taylor did not suffer his humiliation alone since Jarrell, through his character Gertrude Johnson who represented Mary McCarthy, also took aim at Taylor's wife, Muriel Thorne Taylor, in the description of Pamela Robbins. One Jarrell scholar described the structure of Pictures from an Institution as reflecting a "dialectical opposition of two impulses in Jarrell's character: to judge and to love, damn and praise."[3] For the Taylors, the impulse seemed to be judged damnation as Jarrell's narrator "impal[es] the errors and asininities of progressive education on a thousand barbs of aphorism, after dissecting the 'wicked' inhabitants of the institution with his comic scalpel."[4]

It would seem only natural for Taylor to include a chapter in his memoir about his role in The Groves of Academe and Pictures from an Institution, even without the prompting by Decca Mitford that such an account would be "the major interest of your forthcoming book."[5] Taylor offers his impressions and experiences with the authors and a general assessment of McCarthy's work, certainly more positive than Dwight Macdonald's who, in correspondence about The Groves of Academe, wrote, "The trouble is she [McCarthy] is so damned superior to her characters, sneers at most of them and patronizes the rest. . . . You begin to feel sorry for her poor characters, who are always so absurd or rascally or just inferior and damned—she's always telling them their slip's showing."[6] Throughout The Groves of Academe, Taylor's slip shows as he is portrayed as absurd, inferior, and damned. "On Being Written About" meanders among The Groves of Academe and Pictures from an Institution along with Ted Roethke anecdotes and a culminating story about William Buckley.[7]

Taylor began writing this account in July 1979 and, among the other chapters, this essay seems most complete. Yet, one renowned Sarah Lawrence story, perfect for Taylor's wit and narrative abilities, is not included—the famed McCarthy–Lillian Hellman exchange that was said to have taken place during a reception at his home (although Stephen Spender maintained that the gathering occurred at his home).[8] At a 1948 dinner party, Hellman was with a group of students on Taylor's sunporch. When McCarthy overheard her criticize John Dos Passos and his sympathies to the Loyalists' cause in Spain, she proceeded to interrupt Hellman and tell the students to instead read Dos Passos's Adventures of a Young Man. Hellman was incensed by McCarthy, *and the incident is thought to have fostered the 1980s libel lawsuit between the two of them. Why Taylor did not insert a paragraph into this chapter discussing the exchange, alas, is one of the many questions that will never be answered.*

In the fall of 1947,[9] one of our literature teachers decided suddenly to marry and leave the college at Christmas time. We usually took a year or two to make new appointments, but in this case there wasn't time to do more than make some phone calls and go down a short list of people whose work we knew about and admired. I had met Mary McCarthy at a party in New York where we talked about the college and about her stories in *The Company She Keeps*. Mary had taught at Bard College, people I knew there said she was very good at it, she was between novels and had some time to spare. She came up for an interview with some of our teachers, they all got along fairly well, and an arrangement was made for Mary to teach a literature course of her own choosing in the spring term.

The previous academic year, Randall Jarrell taught at the college during his year in New York as literary editor of the *Nation*. I knew that Jarrell was proud of his reputation as a teacher, Lionel Trilling thought well of him, and I had a great admiration for Jarrell's poems. I thought that his war poems were among the best in the language, although too much of Jarrell's critical writing and reviewing seemed to me to be reaching for unnecessary smart remarks. When he came to a writer he could honestly enjoy and respect, there was a precision and a warmth about his approval that made it very hard to disagree with whatever he was saying. In those years, most teachers of poetry and literature had been trained in the graduate schools and brought their graduate school habits for teaching undergraduates to become graduate students, but they often damaged beyond repair the natural delight that students can take in poetry when they are taught without academic constraints.

Most of our instructors in literature hadn't come from the graduate schools. Many of them were practicing writers who loved to teach. Robert Fitzgerald wrote for *Time* magazine, Harvey Breit and Alastair Reid for the *New Yorker*, Max Geismar for the literary magazines and the newspapers, as did Horace Gregory, Genevieve Taggart, and Jane Cooper among others, including Joseph Campbell from whom the books flowed constantly. For the most part they taught what they were writing about and what interested them, their courses were extensions of their lives as artists and writers. Jarrell had the same attitude to his writing and his teaching, and it seemed to me that the work at the *Nation* and at the college would make a good combination. I invited Jarrell up for a talk. He asked if I would like to play some tennis when he comes, since he played a lot at home and had nowhere to play in New York.[10] When I found out later how seriously he took his tennis, it occurred to me that what I had taken to be an urge to teach at Sarah Lawrence was simply a response to seeing two empty clay courts just across from the president's office.

In my office he seemed ill at ease and diffident about talking. His eyes shifted from one object to another around the room, and it was as if he were doing his best not to say anything interesting for fear I would think that he wanted my approval or appreciation. Before very long I began to feel that I shouldn't ask him any questions at all about his teaching or his work in general—it would be an invasion of his privacy. I couldn't find the right words to tell him how much I admired his poetry and criticism since, no matter how I put it, it might turn out to seem condescending or gratuitous. Why should a college president who was thinking of hiring a poet like, or even understand, the work of the poet he was talking to? Do you have to know calculus to hire a mathematician? His manner was one in which he seemed to be acting as my advisor about how to run the college and how to make good appointments.

I steered the conversation around to the problems of teaching at Sarah Lawrence, described Horace Gregory's course in Classical Literature in Translation and Joe Campbell's Folklore and Mythology, and asked Jarrell what kind of course he liked most to teach. Somehow Jarrell thought I was asking him to teach whatever course he would like to teach, and he accepted an appointment before one was offered to him. I didn't mind that since I was inclined to agree with him. He told me that teaching was an art at which he was highly skilled and that he loved doing it so much that he would pay to teach. I told him that with our low salaries that was the impression our faculty already had of what they were doing, and I invited him to teach a course in American Literature at our going rates.

When we went out to the tennis courts, he turned out to possess an overwhelming wish to win and an exaggerated notion of the quality of his own game. He didn't have much of a serve but came to the net on it anyway and then, when he was passed, would either shake his head disbelievingly and laugh nervously as if it were astonishing that a man of his talent could be passed by a man of mine. When he stayed in the backcourt, it wasn't very hard to run him around, and a nice sliced ball wide to the backhand would usually do him in. He liked best to lope back and forth along the baseline, returning balls of moderate pace and convenient location. He gave the impression of thinking that any other kind of shot from his opponent was unfair or at least in bad taste. When he made a good shot, he moved his racket and shouted "Gollie" or "Baby Doll." If tennis playing were part of the requirements for faculty members, we couldn't have signed him up, not because his game wasn't good enough for Sarah Lawrence but because he thought it was so much better than it was. He was one of those people who takes the joy out of playing. A fair amount of the time he showed the same capacity for removing joy in conversation with the faculty.

∾

Richard Savitt, Taylor, and Don Budge at Sarah Lawrence, 1958. In 1951, Savitt won the Australian and Wimbledon men's tennis championships. Budge is best known as being the first player to win the Grand Slam in tennis. In 1938, Budge won the four major men's singles tournaments. Gary Gladstone, courtesy of Sarah Lawrence College.

I had a different kind of experience with Ted Roethke, another poet with a tennis habit. Roethke called one day to ask for an appointment to talk about a job, said he had read some of my pieces, heard a lot about the college, was fed up with Bennington where he was teaching, they were fed up with him, and should he bring his tennis clothes when he came up for an interview. He had heard I could easily beat Jarrell. Upon arriving Roethke announced that he was the best teacher of poetry and literature in the country. He heard I had some room in the faculty at Sarah Lawrence and it was time to make some changes. I had just begun asking him one or two questions about his teaching at Bennington—the books he used, whether his students wrote poems for class—when he began agitating to get out on the tennis court. When I said I had never had a chance to talk to the best teacher in the country and I didn't want to miss the chance now, he said, "We can talk while we're playing. You couldn't tell anything about my teaching by talking to me anyway. I would only tell you lies."

When I said once more that I wanted to talk about our work and his, he simply interrupted and said, "Let's go play some ball. I play a pretty hot game and I feel good today." I gave up. He came on the court wearing a straggly old fisherman's hat, a drooping pair of long shorts, and a heavy brace on his right knee. I regret to say that he was all talk and no groundstrokes, couldn't run much because of his knees, had a peculiar scooped-up backhand, hit his first serve as hard as he could, seldom got it in and hit a second serve with an agonizing wind-up and a ball that came bouncing over as if it had been thrown by a small boy.

I did my best to keep the ball where he could reach it and gave him a chance to win some points. But it was hard to make it look honest. After he lost the first set at love, he offered to bet that he could win the second one—his bet being that if he won I would have to appoint him and if I won he would give me a book of his poems with an inscription recording the score. We played and I got the book, thank God.

While we were dressing, he went on about his teaching and his poetry readings which he said had been a huge success on all the major campuses and would bring a great deal of prestige to Sarah Lawrence if he were at the college. He then started to criticize the Bennington faculty and its president who was a close friend of mine. He explained what a fool the president was, how tedious the students were, and what a dull place it was up there in the woods. He talked at such a clip that even when I interrupted, he didn't notice.

I managed to break through only by saying, "Shut up, Roethke. I couldn't possibly hire you. Your poetry is a gift to the world. You're a fascinating talker. I know you are a hell of a teacher. But you are a lot more than I could handle. In about half a day you would have the whole place in some kind of gorgeous uproar, and we've got enough uproars already."

Roethke let out a happy shout, slapped his thigh, threw his head back, and laughed. "You're goddamn right you couldn't handle me. I can cause more trouble than any president can ever clear up, and I haven't met a president yet who knew what to do with me." We parted good friends. He said he was getting out of the East and going out to the West Coast where the competition was easier. He said if we ever had an opening for a tough poet, we should let him know, and he would come out, work hard, and behave.[11]

~

In Jarrell's term of teaching he gave much less of himself to the students and the college than we would have liked, much like a dinner guest who hurries in late and leaves early for another party. We were a fairly small and intimate community, held together by a common interest in ideas and an unusual amount of mutual affection and respect, without the academic competition and cynicism of the conventional universities.

There were always poets, painters, dancers, sculptors, and artists of all kinds around, and we took pleasure in each other's company and each other's work. We were there because we wanted to be. Randall resisted the idea of joining in. I think he mistook the easy, informal, warm-hearted way the college was organized for an orthodox liberal-progressive stereotype—a do-I-always-have-to-do-what-I-want sort of place—and he didn't want to be identified with it. He made that clear to his students, whose enthusiasm for their college and the life they were leading in it he found naively excessive and misguided. He would have preferred them to be cynical.

This meant that we never did enjoy the full benefit of Randall's attention and talent and that he wasn't a very good teacher in our kind of place. He had his own enthusiasms, most of all for poetry itself and its preemptive place in the life of the mind. We found little warmth of humanity in him, even his laugh had a metallic ring, and he laughed hardest at literary jokes that weren't especially funny. He met his class, kept his office hours, saw his students, played tennis, did his editing at the *Nation*, and that was that.

None of us realized at the time that while they were teaching at the college both Randall and Mary McCarthy were busy collecting ideas and conversations for novels. Hers was *The Groves of Academe*, his was *Pictures from an Institution*.[12] I don't think Mary knew that Randall was going to write a novel about the college, especially one in which she was to be the central character, Gertrude Johnson, a novelist between books.

I took Mary at face value. I thought of her as a friendly sort of person with a serious and informed interest in radical politics who loved to talk and was often brilliant at it. It was only later that I discovered that her frequent smile was more in the nature of a nervous tic or movement of the mouth and eye muscles than an expression of pleasure, amusement, or good will. Her conversations and stories at lunch and her remarks at faculty meetings I had taken to be expressions of a tough-minded, warmhearted writer with a cynical streak which served as a defense against ever being thought sentimental, soft, or gullible.

It did worry me that she told jokes about her students and made fun of them for not knowing Aristotle and not being able to keep track of the names of characters in Russian novels. The jokes often came from the intimacy of private discussions with students who thought she was their friend and who talked to her indiscreetly about other students and other faculty members only to find their words shaped into anecdotes and stories used around town and around the college as a part of Mary's conversational equipment.[13]

When I talked with Mary at the college or with friends in New York, I thought I was dealing with a colleague with common interests. It was not that at all. Mary was simply watching me the way Nabokov might watch a bug he found interesting. The friendliness and openness of the college provided a convenient situation for Mary to put together the caricature of a college president whose manner and ideas, while useful as a source of material for a novel, hardly qualified him for inclusion among serious intellectuals. Life for Mary was a journey through the lives of other people who could produce useable characters and plots.

Here is Jarrell's version in *Pictures from an Institution* of the relation between Mary and my unsuspecting self:

> The President *interested* Gertrude. She realized, suddenly, that she was no longer between novels. She looked at the President

as a weary, way-worn diamond-prospector looks at a vein of blue volcanic clay; she said to herself, rather coarsely—Gertrude was nothing if not coarse: "Why, girl, that Rift's *loaded*." How can we expect novelists to be moral, when their trade forces them to treat every end they meet as no more than an imperfect means to a novel? The President was such invaluable material that Gertrude walked around and around him rubbing up and down against his legs, looking affectionately into the dish of nice fresh mackerel he wore instead of a face; and the dish looked back, uneasy, unsuspecting.[14]

I don't think that Randall was quite fair to my face or to the metaphor. (Can a dish of mackerel look back and be uneasy?) But in the light of what happened, he was certainly fair to the situation. I can usually tell a porcupine from a Labrador retriever and a black widow spider from a daddy long legs, but like nearly everyone else, I tend to accept people at their own estimate of themselves and to respond to people who seem to be friendly by being friendly in return. I don't like to be suspicious or guarded unless it is absolutely necessary. What I didn't know was that it wouldn't have done any good to have been guarded in the presence of two novelists on the hunt for new material. The guardedness would simply have become another side of the president's character, revealing him as a cautious hypocrite pretending to be an outspoken liberal.

∼

The trouble was that I wasn't used to being written about or talked about, and I didn't understand that once you are put in charge of something as visible as a progressive college full of talented intellectuals, you are fair game for writers of all kinds, inside or outside the college. They can say whatever they want, and they don't come to you for suggestions and revisions.

In those days at Sarah Lawrence we had a sense of political responsibility as a college, not only for the education of the students in political theory, history, and social action, but for the role of colleges in the politics of freedom and the domestic issues raised by the Cold War. We also had an active group of radicals and liberals in the student body and faculty who were closely involved in the Wallace campaign of 1948. In the early forties, before I arrived at Sarah Lawrence, the faculty had organized a Teachers' Union affiliated with the CIO, at the urging of faculty members who believed that teachers should accept the responsibility of all intellectuals to join in political action as allies of labor and the trade union movement. The union was dropped in 1946. So many of its functions were already being performed by the regular faculty committees that it became redundant, although a militant attitude in favor of political action by the college remained in the faculty.

Some faculty members felt that the college should be deliberately used by the faculty and students as a political instrument of the left, others were against political involvement of any kind, a few were anti-communist and deplored any action by the college which might be helpful to the communists, including the protection of their civil rights. Because the campus was so close to New York and many of the students and faculty members were close to the liberal movements and organizations which had national headquarters in the city, there was a flow of ideas, in the arts, in politics, in social action and education back and forth between the campus and the city. As a result, whatever was happening in the politics of the late 1940s in the United States or in world affairs was injected into the life of the campus in the form of issues to be debated and actions proposed.

Mary McCarthy was one of the most sophisticated of the anti-communist intellectuals involved in the radical politics of the 1940s. Her knowledge of the tactics and strategy of the Communist Party was based on experience with party members and radical intellectuals in action. As could be seen when *The Groves of Academe* was published, she was also acutely sensitive to the undercurrents of political feeling and the pathology of small college life in which faculty members and their families, students, and administrators are all pressed up against each other in a close community from which there is no escape. From her teaching at Bard and Sarah Lawrence, from knowing people in the faculty at Bennington, Black Mountain, and other places, and having been a student at Vassar, Mary had a very good sense of how, in such communities, all private matters become public knowledge and quite ordinary events take on the character of major crises. She also knew the power of the weak and the power of the protector of the weak in the liberal community, where the highest order of integrity may be granted to those who resist all decisions made by those in authority, including those decisions that seem most sensible. To agree with the people in charge, whether faculty members or administrators, is to sell out.

Sarah Lawrence was a gold mine for a writer of her disposition. As the story in her novel unfolded there were to be found in it no people of clear intelligence, honest motive, or personal virtue, but only innocents who would support anyone who could make a case for being mistreated, or political liberals who could serve a psychic advantage and enjoy a moral pleasure by supporting the cause of a colleague they knew to be a liar. In the world which she constructed, virtue not only could not triumph, it was reduced to a name for hidden motives.

First there was Maynard Hoar, the young president of Jocelyn, a progressive college in the East, "the photogenic, curly-haired evangelist of the right to teach, leader of torch parades against the loyalty oath, vigorous foe of 'thought control' on the Town Meeting of the Air" and "lover of the humanities, guitar-player, gadfly of the philosophical journals." The president is faced with the problem of dismissing a member of the faculty, Henry Mulcahy, knowledgeable about Joyce and the canons of modern literature, a genius in the manipulation of student and faculty politics, widely read, clever, malign, unscrupulous, and a careless, slovenly teacher whom the president had originally appointed as a kindly act of rescue from deserved unemployment.

Mulcahy, through a series of lies about the circumstances of his appointment, the condition of his wife's health, and his claimed membership in the Communist Party, organizes a campaign against the president's decision to dismiss him and against the president himself. The pivot around which his success turns is his lie that he is a member of the Communist Party, a lie uncovered by the president's question to a visiting poet who assures the president that Mulcahy was asked to join the party but he never did. The president's public reputation as a liberal fighter for freedom is then at stake, since if he dismisses Mulcahy he will be accused by the faculty and everyone else of having betrayed his principles both in "investigating" Mulcahy by asking a party member to name him and by dismissing a faculty member who has confessed to being a party member. To protect his public image, the president resigns, Mulcahy goes on.

In many ways *The Groves of Academe* is a brilliant novel, especially in its perceptions of the political operation of colleges and the way in which opinions and feelings and lies can so easily be organized into modes of political action.[15] I could appreciate the satire and the insight, but found it hard to cope with the identification of the president of Jocelyn with the president of Sarah Lawrence. Maynard Hoar of Jocelyn came off as a plausible fake. He was an opportunist who delighted in his public image as a defender of freedom, yet by a combination of stupidity and fuzzy-minded liberalism failed to deal with the reality of his own opportunism. Since in the novel his credentials included most of my own, the philosophical journals, my youth, articles about academic freedom, friendship with Alexander Meiklejohn, guitar playing (substituted for the clarinet), the *Town Meeting of the Air*, there was a period in which the image of Jocelyn's Maynard Hoar was superimposed on the president of Sarah Lawrence.

Readers and talkers in the American academic and literary community found it a fascinating possibility that Taylor *was* actually Hoar and that Taylor was probably just as big a fake as Hoar was. It gave quite a few people something to talk about, and there wasn't much I could do to join the conversation. It was quite like the American Legion and right-wing columnists attacking me as a communist sympathizer who supported communists on his faculty and showed signs of being an Alger Hiss–like figure with a set of proper liberal connections and a hidden record in subversive politics. You can't just stand up and tell the American Legion or Mary McCarthy's readers that they are missing the real you. Since those days in the 1950s, the line between factual accounts of events and the transformation of the same facts and events into novels and TV shows has become very thin. Putting real events into novels is the easier course to take. The writer always has the permanent alibi that after all it is fiction and if you want to identify yourself with any of the fictional characters, that is up to you.

What it can do to personal relations between oneself and any writer, or any group of people which includes a writer, if not quite as frightening, is chastening, and teaches people they should never talk to Truman Capote. In the long run it can mean that no one will ever be able to afford an intimate conversation or any other kind of intimacy, even with nonwriters. It can also serve as a warning to college presidents not to appoint novelists to their English departments. In my case, I was horrified to read the McCarthy account of my character, and I resented the sense of powerlessness it left with me. What struck me as most unfair was the way in which an uncomplicated and honest effort on my part to defend academic freedom against the bastards who were out to destroy it was twisted into a means of getting public attention and public credit for being brave. I kept wanting to correct the character, as if it were in my power to rewrite the parts of the novel which distorted my version of my own reality. When I now look back at that state of mind, I realize that in those days I took everything, including appearing in novels, very seriously, and didn't seem to understand that characters in literature really do have a life of their own even if it is not the one you think they should have.

~

After *The Groves of Academe* came Jarrell's *Pictures from an Institution* with a central character named Dwight Robbins, the youthful president of Benton College, a progressive Eastern college for women. I hadn't yet recovered from being confused with Maynard Hoar of Jocelyn College when the new character was circulated up and down the East Coast. This time he was an Olympic diver instead of a tennis player, a Rhodes scholar who kept being proud of it, a witless spellbinding speech maker with intellectual pretensions; anxious to please; publicized in *Time*, *Life*, and *Newsweek*; an extroverted, solicitous phony; and "about anything, anything at all, he believed what it was expedient for the President of Benton College to believe."

I welcomed with relief the fact that after the first two or three chapters Randall seemed to lose interest in Benton's president, although by that time he had already managed to make him recognizable and quite revolting. Randall turned most of his attention to the character of the novelist, Gertrude Johnson, who had accepted a teaching appointment at Benton, the better to collect material for a new book about politics in a progressive college.

I was even more grateful that Randall's interest in me faded fairly early in the book since he showed the same delight in caricature that Mary had shown in her book and was also much more ruthless. He lacked Mary's professional skill in building a plot and telling a story about situations close to reality. His book was in fact a series of fairly disjointed episodes, conversations, and descriptions of life among intellectuals pinned together in colleges. He seemed to have put into the book whatever occurred to him about Mary McCarthy, along with things he remembered about college professors he had known in the past. But what he lacked in narrative talent he made up for in the single-mindedness, even vindictiveness, with which he pursued his mission of tracking down a colleague.

Here is Jarrell's novelist, Gertrude Johnson, at work:

Gertrude said, in private to the world, very ingenious things about President Robbins; if you have ever heard any you will think me another Parson Weems. Gertrude not only told big lies like Hitler's, she also told a kind of lie that she had learned, I think, from Chekhov—a kind of this-must-be-true-for-who-in-God's-name-could-have-made-it-up lie. . . . How many of our novelists could have matched Gertrude's account of how President Robbins was expelled from the nudist camp? How her eyes rolled when she had him say, "Believe me, *I* have nothing to hide," when really . . . Surely you have heard that story; Gertrude has told it five hundred times. Once, after it, I heard someone say quietly to a friend: "She may be a mediocre novelist, but you've got to admit that she's a wonderful liar." But this was unfair to her; her novels, too, were wonderful lies.[16]

Whether Mary's novels were wonderful lies or fascinating truths, I must say that in the case of *The Groves of Academe*, Mary led her readers into the territory where the real problems about faculty members and their politics were to be found. At the time Mary was teaching at Sarah Lawrence in 1948, the congressional investigating committees and Joe McCarthy had not yet swung into full action, although the Un-American Activities Committee was fairly busy all through the late forties, the right-wing organizations were building up their files getting ready for their leader in the Senate to appear.

But Mary's descriptions of the emotional tension, the intricacies of maneuver, the dangers of moral betrayal, and her grasp of the politics of anti-communism in its relation to the liberal movement in the colleges gave her book the quality of prophecy. Variations of the situations developed in the colleges and universities in the early 1950s from one end of the country to the other, sometimes with a Maynard Hoar sort of weak president and a secretive faculty member, most often with a strong and conservative president and board of trustees and ineffective support by the faculty for colleagues who were attacked. To read the novel now is to realize how much Mary knew about what could happen. The book was widely read at the time, and as one of the first important novels to be written about academic life by a serious writer, it has stayed in the literature as the forerunner of what has become a genre. I've seen Mary since. I mean, we're not sworn enemies or anything. We didn't know each other awfully well. I told her that the next time she was writing a novel about a college, to please leave me out of it.[17]

~

I can report that the Jarrell novel has also been surfacing in later years, this time with more pleasant effects from my point of view. I had written about William Buckley Jr.'s *God and Man at Yale* and found the book to be a sneak attack on some of Yale's best scholars and teachers through the use of distorted material drawn from Yale campus life and the classes Buckley had attended. I recall referring to him as a bigot disguised as a Yale man.

Over the years of the 1950s I was often asked to appear with Buckley on panels or in public debate and always refused, on the grounds that I did not want to spread the idea that he was worth debating. Later on, when he had become a little more careful with his facts and his accusations, I did agree to appear on his television show, *Firing Line*.[18] It turned out to be fairly dull. In his effort to make liberals into people who support communism and the Communist Party, Buckley went back again and again to the old 1950s circle of questions, Do you believe that communists have a right to teach? Would you appoint a member of the Communist Party to your faculty? Would you dismiss one if you found him in your college?

I pointed out as I had been pointing out for twenty years or so to people who asked me that question that when I appointed faculty members I did not ask them what political party they belonged to, and neither before nor after an appointment did I run a political investigation to find out. I said yes, I would appoint Picasso to the art faculty, or Neruda in literature, but was unlikely to appoint a person who listed Communist Party membership on his resume unless he had most unusual qualifications. As for dismissing a present faculty member who was suddenly (or slowly) revealed to be a party member, that would depend on those qualities as a teacher and scholar, not on political affiliation. It all seemed so stale and pointless, as if Buckley had not learned anything about education since he wrote his *God* book.

But then one day in 1962 I had a distressed call from my friend Sarah Blanding,[19] then president of Vassar, with the news that the college had arranged a debate on liberalism and conservatism in education with the controversial William Buckley and that the liberals at Vassar were up in arms about having him come to the campus at all, especially if there was no one who could be counted on to give him the hardest possible time and win the day for the liberals.[20] I accepted the compliment and the invitation, and for the next two weeks before the debate was scheduled had a series of phone calls from Buckley's office wanting to know what debating rules I would agree to, who would speak first, how much time would be given to rebuttal after the opening statements, how much time for questions, whether both of us would be allowed to answer questions addressed to the other, and would I please send him a manuscript. I declined that request and agreed to speak first, knowing that if I sent a manuscript he would concentrate on taking it apart, and I saw no reason for helping him do his homework.

I prepared a very careful statement on the definition of liberalism in education, beginning with,

> It is my belief that education has as its chief task the cultivation of those qualities of mind and character which can sustain the capacity for nobler feelings and the will to carry out humane action. Among the noblest of feelings is the commitment to the use of reason. It is true, as Mill says, that individuals lose their high aspirations, and their powers of intellectual discipline and taste, because the situations of society too often demand that they give them up in favor of lesser goals and easier conceptions. . . . The most dangerous person to the authoritarian state is a free-thinking and tough-thinking liberal intellectual, one who holds a deep compassion for the weak and the defenseless, who is sensitive to the principles of social justice. Such individuals rest their lives on a self-imposed obligation to maintain the integrity of their own thought. They insist that to maintain such integrity against all tyranny and all dogma is a moral obligation of a higher order of value than submission to popular opinion, to unreason, or to the authority of the state. This is the deepest point in the philosophy of liberalism—the conviction that individual human reason is the ultimate source of truth and moral judgment.[21]

I then went on to point out that the basis of Senator McCarthy's attack on liberalism was to denounce reason and compassion and to accuse anyone who cared for social justice and wished to work on behalf of beneficent social change of being a communist. I said that McCarthy was not a conservative but a totalitarian and a political, intellectual, and moral midget. I figured that if Buckley wanted to win an argument against liberalism in that context, he would have to come out against the use of reason and the application of moral judgment.

The chapel at Vassar, the largest auditorium on the campus, was jammed the night of the debate, the entire student body and faculty were there, and although it was 1962 and presumably the battle against McCarthyism and Buckleyism had been won, there was a high degree of tension in the room. I made my opening statement and sat back to listen to what Buckley had to say.

To my astonishment he opened with a reference to the fact that as president of Sarah Lawrence College, I had been the subject of a satirical novel by Randall Jarrell who had been a member of the faculty. He then proceeded to read passages from *Pictures from an Institution*, some about the fictional character Jarrell used to represent me, others about Benton, the name he used for Sarah Lawrence. For example:

> Their education was, for a good many of the girls, what they themselves would have called a traumatic experience. Two of the psychologists of the school talked of education not simply as therapy but as shock therapy: "The first thing I do with a freshman," one of them said, "is to shake her out of her ignorant complacency."
>
> The people at Benton had not all been provincial to begin with, but they had made provincials of themselves, and called their province, now, the world. And it was a world in which nothing happened, a kind of steady state. Benton was a progressive college, so you would have supposed that this state would be a steady progression. So it had been, for a couple of decades; but later it had become a steady retrogression.[22]

Since the Jarrell book had appeared nearly ten years before, almost no one in the student body that night knew about it or the fact that Sarah Lawrence and its president had been made part of the history of American literature by a poet and writer whose name they recognized. A good many of the students and faculty were finding the Vassar of the early 1960s a little tiresome, and the idea that education in a college could be a traumatic experience was enormously attractive. The result of Buckley's reading from Jarrell was that nearly everything I had previously said took on more significance, having now been seen to come from a man who was a character in a novel. The students didn't care how progressive the college was as long as it had at least some capacity to shock.

But that was not all. Buckley went on to say that I and people like me among liberals admired Bertrand Russell as a philosopher of liberalism who propagandized for world peace, in spite of the fact that Russell had been dismissed from the City University of New York for his scandalous views on morals and had been married four times. If this be liberalism, it was bad for college students. What they should have were required courses in the Great Books in order to get in touch with the best thinking of the ages.

I had never thought to be aided by Randall Jarrell, except through the pleasure of reading his work, but this time he was inadvertently on my side. Once he appeared there, I used the opportunity to point out that the mere fact Jarrell was on the Sarah Lawrence faculty and showed such talent for teaching and for writing about teaching was a tribute to the philosophy of education which Buckley took such pleasure in attacking. As for Bertrand Russell and his marriages, his problem was that although he seemed quite intelligent in so many ways, he was simply a slow learner.

And so the day was saved for liberalism, at Vassar and up and down the Eastern Seaboard. If there were any conservatives in the audience who were sympathetic to or moved by Buckley and his views, most of them were finally alienated by his lighting up a fairly long cigar during the question period. In the Vassar chapel.

Chapter 8

Dewey, Meiklejohn, and the 1950s

> In meeting John Dewey for the first time, I discovered in him an example of selflessness, humility, and integrity which has served as an ideal ever since. I admire, respect, and cherish that image of a man committed to independent thought, to the discovery of new social ideas, to the use of ideas for human welfare, and to the defense of the individual mind against all forms of oppression. He gave to me, as he has to so many others, the sense of belonging to a tradition of humanism.
>
> —Harold Taylor, "Thinkers Who Influenced Me," 1952

Harold Taylor's beliefs as a professor of philosophy and college administrator were guided by three mentors—Max Otto (1876–1968), John Dewey (1859–1952), and Alexander Meiklejohn (1872–1964). Otto, chair of the Department of Philosophy at University of Wisconsin, would hire Taylor in 1939 to serve as an instructor at the university. While Dewey's writings were first introduced to him by Otto, Taylor would not officially meet Dewey, then professor emeritus of philosophy at Columbia University, until 1945 shortly after taking the Sarah Lawrence presidency. It is unclear when Taylor first met Meiklejohn, since he had left University of Wisconsin before Taylor's arrival and had subsequently founded the School of Social Studies in San Francisco.[1] Taylor certainly would have had contact with Meiklejohn, who was an expert on First Amendment issues, by the late 1940s and early 1950s as he became embroiled in the issue of communists on college campuses and the investigation of Sarah Lawrence faculty by the US Senate Subcommittee on Internal Security.

All three philosophers did not live lives of abstract philosophy, and their careers clearly guided Taylor's image of himself as an academic engaged with the world as he drew upon their teachings and philosophical positions. His personal correspondence with Otto, Dewey, and Meiklejohn displays great affection and appreciation for their help and guidance; yet, he would have also trod carefully among the friendships. While Otto and Dewey were quite close and, according to Taylor, Dewey viewed Otto as one of the greatest teachers of instrumentalism and pragmatism, the views of Dewey and Meiklejohn were at odds, leading to tensions between them in the mid-1940s.[2]

Taylor's devotion to Dewey took many forms. He served as a toastmaster for the 1949 Dewey ninetieth birthday banquet at New York City's Commodore Hotel with 1,500 attendees, coordinated efforts to publish the collected works of Dewey, assisted with Dewey's nomination for the Nobel Prize in Literature, was instrumental in saving the Dewey professional papers and securing their archival home at Southern Illinois University, and prepared a foreword for the first comprehensive biography of Dewey, The Life and Mind of John Dewey by George Dykhuizen.[3]

Taylor had always planned to write a chapter about Dewey for his memoir and, at my invitation in 1986, prepared the speech "Dewey, Meiklejohn, and the 1950s" for the 1987 American Educational Research Association conference as a draft for this collection. He wanted to rewrite the presentation so that it would better fit into his memoir; yet, this was never finished. I have grafted the original speech with excerpts from Students without Teachers, "Thinkers Who Influenced Me" in Moments of Personal Discovery, and comments taken from a 1966 oral history session held at the Center for John Dewey Studies where Taylor described further his impressions of Dewey as well as Robert Frost and Bertrand Russell.[4]

Taylor's essay seeks to dispel the myth that progressive education ended after World War II and underscores an important and overlooked aspect—the real secret—of a successful progressive school. "The teachers in such schools were activists in the field of educational experimentation and artists in the creation of new educational environments congenial to the growth of children in their intellectual and emotional capacities. At the same time, the teachers were practicing scientists, keeping track of the results of the work they were doing, and finding better ways of judging the quality of student accomplishment than the assignment of letter-grades and numbers from conventional standardized tests."

> I tried to work out what Dewey really meant, how the ideas had been used, and what might happen next. I am a little tired of all the fast-talking laymen and others who dismiss everything which could be called progressive as the work of fools and make the assumption that the only people who care about the intellect or about learning are those who are stuffy about it.
>
> —Harold Taylor, correspondence to Margaret Marsh, 1955

When I first arrived at Sarah Lawrence, I knew very little about the East Coast or its universities, although in six years of teaching philosophy in Wisconsin I had learned a good deal about the difference between progressives and conservatives. Nor did I know much about college presidents and what they did and how they did it. The lack of knowledge was in fact a boon to me in a quite personal way. In the absence of any clues or precedents I found my way to being my own kind of president and learned to plunge ahead in whatever direction seemed like a good idea, whether or not it was progressive, conservative, or radical. In many instances I did not know enough not to do what I did.

In the earlier part of this century, college presidents and professors were considered to be, and considered themselves to be, members of a separate community of the academically inclined, entrusted with handing on the conventional wisdom in matters of moral, political, social, and religious beliefs. They were seldom expected to have anything to do with changing society or with changing the educational system either in their own colleges or in the world at large. In the 1910s and 1920s, college presidents were quite often ministers of the gospel; others gave a basic course in ethics or religious philosophy to the graduating seniors. But it would be a rare one, clerical or nonclerical, who ever said anything very interesting or in any way upsetting, even on his own campus about his own college.

William Allan Neilson of Smith College was one such rare one.[5] He involved himself in the Sacco-Vanzetti case. He spoke every morning at 8:30 a.m. to the assembled student body out of a sense of duty toward their education in contemporary affairs. In matters of public policy—the rights of minorities, academic freedom, foreign policy, social justice, economic change—college presidents were not expected to have deviant views, or if they had them, to express them publicly.

Neither were the faculty members. They were in charge of a given body of knowledge which they were obliged to teach through lectures, textbook assignments, and examinations. Even the illustrious Nicholas Murray Butler, president of Columbia University when John Dewey was there and another exception to the general rule about college presidents and their lack of social involvement, took the position that any faculty member who disagreed with the policies of the university on public issues "should, in ordinary self-respect, withdraw of their own accord from university membership." Translated into ordinary discourse, this would read, "If you don't agree with the president and his trustees, you are fired."

John Dewey and Alexander Meiklejohn with equal degrees of intensity rejected this view of the role of the university scholar as a return to the idea of the Inquisition. Both men had learned to enjoy controversy and to use it as an educational instrument. They believed that philosophers as educators and citizens had a duty to say publicly what they think. If, as was the case with Socrates, this gets them into danger, it is simply the risk that all philosophers and scholars must take.

For Meiklejohn, colleges were places where everybody, including the president, should share in a lively intellectual life, and it was the president's responsibility to make sure that the faculty, student body, board of trustees, and alumni were stirred into active thought on educational and philosophical questions. Meiklejohn was a genius in stirring things up. When he began urging me to take an active part in such stirring, I pointed out that the result of his own addiction to this idea was that he was dismissed from the presidency of Amherst and was voted out of office in his own experimental program at the University of Wisconsin.

As president of Amherst College from 1912 to 1923, Meiklejohn held a clearly defined idea of what a college of the liberal arts should be and what it should do. A college, he said, is "fundamentally a place of the mind, a time for thinking, an opportunity for knowing," and the faculty should see themselves, "not only as the servants of scholarship, but also, in a far deeper sense, as the creators of the national intelligence."

It was fairly clear to the Amherst faculty and trustees that Meiklejohn did not feel that the faculty or the curriculum of the Amherst of 1912 was serving the cause of true scholarship or was interested in creating a national intelligence. The faculty members, twenty-seven of them, were tenured professors in a small town, and they couldn't be fired nor be forced to make a new curriculum if they didn't want to. Meiklejohn's answer to the problem was simply to wait with unconcealed impatience for retirement of the lethargic ones and to make new appointments of young people like Robert Frost as soon as he possibly could.

The alumni in their turn were irritated by Meiklejohn's criticism of the Amherst of the past—their Amherst—and by the moves he was making to change it into a serious college. They wanted, among other things, coaches for the Amherst sports teams so that Amherst would win and the college would gain prestige for itself and its athletes. Meiklejohn, who was himself an athlete with championships in tennis, squash, and soccer, had his own answer for that. He wanted the students to run their own teams, and he told this to the alumni in a statement that should be passed around at every alumni reunion of every American college: "When you look at our team on the field you will see college students playing football, not football players attending college in order to play. . . . The victory must take care of itself. If you win you win. If you don't win, somebody else does. I don't know what more can be said."

Having irritated the trustees, the alumni, and a good half of the faculty, that left the student body as the only section of the college in which Meiklejohn's ideas were persuasive and acclaimed. The day before commencement in 1923, after he had spent the previous year on a sabbatical in Europe, the trustees told Meiklejohn that they had lost confidence in his presidency. He resigned at once and went through commencement without a trace of bitterness or resentment. He merely questioned their judgment, and he told the alumni in a speech the next day, "I differ from you on most issues of life, and I shall keep it up." Twelve students in the graduating class publicly refused to accept their diplomas on the grounds that any college which would dismiss a president of Meiklejohn's quality did not give out diplomas that were worth having. Eight members of the faculty resigned in protest.

Four years later in 1927, Meiklejohn had started his Experimental College at the University of Wisconsin with the help of three Amherst faculty members who left to join him in Wisconsin. At the invitation of President Glenn Frank and after a unanimous vote of the Wisconsin faculty, he organized a two-year program as an alternative to the regular freshman and sophomore curriculum. The first year involved an intensive study of Greece in the age of Pericles, its philosophy, literature, politics, history, and social organization, with a second year spent studying the United States under the same general categories. There was usually one lecture each week which the whole college attended; the rest of the faculty and student time was spent in tutorials and discussion groups. The faculty members read the same texts as the students and led the discussions each week. At some point between the two years, students carried out a field study of an American community, preferably their own. After that, the student entered the regular courses of the junior and senior years.

Five years after his arrival at Wisconsin, the faculty voted Meiklejohn and his college out. There was no doubt about the intellectual vitality of the Experimental College or about the impact on the students of their involvement with Meiklejohn and his program. The effect lasted through the whole of their lives. But once more, Meiklejohn had alienated the faculty by insistence on the superiority of his way of doing things, his sharp tongue, and the critical view he took of the humdrum courses being taught in the rest of the university. As Robert Frost once said, "Alex enjoyed his failures the way most people enjoy success."

There was a purity of motive in Meiklejohn's effort to get his students and the wider public involved in critical thought and enlightened action. Few educators inspired stronger feelings of loyalty, not merely to himself as teacher and friend, but to the principles by which he lived and the commitment he made to the life of the mind. He had the physical frame of a flyweight boxer with a style of argument to match. It was a pleasure to argue with him even though he was relentlessly rational. He would never think of trying for a knock-out. That would spoil the argument when the idea was to keep the discourse going at a high level of intelligence. At the age of eighty-five he was still playing cricket and tennis and teaching the Berkeley students the ground rules of the First Amendment. He wanted the students to know that freedom of speech didn't matter very much unless you put it to work on behalf of ideal causes.

He also wanted the students, and the rest of the nonstudent world, to share his own infatuation with the Constitution of the United States, in particular its First Amendment guaranteeing freedom of speech. Unlike most of the university advocates of free speech, Meiklejohn became directly involved in political action on its behalf. He was one of the early members, in 1927, of the American Civil Liberties Union and testified before congressional committees on the meaning of the First Amendment. In 1957, he petitioned Congress for a redress of grievance, his grievance being that the establishment of the House Committee on Un-American Activities was a violation of the Constitution and his own rights as a citizen and, in 1962, at the age of ninety, he became chair of the National Committee to Abolish the House Un-American Activities Committee. He was fearless, provocative, eloquent, and prolific. He became a leader in the search for sound legal arguments in support of individual citizens and was published in law school journals. Justice Felix Frankfurter, with a touch of annoyance, at one point suggested that Meiklejohn would benefit by spending three years in a good law school. To which Meiklejohn replied that he would do it if Frankfurter would spend three years in a good school of philosophy.

Over the years of the 1950s and 1960s Meiklejohn and I kept up the flow of genial agreements and disagreements. In the meantime the 1950s had become a period packed with controversy about everything from the cryptofascism of Joseph McCarthy to the necessity of reconstructing the college curriculum. "The curriculum," said Meiklejohn, "has now become merely a vast collection of mutually unintelligible subjects. The members of the faculty have, professionally, little if any intellectual acquaintance with one another." The elective system and the open curriculum of the progressives, he said, had undermined the structure of the liberal arts and produced a national disaster. What was needed was a return to the fundamentals of Greek and Western culture, in short, a curriculum quite a lot like the Meiklejohn Experimental College coupled with the Great Books program as developed by St. John's College.

I pointed out that the Meiklejohn plan involved a paradox in his thinking. On the one hand he held the view that students must be taught the meaning of freedom in their lives as citizens of an egalitarian society. On the other hand he allowed little exercise of freedom in their intellectual or social lives and in the planning of their own education. It was a paternalistic system which taught its students to argue endlessly about abstractions and confined the range of their knowledge to a narrow sector of Western thought. He was throwing in his lot with Mortimer Adler, who in Nelson Algren's phrase, was "the Lawrence Welk of the philosophy trade," and with Robert Hutchins, president of the University of Chicago, and Stringfellow Barr, president at St. John's.[6] These were men who felt that students were students, too immature to take a hand in finding prescriptions for their own education.

~

At the time of my going to Sarah Lawrence as president, Max Otto wrote to John [Dewey] and said that I would be writing to him and hoped that John could spend some time with me. It was that simple open invitation to which John had replied, "Sure, when he comes tell him to look me up."

With a certain amount of anxiety and reticence I wrote to John and announced my arrival in the East and asked that if he could sometime spare a moment I would love to pay him a visit. I was coming across a figure in history, and it was in that mood that I visited him. His apartment was on Fifth Avenue where he lived with Robbie [*Roberta Dewey, his wife*] and the children.[7] After having raised one family, he adopted two Belgian children who were refugees. I went down to the apartment and just sat and talked. Robbie invited me into the living room and the three of us spent some time for a while. Then John and I settled down for an hour and a half in his study and talked, and from then on we became quite personal friends. I think that at that point in his life, having lived through three careers, his philosophical colleagues of the great Woodbridge group had all died.[8] Of course Bertrand Russell was still alive at the time, and George Santayana was living in Rome, both of whom he disliked. His immediate friends he had outlived and the middle group of people who could be called Deweyans and instrumentalists had either disappeared from his life or in one way or another were not closely attached to him.

At that point I was young and was president of a college which, while not designed deliberately to reflect a Deweyan conception of education, represented most of the educational ideas which he believed. That is to say that at Sarah Lawrence the progressive spirit and the progressive program was a direct operational model of most of the things Dewey had been working on all of his life. This appealed to John as an educational program which represented the sort of thing he had admired. I think with the combination—that I just turned up in his life at that time when it was rather empty of personal relationships of the sort which used to crowd him and that we had so much to talk about in terms of education and philosophy and he had so much to give me—I became in a sense a student as well as a nephew and son. It is a continuing regret to me that the preoccupations of the presidency prevented my seeing him more and corresponding with him when I couldn't see him. But during the period from 1945 through his death in 1952, I had the sort of conversations with him that I had that first day, informal, direct, unscheduled, no agenda talks dealing with education, philosophy, and contemporary politics. Again I blame myself for not having just carved out sections of time, since Dewey was so interested in talking about these parts of his life, that I did not take the time and make myself available for this sort of conversation and then done something with the result.

Philosophers at that period near the end of their lives need concerned, interested, sympathetic persons to talk to who can then draw out of them the warmth of ideas which comes from reminiscences.

John felt that of all the people who maliciously misinterpreted what he really meant, Bertrand Russell was the worst offender. It may have been our special relationship which made this sort of comment possible in that I don't think John had anybody to say this kind of thing to, whom he trusted well enough. But I can recall the sharp critical attitude he took toward Russell, who was the person who in a sense deliberately refused to understand what Dewey was saying and, with his smart-aleck attitude, his critical posture, his style of writing critically about other philosophers, was at his sharpest when he was dealing with Dewey. I can recall stretches of discussion between us about Russell's basic philosophy and contributions and that Russell was the person most likely to do you in, whether it was Dewey or someone else. Russell was trapped by the brilliance of his own style and by the particular attitude which he took toward other philosophers. If he did not agree with another philosopher's views, Russell would in a sense attack them in the way he described their ideas. This annoyed Dewey. We also talked some about Santayana, for whose work he had a kind of amused tolerance. Santayana's relationship to Dewey was better intellectually than that between Dewey and Russell.

Dewey felt that at this stage of his life there never had been a time in his entire career in philosophy at which there were more misinterpretations of what he was saying. He was quite discouraged in those years—in the 1940s—about the fact that here he was alive, able to read the interpretations of his work which usually came after the obituary, and powerless to correct the misinterpretations of what he was saying both in his theories and practices of education. People were implementing a kind of education in his name for which he violently disapproved, and he couldn't keep going around saying, "No that isn't what I mean, no that isn't what I mean." In another sense, the criticisms of Dewey and the 1950s' attacks on progressive education were attacks on liberalism in social thought and action when a great many people were seriously, and justifiably, worried about a deterioration in the quality of science education and in the ability of school children and college students to read and write. It was also true that there were a fair number of teachers who took to heart some form of progressive ideology at the expense of common sense and educational imagination. The less sophisticated progressives were intent on breaking the chains that bound children to their nailed-down desks, but they were not as clear as they should have been about what to do with students once their desks became moveable. I think that one of the reasons he delighted in his awareness of what was happening at Bennington and Sarah Lawrence was that he thought, "At last I have encountered somebody who understands what I really do mean and is putting these views into practice."

In his personal characteristics, he was one of the sweetest, and gentlest, and most generous men I think I have ever met. There was a saintly quality about him which was flavored by a wit and a caustic reference to persons whose views and attitudes and ideas he didn't especially like. His saintliness was not saccharine—it was an openness of spirit and a concern for others which was just instinctive and beautiful to see. For example, he would take the time to write letters to graduate students who wrote to him asking questions. I kept running across people as I went around the country who had letters from him, which astonished them, written with his own peculiar kind of typing and sometimes written by hand. He replied simply because they had written to him to say here is a question they wished to raise. Several times during our talks together we were interrupted by young people to whom Dewey had said, "Well, come on in when you're in New York, come and see me, and we'll talk about it." When they did come, he would talk to them. It was a kind of affectionate attitude toward the young. He was awfully fond of children, and his philosophy reflects that fondness as well as his fierce indignation about people not paying attention to the sensitive periods of a child's life. One can take from this his philosophy of education as the continuing, emotional, intellectual protection in the development of the child, and this kind of philosophy could be written by no other person than one who was intuitive in relation to children. He just loved them.

He lived a particular kind of life which was, I would judge, atypical of the American academic—and was closer to the life of a European academic. I came into his life at a time when this particular way of living which I saw might not have been typical. He lived so long that he could have lived four or five different styles. But when I knew him, he had the continuing concern to stay in his study and write letters and read, and his interest in ideas was, if anything, more intense than ever.

Upon meeting Dewey, one would have a preconception of a dull person since his literary style was rather wooden and to some extent sententious with only occasional flashes of brilliant writing. But you would find sentences which just shine embedded in whole paragraphs.

His was an academic style without much to it. In my case, I wasn't ready for the simplicity and affection in the way in which Dewey dealt with me. I would have assumed a more distant kind of person who was not as warm and direct in his personal relationships. Again it may have been that his relationships with other people during this phase in his life might have been different. But I have my own corner of direct experience of knowledge about John which was just mine, and I never really saw him much with other people.

He would slide little references to persons and events into his conversations, and he followed the news quite closely. He talked about politics and world affairs and current references would come in. It was a very easy style of conversation and quite amusing when he would start telling stories. He loved to illustrate his points with stories. It was never penetrating or a wit of the sort one might get with a more brilliant conversationalist. I should think that Whitehead's conversations were at a level of wit and literary style which Dewey never reached. His was the plain, Vermont farmer kind of thing. The appearance of that rugged face had in some characteristics a similarity to Robert Frost's face, and there were other similarities between the two men in terms of habitat, a tough country character, and the simplicity of the farm boy who doesn't pretend to be anything but what he was. In Frost, it became, to some extent, an act. I had the privilege of knowing Robert Frost in his later years, too. Although Frost was direct and could talk to you straight, when he was in company he was being Robert Frost. His face became part of the total act of being Frost. I think he may have read his poems a few too many times to audiences, so that he began in personal conversations and discussions saying things that you might hear him say in his comments throughout his lectures and poetry readings.

But in the case of Dewey, the character of grace, of generosity, of heart, and of mind was quite direct, and his conversation was of that kind of simplicity. I wasn't ready for the directness of his discussions in philosophy, without the use of an academic vocabulary, which I found in our personal conversations when discussing philosophical points. He would pause and there would be a momentary silence, which I saw no reason to interrupt, but the flow was there. I remember one time we talked about what was radical in philosophy. He had said, "I consider myself to be more of a radical now than I was twenty years ago." I said, "What do you mean, John, what is radical then, what preconceptions do you wish to sweep away, since the radical means that we're going to fundamentals and we want to change the roots of things. What are you doing now that you didn't do twenty years ago?" He said, "I'm more radical in my separation from the psychologists. My views in epistemology are more radical than they were. I think I was right at the start, and I'm more right now." I had read John Dewey's books in the context of Whitehead, Russell, James, Bergson, and Santayana. I had found a greater strength in Dewey's position than in the others and had come to feel that although Santayana, James, and Whitehead shared many of the same naturalistic convictions, it was in Dewey that these convictions were pressed to their ultimate meaning and thus yielded a greater variety of insights. But until I met Dewey I had not seen how serious a commitment one could make to philosophy, nor had I seen such honesty, clarity, range, and depth in any mind before.

∼

In those years of the mid-1940s and early 1950s when I had just come to know Meiklejohn and Dewey, the lines of battle were already drawn between the progressives and the conservatives, and the progressives were on the defensive. Then as now, progressive education and Dewey's ideas were blamed for everything from the spread of illiteracy to the superiority of the Russians in space science. The focal point of the attacks on liberalism was the philosophy of John Dewey, although in the 1980s in the mouths of the money-grubbing TV evangelists, it was called secular humanism. Back in the 1950s it was a fairly simple matter to attack Dewey's philosophy, since so few people knew what it was, and those who did and disliked its radicalism found ways to misinterpret it. One of the most powerful instruments of misinterpretation was Henry Luce and the Luce publications, in particular *Time* and *Life*. Luce asked his editors and writers for articles, editorials, and reports which could link progressive education and Dewey to American failures in cold war diplomacy and educational practice. Alfred Kazin reported that at one of the Henry Luce office luncheons with intellectuals, Luce announced in a loud voice, "John Dewey sold philosophy out." Two of the more powerful critics of Dewey and the progressives were Admiral Hyman Rickover and Robert Hutchins.

I found Dewey impatient with much that was done in his name in the schools and much that was said about his philosophy of education.

He was baffled by the fact that his educational ideas were being systematically distorted in the national press and at the same time were widely misunderstood by teachers and educators who were putting them into practice in the schools and colleges. He didn't quite know what to do about it. He said that one of the primary ways in which he had been misunderstood was in his concept of growth and experience. What he meant by growth and what his critics meant by what he said about it seemed never to be understood. The critics said that he was confused, ambiguous, and hopelessly optimistic, and that his idea of growth made no distinction between the growth of weeds and the growth of flowers—it was sheer growth in whatever direction the individual psyche cared to go. In fact, Dewey was hardheaded, realistic, and profound, all at the same time. His criterion for measuring growth was whether it led to further growth, and the institutions and practices of education were to be measured by the degree to which they freed students to discover truths, ideas, and experiences of their own. There could be no intellectual or personal growth until individuals learned to make their own discoveries and injected themselves into their own education.

Through his lectures, articles, and books he had already made most of the same criticism of current education that Rickover and Hutchins had made, and he didn't want to dignify Rickover or Hutchins with a serious reply. He thought of Hutchins not as a philosopher but as a cultural entrepreneur unduly influenced by Mortimer Adler. He considered Rickover a publicity-seeker and a military autocrat who was giving orders to the country.[9] He felt that to reply would be to promote him from busybody admiral to educational philosopher.

I disagreed. I felt that Hutchins was being taken seriously precisely because serious scholars had not set out to refute him and he had developed a successful public relations formula for his public statements and speeches. His opening paragraphs would contain an obligatory and extreme denunciation of American education, designed to catch the eye and ear of the reader or listening audience, with variations on the theme that the present educational system was rotten to the core. Then he would follow a set of admonitions about the ideals of higher education with the general conclusion that the whole thing could be remedied by reading and discussing a set of well-known books.

Instead of leaving the case for the progressive cause to be made by others, I felt that Dewey should have done a short series of articles which met the criticisms head-on and redefined rather than defended progressive education and that this would be the most effective way not only of dealing with Rickover and Hutchins but of giving an injection of new ideas into the educational system. Dewey decided finally that after sixty years of explaining, proposing, redefining, and stating the case for liberalism in education and social change, he would leave the field to the younger ones and get on with his own work. "It's getting pretty late for me, and I've got a lot more to do."

In fact, at eighty-six he *was* old. But more than this, the study of philosophy itself had shifted under the influence of the linguistic analysis and had become a technical subject for linguistic experts. The new generation of graduate students was being taught that analytic philosophy was the only kind worth doing and that Dewey's ideas were outdated and were either irrelevant or too obvious to be bothered with. Dewey went on to deplore the development of a current breed of academic professionals whose competition for prestige and status within the profession led them to write papers on technical subjects, publishing them in journals and reading them at philosophy conferences. He said that most of the professional philosophy was not worth reading and most of it consisted of papers written in reply to other papers by one person about another person's book. He predicted that if academic philosophy continued in its present path now that the colleges and universities were expanding, with enrollments doubling and tripling every few years, no one would be studying philosophy. The students would refuse to become trapped in courses with almost total irrelevance of subject matter and would turn toward psychology, sociology, history, and the creative arts, leaving the philosophy professors to go on talking to themselves.

I was happy to be able to tell Dewey that in Wisconsin the philosophy classes were overflowing with students and that his dear friend Max Otto was still flourishing with his course "Man and Nature," having grown to more than five hundred in size, and was generally considered to be the most exciting intellectual experience available in the entire university. I also explained to Dewey the extraordinary practice of the Wisconsin students in expressing their approval of a given lecture by something more convincing than a standing ovation. At the end of a lecture the entire class would begin a low hissing sound which rose to a crescendo, transposing itself into a loud "BOOM," then turning into a reverent "aaaah," finishing off with the shouted name of the professor. (SSSS, BOOOOOM, AAAAH, OTTO.) It was the academic equivalent of a football cheer. There were only a few professors in the history of the university who ever evoked this kind of response, and the faculty members who were critical of Max Otto's country style of teaching referred to the "Man and Nature" course as the largest and the worst philosophy course in the whole United States.

Dewey's disappointment with the state of philosophy was matched by his embarrassment with the Columbia University trustees who in his view had disgraced the institution by putting a five-star general into the president's office, obviously to demilitarize his public image and to help him on his way to the US presidency. Dewey was delighted with the story that circulated around the Columbia faculty that if Eisenhower ran for office, a faculty member who voted for him would be showing that he cared more for his university than he did for his country. Dewey was also delighted with the story about his ninetieth birthday dinner which Eisenhower found impossible to attend. The reason given was that were he to attend Dewey's dinner, he would then be obliged to go to all the other dinners for ninety-year-old faculty members. Hundreds of other guests of various ages and degrees of importance, including Nehru, then prime minister of India, managed to get there.

∽

The birthday dinner itself had certain elements of suspense, drama, and humor in that John had been asleep that day [*October 20, 1949*] and Robbie, taking full care of him, didn't want to wake him up because he had a cold and to root him out and bring him to the dinner she considered not to be very good for his health. So, we waited and waited for John to come. As chair, I had the responsibility of deciding what to do about his absence and whether we should postpone the program until he did come. Harry Laidler [*executive director of the League for Industrial Democracy who arranged the event*] called on the phone to see if John was awake yet. There was the empty seat beside me and people at the dinner were wondering whatever happened to John.

Finally we couldn't stand it any longer since we knew he was going to come, but if we had stopped the program until he arrived we might then postpone it until so late that people would have to leave. So I stood up and announced the fact that we were going to start the dinner, the speeches, and the rest as soon as we reasonably could. But since it would be rather like a marriage ceremony without the bride, perhaps we could do something which is so often done before marriages—discuss the bridegroom informally before the formal ritual begins. I called on people in the audience who were not on the program. We did that until John turned up.

John finally arrived, and, of course we all made a big fuss, and he made a lovely speech. He was in full cry, no hesitancy, and it was, in my judgment, the best speech made at the whole dinner. Simple, direct, he spoke of the meaning of democracy and referred to the basic notion of democracy as being the way in which a minority comes to be a majority, that ceaseless flow of minority views infusing the social system and becoming the views of the majority, the way society regenerates itself. It was grand.

Then, as the dinner drew to a close, we had celebrated his birthday, we had said all the things about him, he had responded, but Nehru wasn't there yet.[10] Just as I had the horrors of John not coming at the start, then I had the horrors at the end. The question was whether we all were going to wait there in case Nehru came, or should we all go home? So I stood up and asked John if he would mind waiting a little while to see if Nehru came, and he said he wouldn't mind. Robbie said that it was all right, that his health would stand since he had had a sleep that afternoon.

So I said to the audience, "Just as we had some problems at the beginning of this dinner, we have some at the end because Mr. Nehru is coming over if he possibly can. But I can't tell you at this moment if he is or is not coming because there is the question of how long his dinner goes. I suggest that you all sit down and discuss the speeches or John Dewey or anything else. Just trust that Mr. Nehru will come and then if he doesn't come we will have discussed John Dewey, which is always a worthy thing to have done."

So we waited, and in came Nehru with his rose in his tunic and with his white hat on. He made a delightful statement about Dewey's influence on Gandhi and the fact that he as a student and as a person in later life had read Dewey and admired him, and he was so proud to have this chance to be associated with him publicly. It was a gracious speech which had the ring of truth in it.

John Dewey with children at his ninetieth birthday party; Taylor appears in the upper-right-hand corner, 1949. Alexander Archer.

~

My conversations with John were a revelation to me in understanding the ways in which his ideas had so permeated the American culture and modes of thought that they had, so to speak, disappeared into the American collective unconscious where even Dewey himself had forgotten them. He had lived his way from the middle of the nineteenth century into the middle of the twentieth, and as he worked he had a major part in shaping the intellectual character of the time through which he lived. Beginning with a redefinition of scientific knowledge and its place in the philosophy of pragmatism, Dewey went on to apply the attitude of the true scientist to every dimension of moral, political, and social inquiry. The start of the twentieth century and the years following the First World War were a time of opening up and overcoming the past, when painters, playwrights, sculptors, composers, psychologists, architects, dancers, and novelists were breaking with tradition and inventing their own styles, forms, and subject matter in a continual flow of fresh hypotheses. Nothing need be done according to convention. You could try it out—a new curriculum, a new school, a new conception—if it didn't work, invent another hypothesis. That was the real secret of the successful progressive school. The teachers in such schools were activists in the field of educational experimentation and artists in the creation of new educational environments congenial to the growth of children in their intellectual and emotional capacities. At the same time, the teachers were practicing scientists, keeping track of the results of the work they were doing, and finding better ways of judging the quality of student accomplishment than the assignment of letter-grades and numbers from conventional standardized tests.

As I look back on the 1950s and the public debates on the nature and purpose of American education for those years and for the 1960s, I am struck by the number of ideas which bear the marks of Dewey's philosophy. Consider, for example, the programs organized by college students in the early 1960s through the Student Nonviolent Coordinating Committee (SNCC). Students with the courage to put their lives at risk went to the deep South and organized Freedom Schools to teach their contemporaries the rudiments of American history, the skills of reading, writing, and voting. These students, without formal instruction either as teachers or as scholars, set to work to apply their conception of democracy to the existing social system which for the period of revolt, roughly two to three years, had opened up enough to allow for a wave of new experimentation. In one sense the spontaneous experiments were improvisations to deal with the emotional and political conditions of the anti-war and civil rights movement. It was not the regular set of required courses assembled by faculty committees that made 1960s Freedom Schools, free universities, and teach-ins, for example, so powerful a set of instruments for reaching new goals for education.

This was the application of progressive ideas to new social situations and a magnificent demonstration on a national and international scale of the wisdom of Dewey's principle of learning by doing. Few precedents were to be cited and followed. There was only the work to be done and the men and women of good will who volunteered to do it. As the first years gave way to successive efforts in training and performance, programs became more sophisticated and effective. I think it is fair to say that the cumulative body of experience of the Peace Corps, Head Start, Vista, and the Teacher Corps confirmed the validity of progressive ideas in the reform of the schools and colleges. The apparent defeat of the progressive movement of the 1950s has been countered by the response of a new generation of critics and a renewed sense that something is seriously wrong with the system.

The contribution of Dewey and Meiklejohn in the 1950s was to clarify the issues and to provide two sets of ideas for the reform of the schools and colleges. I think we can assume that as the cycle of history moves into its next phase it will work its way out of the conservative period in which it now finds itself and recapture the social and moral energy of John Dewey.

President of Sarah Lawrence College, 1947. Charles Trinkaus, courtesy of Sarah Lawrence College.

There are few men and women who receive as much advice as the president of an American college. The advice comes from politicians, journalists, radio commentators, Congressional committees, businessmen, alumni, trustees, students, parents, deans, faculty members, and people he meets on buses. Much of it does not reach the president directly but is blown on the winds of private talk. There are people, some of them strangers, who will quickly advise him about raising money, how to get rid of subversives, how to aid free enterprise, what to say and what not to say, what subjects to teach, how to discipline the younger generation, what to do about communism, and how to encourage free thought without worrying anyone about its consequences. The inner content of a great deal of this advice, no matter what its outward form, is, Don't do anything. It will be either expensive or dangerous.

—Harold Taylor, *On Education and Freedom*, 1954

Chapter 9

Thoughts on Leaving Sarah Lawrence and Life Thereafter

I think if we continue to load the fund-raising on our presidents, we will either kill them, drive them out of office, or sterilize their intellects. I enjoyed my fund-raising experience and I think that any president who takes a stand-offish attitude to financial problems of his college is lacking in a basic qualification. But let's have our educators do education, otherwise the businessmen and fund-raisers will be doing it for them.

—Harold Taylor, Correspondence to Millicent McIntosh, 1959

Taylor brought much attention to Sarah Lawrence during his fourteen years as president but made references to being worn out by the expectations of administration and fund-raising as well as feeling detached from students and faculty. This is not to say that he did not successfully raise funds for the college. In the early 1950s, Taylor oversaw a capital campaign to secure support to build the Reisinger Concert Hall. Upon his resignation, however, he wrote an essay for the New York Times, *"College President—Idea Man or Money Man?," where he questioned the expectations for the new college president who was enmeshed in a public relations culture. In contrast, he maintained that the college president "must have time to read, to talk with students and faculty, to listen, to learn" since leadership was not merely the act of making a public statement but, rather, represented "years of continual study and critical thinking through daily association in the university with those who are themselves concerned with such issues."*[1]

Taylor's final years at Sarah Lawrence were not without tensions. Faculty and students objected to the college's decision to increase student enrollment by 38 percent; ill-timed resignations of deans caused some to question his leadership; rumors of promiscuity were whispered; and some resented his efforts to establish a "coordinate college," a proposed Eugene Meyer College for men at the Meyer mansion in Mount Kisco, New York, approximately twenty-five miles from the Bronxville campus.[2] Taylor recognized those difficulties during his final year and, in early January 1959, submitted his resignation to the board of trustees.

[When I decided to leave Sarah Lawrence] there were a lot of internal factors. I had become so busy that I'd bungled some things inside and become less patient, and I was becoming physically and intellectually and emotionally exhausted. It was not a decision which I had planned a year ahead; the situation for me had become, in a sense, untenable. I had no patience to go on dealing with the complex problems which arise at any institution that has to be supported from new funds. I entered a different dimension of administrative responsibility, since I had been trying to do more than I reasonably could and had lost touch with the sort of central concerns which had formerly been mine.

I was no longer on the educational side of the college. The situation had become such that, partly because I'd made some administrative mistakes which could not be corrected and partly because I had done about all I could for the place, to have tried to do more would have, even if the situation had been entirely comfortable, been stretching myself against too great of odds.[3]

On January 2, 1959, Taylor submitted his resignation to Lloyd Garrison, chair of the board of trustees.

Dear Lloyd:

I am writing to resign from the presidency of Sarah Lawrence College.

I respect the college and am completely devoted to it. There is no finer teaching anywhere. There is no student body more interesting, more loyal, or more committed to the ideals of an enlightened community than this one, no alumnae body more alive to the values of the mind.

However, the steadily increasing burden of responsibility placed upon the American college president for administering and financing education has become so great that it removes from him the opportunity to share in the intellectual and educational life of his institution. This raises special difficulties for a college president whose deepest interest lies in the content and process of learning rather than in the problems of its external organization.

We at Sarah Lawrence believe in the right of the members of a scholarly community to govern themselves, to teach what they know, what they believe, and what interests them most. This in itself produces a variety of administrative problems which develop from the nature of a fully democratic community of the kind we have here. That these problems are worth taking any amount of trouble to solve, I am certain. But I am less certain of my ability to solve them without relinquishing the opportunity for a personal and intellectual life of my own.

I have tried over these past fourteen years to act in ways which can secure the freedom of our faculty to teach, to create, and to work together in their own terms to achieve ends of their own making. I have done what I could to foster new ideas and talents in the students and faculty alike. Whatever of this has been accomplished is a measure of the satisfaction I have found in my work at Sarah Lawrence.

It is thus with regret that I submit to the board of trustees my resignation as president, effective as of June 30, 1959. There are great things in store for this college. My best wishes for its future go with my regret that I will no longer be a part of it.

Sincerely,

Harold Taylor[4]

Taylor would publish an essay, "Some Thoughts on Leaving Sarah Lawrence," for the alumnae in the Sarah Lawrence Alumnae Magazine *in spring 1959. Not only does this represent a farewell to his former students, but Taylor underscores an important yet overlooked perspective for educational reform—addressing issues and problems in fresh and original ways rather than by today's conventional best-practices approach.*

"Having grown up in Michigan, in pioneer days before railroading, father had a habit of regarding every problem as though it were original, to be thought out as if no one had ever thought it out before." This is how Louise Lawrence Meigs describes her father, William Van Duzer Lawrence, the founder of the college. It seems to me that the founder's habit of mind has been central to Sarah Lawrence's way of thinking ever since the college began. It seems to me, too, that this way of thinking is essential to progress in human affairs. Unless every problem is thought out as if no one had ever thought it out before, we are likely to accept conventional solutions, simply because someone else has done the thinking for us.

The original problem the college set out to solve was how to bring the liberal arts and sciences into the lives of young people in such a way that the knowledge and insight thus gained can become a natural part of the lives they lead after college. That is to say, education was considered to be a way of making human life richer in enjoyment and wider in range, deeper in its satisfactions, and greater in its service to humanity at large.

How is this accomplished?

By allowing full rein to the talents and interests of students in fields of study in the liberal arts and sciences where these talents can be put to work most effectively. By thinking of the strengths of young people and building upon them, rather than penalizing them for their present weaknesses. By showing respect and affection for students, by trusting students to do their best. By making a college community in which students are free to give the most that they can and free to enjoy a rich variety of experiences in everyday life.

The particular style of Sarah Lawrence is the result of this philosophy. What it means in practice is that each student is to be regarded as though she were the first student ever to be educated and that therefore an original solution must be found for her education—a solution which no one had ever thought out before because never before was there this particular student. It would be foolish of course to act as if thirty years of educating students had taught us nothing useful to apply to the next student who comes along, or to act as if the history of the human race since civilization began had given no clues by which to construct a college curriculum. But it does mean that one key to educating the young will not fit every lock; each student has his and her own combination.

Over these fourteen years it is this freshness and originality which has struck me about Sarah Lawrence and its students and teachers. There is no more diverse group than the Sarah Lawrence faculty. They vary as much in temperament, interests, and fields of knowledge as do the students. They have their own style of teaching, they have their own courses with their own content, developed from the materials which they have found in their own intellectual and personal experiences.

Our aim is to make it possible for students and teachers to work together closely in ways most suited to their mutual interests and concerns. Whatever regulation and order is put into our curriculum, however the schedule of classes is arranged or the program is organized, it is the result of this primary aim to make learning and teaching a deeply personal experience for those who undertake it.

For a person like myself, this has meant that the life at Sarah Lawrence has had a richness and a completeness which I doubt could be found in any other place. The president of an experimental college with a community of four hundred students is in a special situation. I have the privilege of knowing most of the students and all of the faculty, when in other colleges of greater size and different style the president might have little chance to know many of them at all.

I also have the privilege of sharing with students and faculty the day-to-day life of the campus. One evening it might be a philosophy seminar on Nietzsche, the next day we might hear a Tuesday afternoon concert of new works by members of the music faculty, two evenings later a brilliant new play by a student, the following weekend an intercollegiate student conference on Zen Buddhism. In this sense, the intellectual and social life is diverse enough and big enough to be self-contained even without the wealth of resources offered by New York City. The intellectual currents of Western culture flow through the college. Many of those who visit the United States from Europe or the East come to Sarah Lawrence, either because they have friends here in the faculty, because they are invited by the college, or because they wish to see one of America's experimental colleges in action.

At the same time, the number of student visitors from other campuses produces a constant interchange of ideas on topics ranging from education to the Russian ballet. Aside from the visitors, the intellectual resources of the college faculty are so great that any person in this community can find intellectual companionship of extraordinary variety whether

her interests lie in politics, science, poetry, or theater. I am grateful for what the faculty has taught me.

The single most important difference I have noticed between Sarah Lawrence and any other institution I know is the seriousness with which both students and faculty take the educational program. In most universities there is very little conversation among faculty members or students about teaching or about anything much to do with the curriculum. Faculty teach in their own department, students take their own courses, and that is all there is to it. There are, of course, curriculum committees where suggested changes in educational policy are discussed, but the discourse among faculty members has little to do with the content of the teaching program. Nor is it likely that one teacher will visit another's class, either to join in the teaching or to learn more about the subject being taught. Nor is there much interest in students on the part of teachers.

At Sarah Lawrence there is not only continual discussion of education and the college program, but the discussion itself has to do with students. Ever since the college was founded, research in student development has been a significant part of the college plan, and the publications by the college in this field are a reflection of the continuing interest shown by the faculty in what is happening to the students as their education goes along.

As a result of all these conditions, I find that I am greatly in debt to the college for the education it has furnished for me. The necessity to explain Sarah Lawrence to educators in other institutions and to the general public has been an education in itself, just as the necessity of understanding the college in order to work in it has given me a field of study which has ranged all the way from research projects with the faculty to studying the history and philosophy of education.

I am in debt to the students of Sarah Lawrence for their lively minds, their frank opinions, their gaiety, their loyalty to the college, their affection for its values, and their companionship. Every year for fourteen years I have seen a hundred or more young women come eagerly to our campus to bring their gifts of talents in a spirit of trust and promise. They and their fellow-students have learned what we had to teach. In the time they have been with us, they have left their mark upon the college—it is what it is because of them. This is what education means, and few who have come here have failed to be touched by the spirit shared by all. I know this when I meet alumnae around the country who were here before I arrived and whom I have come to know as

Taylor speaking at his retirement dinner, 1959. Gary Gladstone, courtesy of Sarah Lawrence College.

Taylor with Eleanor Roosevelt and Robert Oppenheimer at his retirement dinner, 1959. Gary Gladstone, courtesy of Sarah Lawrence College.

friends. What we all have in common is an affection and respect for the creative spirit, wherever it may be found—in science, in the arts, in society, in daily life.

I am therefore grateful to the students of the college, those who are here now, and those who have been here before. Each of us has had an experience of importance to our lives and one which in my case will last as long as I live. Thank you for having made that experience possible.[5]

Life after Sarah Lawrence

> I had no idea what I would do, except that I knew I had to get away from everything I had been doing. Which I did with that six-month disappearance into Asia. That took me back into myself and I found that I had taken up where I left off before I went to Wisconsin to teach after London, before marriage, before getting into the sequence of things that took me to Sarah Lawrence and all the rest of it. When I came back from Asia, what I had hoped would happen did. I had broken all the ties and had the privilege of taking up only those that seemed nourishing.
>
> —Harold Taylor, correspondence to Alastair Reid, 1973

After the staging of a testimonial retirement dinner for 1,300 attendees in the grand ballroom of the Waldorf-Astoria on May 21, 1959, chaired by Edward R. Murrow with speakers including Eleanor Roosevelt, Archibald MacLeish, and Robert Oppenheimer, what does a forty-four-year old emeritus president do? Taylor describes his thoughts and activities during his post–Sarah Lawrence College years.

The day that the announcement of my resignation appeared in the *New York Times*, quite a few people phoned and a fair number wanted to know what I was going to do. I replied that I was going to be by myself for a good six months. My friend Alvin Eurich who was at that time vice president of the Ford Foundation called and asked the same question. When I told him I didn't know the answer, he said, "Come down to lunch and we'll talk it over. Whatever you want to do for the next year, the Ford Foundation will back you." By the end of lunch we had decided that I would set off for a trip through Asia, the Soviet Union, and Eastern Europe, talk to educators and political leaders, have a look at what they were all doing about developing their countries, and take along my clarinet and tennis racket.

The Ford Foundation provided a grant for travel, from September 1959 to March 1960, and it was exactly the right thing to do at the right time. Turner Catledge, managing editor of the *New York Times*, wrote to his correspondents in each of the cities I visited, from Tokyo and Jakarta to Delhi and Moscow. They steered me to exactly the people I wanted to see. The US cultural affairs people organized meetings of all sorts, and there were always friends of friends in what was an honest to God global village. The whole experience had a tremendous effect on me. I was much more aware than I had ever been before of the reality of the problems and people I had been talking and writing about. From that point on I knew how to travel and find out about international affairs at first hand. I formed a passion for international education that never left me. The travel and direct contact with the people in Asia and the Soviet Union had exactly the effect I hoped it would. It not only gave substance to the general ideas I had held about the politics and social reality of world society, but it put a complete block of time between my work at Sarah Lawrence and whatever was going to happen next.

After I arrived home, I was invited to speak at a mass meeting of Yale students on the subject of American democratic leadership. Since it was my first expression of what I had learned in my international tour, it gave me a chance to see what I thought about the issues and ideas afloat on the American campus. I found that the life of a lecturer was a suitable one for a person as interested in ideas and public issues as I was. [*See appendix for an example of Taylor's schedule.*] Around two dozen invitations arrived for university posts—as professor, dean, chair of philosophy departments, president, chancellor, and provost. One university president offered me any position I wanted in his institution except his own. Bill Benton even offered me a vice presidency of *Encyclopedia Britannica*.

When I considered the variety of things I was asked to do, I discovered that I didn't want either to administer or to become part of the faculty of a university. In a sense, the fourteen years at Sarah Lawrence had spoiled me for any presidency of another institution, and for the next fifteen years my chief occupation was that of an itinerant intellectual whose main concern was with speaking on national and international cultural issues and writing articles, books, and book reviews on the same topics. The lecture and visiting professor fees provided a modest income.[6]

Taylor speaking to the alumnae at Sarah Lawrence, 1974. Gary Gladstone, courtesy of Sarah Lawrence College.

In 1975, Taylor accepted a full-time university appointment as distinguished professor of social sciences at CUNY–Staten Island and was assigned to teach undergraduate students and to collaborate with the president of the College of Staten Island in merging Richmond Community College with their four-year liberal arts program. He also developed an international studies curriculum and helped to establish a center for international service, a poetry center for the college and the teachers in the Staten Island school system, and a high school for international service. He officially retired in 1982.

Chapter 10

Adlai Stevenson and the 1960 Presidential Campaign

Putting the Public Interest above His Own

> So to try to talk about what happened is easier now than in the days of the [1960 Democratic] convention, one does not have to put everything in—an act of writing which calls for a bulldozer rather than a pen—one can try to make one's little point and dress it with a ribbon or two of metaphor. All to the good. Because mysteries are irritated by facts, and the 1960 Democratic Convention began as one mystery and ended as another.
>
> —Norman Mailer, "Superman Comes to the Supermart," 1960

Harold Taylor first met Adlai Stevenson through Sarah Lawrence College trustee Marshall Field and, in his role as college president, met other nationally renowned social activists including Ruth Field, Agnes Meyer, and Eleanor Roosevelt.[1] Through an informal arena of political influence, Taylor would find himself becoming part of a short-lived kitchen cabinet for Adlai Stevenson where he served as an unofficial advisor and speechwriter for Stevenson's 1960 "not-a-candidate" presidential campaign. Later, in 1962 and 1963, he would work closely with Stevenson, whom he would come to view as a friend, with the Eleanor Roosevelt Memorial Foundation where they both served on its board of trustees and Taylor oversaw the grants program for social justice and civil rights projects.

While Taylor had decided not to include an essay about his experiences with Roosevelt or Stevenson, I came across two documents that seemed appropriate for this collection—a report by Taylor of a 1960 meeting with Stevenson and an early draft of a 1961 essay to be coauthored with Stevenson's campaign aide, Stuart Brown.[2] Both items, autobiographical in nature, are historically significant and offer his account of Stevenson's involvement with 1960 presidential politics. While Theodore White, Arthur Schlesinger, and many others have written about the 1960 campaign and events leading to "the making of the president," Taylor's limited role, while not recognized, is worthy of note.[3]

Adlai Stevenson (1900–1965) is best known, unfortunately, for his two unsuccessful attempts to win the presidency of the United States in 1952 and 1956, losing on both occasions to Dwight Eisenhower. The 1960 campaign is remembered as the emergence of John F. Kennedy and a hard fought battle between him and Richard Nixon for the presidency. Yet, while Kennedy would attend a contested July 1960 Democratic National Convention in Los Angeles and receive the nomination on the first ballot, much speculation involved whether Stevenson, called "the prophet of the 1950s," would announce his candidacy and be selected on a second or third ballot. In 1959 and 1960, Draft Stevenson clubs had been established throughout the country, and Stevenson's "sleeping candidacy" was a force recognized and feared by the Kennedy staff.

Taylor's "Notes on Conversation with Adlai Stevenson" and his "Brown-Taylor Piece on Adlai Stevenson" have been grafted together to form this chapter. In writing to Brown, Taylor mentioned, "There is some confusion as to who the 'we' are, as the piece goes along. Sometimes it is we the followers of AES [Adlai Ewing Stevenson], at other times it is we the authors of this piece, at others it is the group of Agnes [Meyer], Ruth [Field], Tom [Finletter] and me, without either Tom or Ruth being mentioned."[4] I have edited this material to maintain its integrity; however, since the "Brown-Taylor Piece" was drafted solely by Taylor, I altered "we the authors" to singular nominative case and have allowed "the group" to remain in its original form along with "we the followers of AES." The 1961 article is difficult to place into context, and no copy of Brown's subsequent edited version of the original material exists, that is, a second draft returned to Taylor. Brown-Taylor correspondence is archived at Syracuse University Special Collections Research Center as part of Stuart Brown Papers and "includes" letters from June 1961. Yet, while formerly cataloged into the archival collection, this material cannot be located.

Taylor concludes his correspondence to Brown by saying, "I am astonished that persons like ourselves should have become so close to the center of things through Adlai's accessibility to us and his lack of professional staff. If he *could have done that well with just us kids and the few others, think how he could have done if we had had a half million bucks and a real staff."*[5] While the Kennedy campaign staff felt that JFK would have received the nomination under any circumstances, one can only wonder.

With an interest in history, a concern for contemporary events, and an admiration for Adlai Stevenson, I have been turning over Stevenson's nine years as a presidential candidate and the reasons why he is not president of the United States. I wish to make the case for Adlai Stevenson and to clear away misconceptions about Stevenson's character and his behavior during the [1960 Democratic] preconvention and convention period.

I admit that he had no chance against Eisenhower and that the country in 1952 and in 1956 was not ready for him. Reasons for his not being nominated and elected in 1960 were not, as is so often said, that he was indecisive, that he lacked political realism, that he was soft on hard issues, or that he was unable to come to grips with the details of political operation. Stevenson was a decisive man. He understood himself and his own political strategy very well, and he had had a firmer and more decisive grasp of national and international affairs than any other American in public life, including Mr. Kennedy and those associated with him in his administration.

If the country was not ready for Stevenson in 1956, it was ready in 1960, and it is said by some Stevenson supporters that if he had campaigned he would have been nominated, and if nominated, elected. Why then did he not campaign? His critics said that he could not make up his mind about whether he wanted to be president or about how to act if that was what he wanted. Since he did not take himself out of the running, it was clear that he wished the office. But if he wished the office, then the only way to get it was to run. By not running, he made certain that he wouldn't get it. Yet he stood around waiting to be asked, without giving his supporters what they needed if he were to achieve the goal implicit in his public conduct. Under this explanation, Stevenson becomes a man who is continually uncertain of himself and whose failure to act was a constitutional weakness which would have served his country ill had he ever been elected.

I wish to present a different conclusion based on my experience in the 1960 Draft Stevenson movement—that Stevenson acted consistently and decisively from the moment he was first approached to run for president in 1952 to the Wednesday evening of the Democratic

National Convention in July of 1960. His conception of the presidency was that the office seeks the man and that the man then demonstrates his capacity for the office.

Stevenson's conception of the office was one which endowed it with responsibilities and powers greater than any public office in the world. His conception of himself was of a man who could and would do his utmost to carry out responsibilities assigned to him. The question of whether he should occupy the highest political office in the world was one which he had never felt ready to answer only for himself. He had believed that if the time were to come when in the judgment of America, as that judgment asserted itself in the regular process of American politics, he should be called to office, then he would serve. If not, not.

By definition of temperament and choice of principle, this precluded for Stevenson the practice of operating in his own interest. In this he was fastidious. It was this quality of honesty of motive and clarity of aim toward the public interest which marked him as a man who could be trusted and a trait which endeared him to his supporters. One way of describing his failure to be elected president is simply to say that there were not enough citizens who understood how valuable in political life is the man who honestly puts the public interest above his own.

∽

Stevenson campaigned in 1952 and 1956 for the Democratic Party, not for himself as the man who had thrust himself forward to serve as the national leader. When he said in the 1952 campaign that only men who confused themselves with God could pretend to know exactly how to steer this country through the problems it faced, he was speaking the truth about the presidency, about presidential candidates, and about himself. Mr. Eisenhower's reply was at a completely different level of discourse. "Remember your own power," he told the electorate, "and be not dismayed, because you can do anything." The truth is that the American people could not and can not do "anything." Stevenson was the man who spoke the truth and wished to deal with the issues. Eisenhower covered the issues with rhetoric and smothered proper anxieties with a marshmallow of optimism.

When Stevenson pointed out that in foreign affairs it was necessary to be patient and forbearing, he was shouted down by his opponents who called the courage of patience and the strength of forbearance as the weaknesses of one who was soft toward the enemy. The truth lay with

Stevenson; the softness, as was quickly revealed, lay with Eisenhower. The slow erosion of the truth of America's situation in the world was the result of the Dulles-Eisenhower combination of impetuous talk and intellectual softness.[6] The country was taught to consider foreign affairs to be a battle between two tough opponents and was instructed that the basic policy was to be tougher than the opponent. Thus, Stevenson, who wished to be intelligent and not angry, who wished to deal with the reality of the issues and not with the emotion of a blind patriot, was said to be a man who was soft with the enemy.

But in 1952, the office truly sought its candidates, and Stevenson was one of them. The accusation of indecisiveness began then, when Harry Truman wished to name his successor and finally settled on Stevenson. Stevenson had already begun his campaign for governor of Illinois and told Truman that he did not care to announce his candidacy for president in January of 1952 when he was already committed to the campaign for governor, a post which he was proud to occupy. What he did not tell Truman was that he was not ready to believe that he had the qualifications to be president of the United States and that it seemed improbable to him that there was very much chance of enough people thinking he had those qualifications to get him nominated and elected.

Later that year Stevenson called Truman to ask what Truman thought of his running for the nomination. Truman was understandably angry and wanted to know why Stevenson could not have started when Truman first asked him, giving everyone time to get the campaign moving. They were both right, but Stevenson's course of action was the only one for him to take. Had he agreed to Truman's suggestion when it was first made, he would have had neither the support of a political party which finally closed ranks and came to one conclusion as to the candidate they wanted, nor would he have had the assurance he needed that he was the man who could do the job that needed doing. In any event, Stevenson's record of decision-making while he held the governorship of Illinois was enough to kill the notion that he was too introspective to act decisively.

In some ways, the Stevenson candidacy of 1956 was 1952 all over again—the same Republican candidate, the same confusion in the Democratic Party over a course of action, the same reluctance by Stevenson to commit himself in advance of any clear indication that his nomination would be successful. Adlai said that he had been urged by nearly all the democratic governors in July of 1956 to run. The most decisive thing about Adlai had been the way in which he clung to the decision not to run as an active candidate but to wait for the party to run him. This was sound political strategy, but it was also typical Stevenson in terms of his own integrity. Truman on the one hand was telling Stevenson to become an active candidate, otherwise no one would have anything to do with him unless he did, and on the other hand he must let the Democratic Party pick its own candidate from all those available. It seemed clear to me that Truman refused to accept any act or decision by Stevenson or anyone else which might diminish his own power in politics. His was a political strategy based on personal egotism and a wish to manipulate Democratic Party politics against the idealists and eggheads who, in his judgment, could not be elected to office.

If Adlai had done as Truman requested, he would have been a dead duck in 1956; the party regulars would probably have gone after him as a one-time loser, unable to carry crucial states, and he would never have been nominated. Even as it was, the caution and circumspection which was forced upon him by the party line on civil rights and foreign policy made him much less effective than he could have been. My conclusion was that rather than being indecisive in Truman's terms, Adlai acted in the only way he could, according to his temperament and according to a political strategy based on that temperament and on the real facts of Democratic Party politics.

There have always been these two strands to Stevenson's political strategy—the one of holding back until commitments were made, the other of using this reluctance of a man sought for office to clarify and to strengthen the reasons for the choice. Certainly if one looked at the opposite strategy as employed by the unsuccessful candidates for nomination, there was more to recommend a policy of reluctance than one of pressing one's candidacy forward. A rough and tumble coonskin cap of a man like [Estes] Kefauver [senator from Tennessee] could sustain this kind of defeat without loss of position, since in national and international stature there had never been that much to lose. For Stevenson to have put himself into the running prematurely would have removed him from his special category and in all probability have resulted in the loss of the nomination. He was not that kind of candidate.

∼

Now to the crucial question of the 1960 nomination. The seeds for this action were sown in 1956 when, after the Eisenhower victory, Stevenson was asked about his plans for the future. In a statement issued in November of 1956, Stevenson said that he was no longer a candidate and that he would confine himself to working with the Democratic National Advisory Committee in making opposition policy and providing some alternatives to the Republican administration. From that moment on, Stevenson took no part in Democratic Party politics as such. He addressed no rallies, engaged in no caucuses, attended no meetings except of the Advisory Council, and when asked, both inside and outside the party about his candidacy in 1960, said that he had no plans and that it was time that the others had their turn. During the primaries, Stevenson was deliberately out of the country in South America, had agreed to support none of the candidates either before, during, or after the primaries, although his support was sought by several of them including Senator Kennedy.

In February of 1960, the press had begun to write Stevenson's political obituary. Since he was not a candidate, no one among the party delegations was prepared to try to make him one, and the Kennedy machine had started to roll. Yet Stevenson's candidacy was reborn in the public opinion polls while he was absent from the country. In the meantime, the American position abroad had deteriorated. Eisenhower had been rebuffed in Japan, and America had a genuine recession. There was rumbling of discontent among Democrats with the quality of the Democratic candidates. Then Stevenson arrived back in the United States, having agreed a year in advance to speak in Charlottesville, Virginia, at a celebration in honor of Thomas Jefferson [on *April 12, 1960*].

There were many among his friends who pressed him at this point to enter the race for the nomination, using the Charlottesville speech as the beginning of a fresh campaign. One of his friends, Agnes Meyer, knowing that Stevenson had no staff except the informal help of the members of his law firm, put up the money to supply a speechwriter, William Attwood, an editor at *Look* magazine, who felt so strongly about the dangers of a victory by Richard Nixon that he volunteered to devote himself during the period of the campaign to an all-out effort to see Nixon defeated.[7]

Although Stevenson had asked for help researching the parallel between Jefferson's problems and those of the twentieth century, Attwood provided him with the draft of a speech which would have put him squarely in the middle of the campaign. Stevenson scrapped all the notes except those relating to the Jefferson parallel and wrote a stirring and eloquent statement of American political philosophy which, without specific relation to the campaign, automatically put him back in the public eye and started more tongues wagging about his candidacy.

At that point, a number of us approached Stevenson directly with the request that he drop his previous commitment to remain out of the running and declare his candidacy. The grounds for our doing so were that the world situation had changed radically since the earlier commitment was made and that he was the only figure in public life who had the intellectual stature to do what needed doing in the presidency and to defeat Richard Nixon in the election.

Stevenson's reply was characteristic and in essence the same reply which he gave to Truman in 1952. He said that he had never refused a call to serve his country in whatever capacity he could and that if he were called up now to serve as the Democratic nominee, he would do so. But having committed himself to a position of neutrality about the other candidates and having taken himself out of the active running, he would not declare himself to be a candidate.

Then came the U-2 incident and the disaster of the Summit Conference [*on May 1, 1960, an American U-2 reconnaissance plane was shot down over the Soviet Union causing the collapse of a Paris Summit conference among the Soviet Union, United States, France, and the United Kingdom*]. It was, among other things, a period of incredible confusion, with a mixture of emotions and arguments from those who called for our rallying around our president to support him against the Russians, from others who proclaimed our right to fly reconnaissance planes over any territory we chose, and from those who found our public dishonesty deplorable and our situation in the world one of desperation.

Stevenson had intended to make no more speeches until after the campaign. But the urgency of the world situation and the need for national clarity as to the meaning of the U-2 and Summit incidents persuaded him to speak clearly, decisively, and directly to the issues, pointing out the central failure of the Eisenhower policy. No one else spoke in the bold style, and once more Stevenson was seen to have the qualities of mind and courage to talk sense and to speak the truth to the American people. He was in the presidential running whether he wished to be or not. Once more his friends pressed him to declare his candidacy and to give the millions of people in the country who looked to him for leadership a chance to work on a national scale for his nomination and election. Once more he was adamant. The problem from our point of view was not that he was indecisive but that we couldn't budge him from his previous position.

We decided that whatever kind of candidate we had, declared or undeclared, we were going to do everything in our power to win him the nomination. Just at that point, Arthur Schlesinger Jr., Kenneth Galbraith and Henry Steele Commager, and Joseph Rauh of Americans for Democratic Action, all of whom had been close friends and supporters of Stevenson in the two previous campaigns, issued a statement which confirmed their previous decision to work for Senator Kennedy's nomination on the grounds that, although Stevenson was the best candidate for the Democrats, in Kennedy they were supporting a man who was an actual candidate in place of one who refused to commit himself. In private they pointed out that nominations were won, not at the convention, but in the preconvention period where the delegates were lined up for the man they thought could win. This was a blow to those of us who felt that a national Draft Stevenson movement now, for the first time, had a chance of winning. We believed the Cambridge group to be wrong and that the best way to get the best man elected was to make him de facto a candidate.

∼

I came into direct contact with Adlai originally because Ruth Field invited me to lunch at Lloyd's Neck with Adlai, Ronald and Marietta Tree, and Buffie Ives.[8] Adlai at that point was so busy with everything he was doing that he had no time to think, no time to write, no staff to deal with his mail, and he had Agnes Meyer and Bill Attwood on his neck, having suffered from Attwood's loose mouth and strong prose style. Ruth thought that I could be helpful to Adlai both in writing some things for him (he had seen and liked my "Crisis in Liberal Democracy" speech) and in acting as a general assistant, advisor, or whatever needed doing.[9] Attwood wasn't the kind of writer who could think his way into another man's mind and then write his way out again. He felt, I believe, that his mission was to make Adlai an active candidate whether he wanted to be or not, and he was a dangerous man to have talking all round the place about what he was doing for Adlai. He was also a psychological menace, since here he was, hired by Agnes to work full-time for Adlai, with Agnes also convinced that Adlai should be an announced candidate. And if my theory of Adlai's way of running is correct (that is, he couldn't be nominated *and* elected if he ran hard because of the split this would make in the party and he therefore, both temperamentally and politically, had to go on holding himself apart from the rough and tumble), then Attwood would thwart Adlai at every turn by a lack of sympathy with Adlai's inner nature and outer behavior.

We had a very amusing luncheon, with nothing too serious discussed, and afterward Adlai and I spent an hour and a half together by ourselves and he told me directly how his problem as a national figure centered on the fact that he was a private citizen, involved in Democratic politics only as far as the Democratic Advisory Council was concerned, and that he had no staff except his dear friends in his law office who did the best they could with the mail but could not be expected to deal with administrative problems of the sort that a public figure like himself had to contend with. I offered to do anything I could to help, and Adlai suggested that I write him some memos, starting with a short statement about Truman's accusation of his indecisiveness which would be published in ten days [*to be published in* Look *on June 7, 1960*]. He also said he would be happy to have me help him with his speeches and his writing, and I might give Attwood a call and talk to him about what needed doing. This, of course, meant that I really could not do much for him, since it seemed not very dignified for me to call Attwood and offer to help him help Adlai. It bothered me that Adlai, having had such a bad time with Attwood, should not have cut loose and taken fuller advantage of what I and others might have done for him.

I got an advance copy of the Truman attack from Leo Rosten at *Look* and wrote a short statement for Adlai to have ready for the press and an explanatory letter saying that I didn't think he should tackle Truman on the facts but should simply finesse him by saying that Mr. Truman had strong opinions about a number of things and that this was simply another of his opinions. I then became active with Ruth Field and Agnes Meyer in drawing up a list of those who should be asked to sign a Stevenson for President statement to be published in the *New York Times* as an advertisement. I wrote the statement for the advertisement, arranged to have it published through an advertising agency, and worked with Ruth at her office in lining up the signers.

I also conferred with the Garth group [*political advisor David Garth with others who were preparing their own statement to be published in the* New York Times] at their headquarters about what we were doing, in order that they shouldn't feel that we were in any way undercutting them by organizing our own committee. They understood that we would stay in touch with them about anything that we were doing but that the two operations were separate. They also understood that what we were doing was without Adlai's participation and that although we would like to have him be more forthright in the candidacy, we did not wish to push him into it but would work on our own.

I had also been conferring with Tom Finletter about the Stevenson for President statement, in order to get his ideas, and had a meeting with Agnes, Bill Attwood, and Ruth Field on strategy. Following this, Agnes and I held a press conference where we released the statement relating it to the move of the Galbraith, Schlesinger, Commager group to the Kennedy side. (We also thought that their statement that Adlai was the best candidate but they were going for Kennedy because he was the declared candidate was weaseling on the issue. We believed that a person should go for the best candidate, rather than for the one who is running.)

About this time, Tom Finletter, Ruth Field, and I had been talking on the telephone about how we could get some help from Adlai if he clarified his position about his candidacy. We agreed that unless we could obtain a stronger statement from Stevenson than anything we had been able to get so far, there was little hope of influencing any delegates or any large section of the public. I had a luncheon appointment with Mrs. Roosevelt to talk about my recent Asian trip and, since Ruth, Tom, and I wanted to confer with her about strategy, we changed the luncheon date into a conference about Adlai.

Halfway through the luncheon we had figured, under Mrs. Roosevelt's leadership, that the question of his candidacy should be raised to Adlai in Mrs. Roosevelt's column [My Day] and that this would be the best means of springing it into the open. Tom left the luncheon table to call Bill Wirtz in Chicago to tell him what we wanted and to give him the kind of reply which we felt would do us the most good.[10] Tom had a reply written in a notebook, and after working it over a little at the luncheon table he gave it to Bill over the telephone. Things went according to plan, Mrs. Roosevelt's text was either telephoned or wired to Adlai on Thursday night or Friday morning and the reply was sent. We got our answer. Stevenson would not refuse to serve his country if called upon to do so.

In *Eleanor Roosevelt's June 11th nationally syndicated newspaper column, My Day,* she stated, *"This led me to decide that it would be wise to ask Mr. Stevenson to clarify his position on being a candidate, and I hope in my next column, or perhaps before that in a statement, to be able to give you his answer."*[11] She then goes on to mention the strength of a Stevenson-Kennedy *presidential ticket. In her June 13th column, Roosevelt reported that she received a telegram from Stevenson stating, "I have declined repeatedly to comment on questions about a 'draft.' I think I have made it clear in my public life, however, that I will serve my country and my party whenever called upon." She concluded from this, as printed in her column, "This is clear. If there is the call on the part of the party and the country, he will be a candidate."*[12]

We could have rested content with this, but unfortunately Adlai embroidered his statement with some comments to a *New York Times* reporter over the telephone.

Stevenson spoke to New York Times *reporter Wayne Phillips resulting in the June 13th article, "Stevenson: Not Candidate; Mrs. Roosevelt: Yes, He Is," and concluded with a quote from Stevenson:*

When asked by telephone if he [Stevenson] agreed with Mrs. Roosevelt's interpretation of his statement, he dictated this additional statement:

"My message to Mrs. Roosevelt speaks for itself. I reiterated the position I have taken for several years that I will not seek the nomination for President at the Democratic convention. Therefore I am not a candidate."

When this was read back to him for confirmation he added, as though to himself: "Oh, dear, I suppose that will get me into it with Eleanor, won't it?"[13]

We were right back where we started. Mrs. Roosevelt argued publicly that Stevenson was now a candidate. Others, quoting Stevenson, argued that he wasn't. I think that cooked our goose right there, since no matter how hard Mrs. Roosevelt worked to make this into the sort of candidacy we all had in mind, it still remained fuzzy. I hold the conviction that if Adlai had just shut up and let his statement stand, we would have been off to the races. A good many more people would have rallied round and worked on delegates from various states, at least to have them hold out until the second or third ballot.

Adlai said that his statement to Mrs. Roosevelt's question had gone as far as he wanted to go and to have gone any farther would have been against the position he had taken all along. This reply of course avoided the possibility of his saying that with the world in different shape and so many people after him to run that he had decided to jump in. It also avoided a different kind of statement which could have gone farther without compromising him, for example, to have said that he would not be an active candidate and seek delegates but that if the country wanted him, let the people speak. This was my preference at the time. Adlai's account was that he simply got a request from Mrs. R. and handled it in his own way. Again, he seemed to me to be concealing from himself the degree to which he was committed to helping his own candidacy along, since there was clear collaboration between him and us on this point and he said nothing of our part in it, even when telling the three of us what happened.

There was also irony in the fact that Mother Roosevelt and all us friends had to take him in hand and try to get him to act in such a way that he could get the presidency, since he seemed not to be able to figure it out for himself. But this, too, may be part of a philosophy of allowing fate to carry him along. Although as things turned out, he sure didn't help fate along by anything he did that weekend. When Agnes saw what he had done in the *Times* the next morning, she called me in tears to be comforted and to cuss him out. "He's such a dope," she said. Then, after a pause, "But he's *our* dope."

~

I did some more work for the campaign around New York, spoke at three or four Stevenson for President rallies, and did what I could by writing memos and letters for Adlai. The Friday night [July 8] of the Monday before the convention, Adlai called me from Los Angeles to ask if I would write an acceptance speech which could be used two ways, first as an acceptance speech in the event that, as he put it, the thousand to one chance emerged that he would be nominated, and second, as the charge to the new nominee if it were one of the other people. I sent off a text which I believe reached Adlai on Tuesday or Wednesday of the convention week. It was a rough assignment, since he really needed two different speeches.

Later, in August, when Tom, Ruth, and Adlai and I talked about Adlai's next moves and his stance before the public, we came to the general conclusion that Kennedy was not going to do any more than absolutely necessary to bring Adlai into his administration. I felt that he would not offer the secretary of state job because Adlai was too big for Kennedy to handle. My counsel was that Adlai play his own game from August until November and, when he spoke for Kennedy in the campaign, not to attack the Republicans but to make big policy statements about where the country needed to go in order that he maintain the public image of an American statesman rather than a politician helping another politician. I also said that the possibility of Adlai being useful to his country rested on his retaining his influence in American public and international affairs, since Kennedy would only respect Adlai's power and not have much to do with him on the basis of their past association. Since I felt that the secretary of state job would not be offered, I thought that the UN post would and that Adlai should take it, since this was an arena where he naturally belonged and where he would not be as directly responsible to Kennedy's supervision as he would in the secretary's job. [*Adlai Stevenson served as the US ambassador to the United Nations from 1961 until his death in 1965.*]

~

I would say that the most extraordinary fact about Adlai's candidacy was the utterly personal and simple way it was handled. I had always assumed that public figures of Adlai's stature automatically had working staffs, professional advisors, and all sorts of things going for them. In this case, it seemed to me that Adlai went from moment to moment, improvising as he went, with a central theme underlying all the improvisation—that he was a private citizen who would serve his country in any way he was called upon and that he left it to the luck of the draw and the accidents of history to carry him either in or out of the nomination and the election.

If Adlai had made even a ten-minute statement at the convention about the problems of the country and how they should be solved, he might have taken the whole place by storm. One way of explaining him is to say that it is a tribute to his integrity and to the high standards he set for himself that he refused to exploit such an incredible political opportunity. It would also be possible to argue, of course, that this was the reason he was not president—that he had always refused to act in a tough political way, that he kept compromising himself by his own beliefs until he could not act to win except against his principles. I would argue that unconsciously he knew he didn't want to go up on the cross again and wanted to get as close as possible without winning, but at the same time to be a romantic hero who was too great for the job under the circumstances of its having.

This was probably the last time in American history that a presidential candidate could go so far without running, the last gasp of the amateurs in American politics. No doubt we were foolish to believe that sheer admiration and respect for a man could be mobilized on a national scale outside the regular political party machinery. No doubt we were foolish to believe that a man so committed to principle, so sensitive to the responsibilities of political office, so reluctant to press his own cause could be elected president. But we can testify at least to the fact that in Stevenson we had a man who made decisions and stuck to them, and he held the respect of the country and the love of those who knew that he had never acted out of personal interest or with double motives. I still think he would have been a better president than Kennedy.

Taylor's summer home, Brushwood, in Holderness, New Hampshire, 1972. Taylor was part of an informal group of social scientists, centered around a community formed and led by Lawrence K. Frank at his summer home, Cloverly Cottage, and including Margaret Mead and Gregory Bateson, Lois and Gardner Murphy, Peter Blos, Rollo May, William Perry, and Robert and Helen Lynd (who originally owned Brushwood). Courtesy of the Taylor family.

Taylor at Brushwood, 1960. Courtesy of the Taylor family.

Taylor typing at Brushwood, circa 1975. Courtesy of the Taylor family.

Chapter 11

The Student Revolt Revisited
Students in a Stormy Time

> I think to understand what is radical one must move past the political manifestations of demonstrations, destructions, and assaults into the true meaning of the word, into what the peculiar and unique quality of this generation of student is. They are radical, not merely politically. As a matter of fact, a lot of them never get to politics. They're radical in their attitude to authority, in that, for many of them, they simply deny that any appropriate authority exists for anything. . . . The radical element in this generation of students, among those who are genuine radicals, is that they are testing themselves out in all sorts of ways to see what it is that they believe in, and what it is that's true, what's valid, what they hold precious, what they wish to discard.
>
> —Harold Taylor, "An Interview with Harold Taylor," 1969

During the 1960s, few academics were as supportive of and had as much faith in the college youth movement as Harold Taylor. His 1969 publication, Students without Teachers, *brought further credibility to the social activism of college students that, while now applauded, was held in disdain by most higher education administrators and many faculty at that time.*

In Students without Teachers, *Taylor situated campus Vietnam war protests within the context of social and educational reform and showed how the students' educational critiques—objecting to traditional classes completely* detached from current issues and criticizing common core requirements that were too distant from the interests of students—were within a progressive education ideology and tradition of experimentation dating back to John Dewey. This 1969 publication maintained that the university, as a central institution in modern democratic society, helped to define the quality of American life and insisted that youth could behave with humanity and intelligence (with Taylor's often-quoted phrase "the mark of a true university is whether or not it takes its students seriously"). As he earlier had described Sarah Lawrence's practices within the context of progressivism, Taylor developed a broader framework to situate "the student movement in the total series of social and political changes."

More than a sketch and less than a finished draft, "The Student Revolt Revisited" was conceived but far from being completed at the time of Taylor's death. On a draft page from "On Being Written About," Taylor made a note in the margin saying, "perhaps not this chapter but somewhere the story about SDS [Students for a Democratic Society]; how I got started with Tom Hayden, et al. Use as story of how American politics works." No doubt, this was the beginning of that planned chapter. Begun during the summer of 1987, Taylor describes his involvement with SDS and deliberations of the Port Huron Statement where he would defend Tom Hayden against accusations raised by the League for Industrial Democracy. In his memoir, Reunion, Hayden referred to Taylor as his mentor, and their close relationship lasted throughout Taylor's lifetime.[1]

In Taylor's narrative style, his reminiscences meander with insightful and ironic accounts of the first meeting of SDS at Port Huron (MI), campus speeches at University of Colorado and University of New Mexico, and an exchange with Dwight Eisenhower. Unlike other chapters where I have drawn text from Taylor's interviews and personal correspondence, I have grafted two thousand words of more formal excerpts from Students without Teachers into the body of his original draft along with a postscript including Taylor's remarks at the 1968 Columbia University counter-commencement. I have also added related correspondence with Fred Hechinger, the New York Times education editor, who attacked that event both in the New York Times and later in Change: The Magazine of Higher Learning, referring to Taylor as an aging intellectual and camp-follower of the youth cult.

One of the extraordinary things about the student revolt of the 1960s and 1970s was that so few university faculty members and administrators had any notion that it was about to happen and, when it did, very few notions about how to deal with it. Before it started, at Berkeley in October of 1964 is the date generally agreed to be the time and place,

Harold Taylor, circa 1975. Courtesy of the Taylor family.

I had left the presidency of Sarah Lawrence. While the revolt was going on I was traveling to universities, peace conferences, and international meetings in this country and abroad, doing lectures, writing, talking to students, faculty members, administrators, politicians, and government people about the issues that agitated the students.

I found that the student revolt was a world movement, with outbreaks not only in France, Italy, Germany, and the Netherlands, but in India, Indonesia, South Korea, Japan, Nigeria, and South Africa. It was not a consolidated movement, organized through international bodies, but a collective awareness among the youth of the world's societies that the universities were instruments of social and political control and that students could act on their own behalf to break the grip of governments on their lives and on their future.

In many countries, the mere presence of thousands of youth who held the special status of being students created a new social and political force to be reckoned with. In Thailand, Indonesia, and South Korea in the 1960s and early 1970s, the students were a major factor in the overthrow of tyrannical governments. The developing countries as well as postindustrial societies had never before had to deal with mass numbers of intelligent young people with time on their hands and a social vision in their heads. In Thailand, for example, in October of 1973 the students fought a pitched battle in the streets of Bangkok with the Thai government and its armed forces. By the time the smoke cleared sixty-six students had been killed, more than eight hundred wounded, and the Thai military government had been overthrown.

For the most part my sympathies were with the students, although there was such a variety of situations in which students were acting, and they acted in such a variety of ways—from peaceful demonstrations to violence and arson—that it was hard to make a case for a student revolt with so many different kinds of activists. It was commonly agreed among American college presidents, trustees, and faculty members, for example, that Students for a Democratic Society formed the radical leadership for the American student revolt. They were seen as a dangerous element on the campuses by their physical violence and their advocacy of disruption of speeches, classes, meetings of all kinds and their stupefying refusal to allow any other opinion but their own to be expressed in public.

But Students for a Democratic Society was a completely different organization in 1968 from the form it took at its founding. In its origins, SDS was an idealistic group of student pioneers who developed their own political and social leadership from a general agreement among themselves to support the ideas of a manifesto for American youth which two of their members had written. The basic organizing principle was the idea of participatory democracy. As the organization developed, it did so by spontaneous growth on each campus where a chapter was formed, with a little help from a national central office. Anyone could be a member by sending in five dollars to a "head office" so little organized that it could not supply itself with a list of its own members. SDS was therefore whatever the group of students on a given campus decided it was, and if the chapter at Harvard called for occupying the administration building, or the one at Kent State called for burning down an ROTC building, this was a local matter dealt with by local students and university authorities.

The variety of actions and attitudes, all of them under the ambiguous name Student Revolt, made it very hard for a person like myself to deal accurately with my own feelings and beliefs as far as the students were concerned. Having had a part in getting SDS launched in the spring and summer of 1962 and having defended Tom Hayden and his coworkers of the Port Huron Statement against unfair attacks outside as well as inside the student movement, I had my own conception of the character of that organization and the quality of its leadership.[2] Mine was a conception favorable to SDS but not to everyone's idea of SDS. I summed up my view in a public declaration back in the 1960s that the Port Huron Statement marked a turning point in American political history, the point at which a coalition of student movements had become possible and a radical student movement had been formed. It also marked the coming of age of a new generation.

∽

In the spring of 1962, students at Swarthmore College organized an intercollegiate conference on disarmament, arms control, and American foreign policy to which six hundred students and faculty members from sixty colleges came. Others at Northwestern University created a university-wide symposium, Personal Commitment in the Age of Anxiety. The Student Peace Union with the help of other organizations mobilized a national student protest in Washington against the war in Vietnam to which five thousand students came from everywhere in the country. The Northern Student Movement, a counterpart to the Student Nonviolent Coordinating Committee in the South, was formed to deal with discrimination in the cities of the North. I knew at first hand the quality of effort of the students in these institutions and movements and, being free from the duties of the college presidency after fourteen years, had time to speak at the meetings of the new groups, to confer with them on the issues, and to recognize in them the spiritual and educational allies of Sarah Lawrence students who already held the rights and responsibilities in educational policy and political action for which the students on other campuses were beginning to struggle.

At Sarah Lawrence, the style of education and my own interests made it natural for the president to work more closely with the faculty and the students on educational questions than is usual at other institutions. There were formal and informal meetings with the student council, student committees, classes, student organizations, the editors of the student newspaper, individual students, and with visitors who were either friends of Sarah Lawrence students or others interested in the college's educational program as a possible model for reforms in their own. From the early 1950s on, there were intercollegiate conferences at Sarah Lawrence and elsewhere, on issues in education, politics, the arts, world affairs, and contemporary culture to which students from other colleges sent delegates, dance groups, theater groups, writers, and other representatives. Simply by staying still and listening I learned a great deal about what was happening in the universities and what was happening with the younger generation.

It was not generally known at that time that a national network of students had already begun to assemble itself, not so much by formal organization as by personal friendships and common interests. Students thought nothing of getting a group of six into a car and driving for two days and nights to attend meetings they had heard about through a tattered piece of mimeographing or a note from a friend. An increase in energy could be seen in the National Student Association, which began to collect members and ideas from the informal network of activists, student editors, and reformers previously out of touch with any national organization, some of whom in 1961 and 1962 were beginning to organize SDS.

I had come to know Tom Hayden from his student days at the University of Michigan and to admire his single-mindedness in dealing with the social and political issues which bothered other people, among them the liberal intellectuals, but which did not move them into action. Hayden had a quiet way of doing whatever was necessary to produce some actions and had endless patience with other people, not pushing them to agree with what he said but persuading them by his own behavior that what he believed in and what he was doing was important and necessary. I have known few students who had as natural and easy a way of coming to grips with ideas and of putting them into effect, whether it was a matter of rearranging an administrator's office to improve its operation or examining American foreign policy.

Hayden and some of his friends prepared the draft of a policy statement to serve as a basis for discussion and action among a scattered group of activist students in the Midwest and around the country.[3] They were loosely affiliated with a beginning organization whose name was an accurate description of what they intended to do, Students for a Democratic Society. After reading Hayden's draft of the manifesto and listening to the discussion of the issues it raised, at the first national convention of the organization in June of 1962 in Port Huron, Michigan, it became clear to me that the next phase in a national student movement toward

Taylor with Tom Hayden; Jane Fonda and Hayden were staying with Taylor at Brushwood during the filming of *On Golden Pond*, 1981. Courtesy of the Taylor family.

political action had begun, even though the exact character of a program of action remained undecided and largely unpredictable. Whatever the outcome might be, it was also clear that it would depend entirely on the initiatives taken by students themselves, with little support from the older generation of radicals, trade unionists, liberals, or educators. It was up to the students to find their own political style and their own set of unifying principles.

The SDS manifesto, as I discussed it with the students (there were seldom more than forty or fifty of us together in Port Huron), did not seem to me to be an unusually radical document but a clear and strong statement of the situation of American society—its racial, educational, social, economic, and moral failures and the assumptions on which they rested. It contained a description of the extent to which an interconnected system of government, business and industry, the military, and the universities controlled the social and political direction of the country. The document called for a reconstructed society in which individuals had a chance to exert their right to share in those social decisions determining the quality and direction of their lives.

The manifesto was radical in another sense and served to rally a new generation of activists to work together to achieve their aims. Its radicalism lay in three points. First, it rejected the ideology of anti-communism as a false and pernicious doctrine, false to the historical situation and pernicious in its negative effects on the ideals both of liberal democracy and of democratic socialism. Second, it linked the universities to the economic and social system as instruments of their purposes. Third, it defined a role for students in the political system as a whole, raising them to a level of equality with all other concerned citizens whose lives were affected by national and international decisions over which they had no control. "Do not wish to be a student in contrast to being a man," said Hayden. "Do not study as a student, but as a man who is alive and who cares."

The extraordinary fact then was that the rehearsal of the battle of the generations which has since come to occupy so central a position in contemporary affairs was immediately enacted, in the form of a rejection by the parent organization of SDS of both the Port Huron document and the plan of organization of its proponents. The Students for a Democratic Society was the revived form of the earlier Student League for Industrial Democracy. Its parent organization, the League for Industrial Democracy, had been founded more than forty years before as a coalition of intellectuals, including John Dewey, a principal sponsor, and the left wing of the Labor movement, at that time to be found principally in the International Ladies' Garment Workers' Union.

Within the board of directors of the parent group, of which Norman Thomas and I were members, there were enough persons whose memory of the internal battles against communist infiltration of the organization was still fresh enough to produce a strong set of objections to the free and open way in which the students had dealt with the question of communism and of membership in SDS. The students, in rejecting anti-communism as an appropriate response to the doctrines of programs of communism, had enough confidence in their ideal of participatory democracy and decentralization of leadership to make no political conditions for membership in their organization. Those who wished to infiltrate would have to do their work by pressing their ideas upon the others, not by seizing control of the organization, since it had so little organization built into it that there was nothing much to seize.

In the debates and difficulties which ensued, involving at one point a decision by the board to dismiss the elected officers of the new organization, I was impressed not only by the intelligence and forcefulness with which these young people made arguments which were essentially my own, but by the fact that they showed more faith in the power of democracy and in what they could do with it in political action than did their elders in the parent organization. Two of the students, Paul Potter (who was responsible for organizing the Swarthmore Disarmament Conference) and Tom Hayden had already had the experience of working in the South on voter registration and education projects, had been threatened, beaten, and jailed by white citizens and knew what it meant to be a contemporary political activist, at least in the Southern part of the United States.

The position which Norman Thomas and I took, that the student group had a right to its own ideas and its own style of organization whether or not their elders agreed with it, finally prevailed, although two years later the students were completely on their own. That marked a turning point in American political history, the point at which a coalition of student movements had become possible and a radical student movement had been formed. It also marked the coming of age of the new generation, one which had formed its ideas and political programs as a direct result of its college education.

That is what is so often overlooked by those who condemn all radical students without looking either at their accomplishments or their intellectual character. Potter had learned his way to political clarity at Swarthmore. Hayden had learned about the politics, character, and commitments of the big university by studying at the University of Michigan and editing its student newspaper. His practical experience in social and educational reform came from there and gave him the basis for the views he has since expressed about the university and society, just as his four years in the slums of Newark were the source of his knowledge of how the police and politics work in the American ghetto. The absence of that firsthand experience of American society at work in the lives of the underclasses prevents most American students and all but a fraction of the faculty and administration of the university from understanding the nature of student radicalism or the problems to which it was addressing itself.

Without a firm national leadership policy for SDS, individual power groups formed themselves on the campuses and at the national office in Chicago. I can remember a national meeting of SDS at the University of Colorado in Boulder in 1966 when the SDS officers refused to allow the press or television reporters to cover any of the meetings and had set up their own security officers and police system to make sure that no one outside the membership heard their speeches and discussions. I remember vividly the episodes on dozens of campuses when SDS organizers and their goon squads did prevent, by threats and violent actions, any groups but their own from speaking or from listening. In 1968, some two hundred American students, at the invitation of the Cuban government, went to see the new Cuba and to work in the sugar fields with Cuban students. I can recall a speech at the Boulder SDS meeting by a young returnee dressed in a Che Guevara costume of a young revolutionary complete with a Che mustache. After he had spoken of the joy of working in the Cuban fields, he spent the rest of his speech denouncing the United States for having corrupted Cuban youth into a passion for rock music, Coca-Cola, and American cigarettes. When a member of the audience mildly suggested that Cuban youth were free not to buy American records and could turn off their radios whenever they wanted, she was denounced by the speaker as a counter-revolutionary.

The incident I remember most vividly of all was staged in 1970 by a handful of students to break up a public lecture on education and social change which I was to give at the University of New Mexico during a visiting professorship there.[4] The students, some of them members of the "Radical Transformation of the University" graduate seminar I was teaching, seated themselves around the auditorium at strategic points, including eight or ten of them in the front row. At a given signal, the front row of students would break into irrelevant laughter, at other times those in the middle of the auditorium would release a series of loud boos. The vice president of the university had learned in advance of the plans for serious disruption but had no idea what form it would take. He and others in the university administration were in favor of calling off the lecture in case there was violence. I asked that we go ahead, and that the police be there in full sight ready to move in if anyone tried to remove me from the podium.

In a fairly short time after I had begun the lecture, the situation had become intolerable. There was so much booing and laughter from all sectors of the auditorium that I could not be heard. At that point I stopped the lecture. Referring to the disruptive students by name, I explained to the audience that their exhibition had been planned ahead of time, that they had distributed themselves around the auditorium to create the illusion that this was a general student protest on behalf of a good cause, not merely an interruption staged by a dozen or so students pretending they were revolutionaries. Again calling on the students by name, I pointed out that a thousand people in the auditorium had come to hear a lecture on an important subject only to find that a small band of anti-intellectuals was preventing it.

I proposed to the students that anyone who didn't want to listen could leave, and we would have another meeting consisting of only the disrupters and myself at which they could laugh and boo and interrupt as much as they wanted to. Three students from the front row left. The rest stayed and were quiet. The tactic worked on that particular night, mainly because the designated radicals were in my seminar and I could deal with them in personal terms. By the time we got through the question and answer period after the lecture, the students felt fairly sheepish about having played what amounted to a silly game of political bullying.

But this was a fairly mild set of circumstances which yielded positive results. On other campuses there was often a form of ritual takeover, aside from the regular guerrilla theater of holding administrators captive in their offices, destroying faculty notes and files, stealing personal and university correspondence. To deal with student activism in general with these inhumane and criminal acts was impossible. On the other hand, to talk about the student protest movement as if it were simply a string of violent acts aimed at destroying the university and breaking up the social order was to accept at face value the rhetoric of the radical fringe and to misconstrue the deeper meaning of the changes the student movement was bringing about. As I saw the serious students at work on the campuses and in the communities on the voter registration projects, Freedom Schools, and teach-ins, I was much more impressed by the qualities of courage, imagination, and political accomplishment.

I went from one campus to another and found that the presidents whom I had known in the past envied me for the position of being a former president. I usually stayed for two or three days on a given campus, taught some classes, conferred with the faculty committees on curriculum and educational reform, met with the local radicals, made anti-war and civil rights speeches and public lectures, advised the president and boards of trustees about what to do with the student revolt, and then left town. Many of my friends, the presidents, wished very much that they could come with me. In my public statements in those years, in books, lectures, and articles I concentrated on locating the student movement in the total series of social and political changes that were going on from the Kennedy through the Johnson eras into the Nixon times, and I gave the students credit for taking the initiative and forcing the pace of progress in stopping the war, reforming education, and breaking new ground in the field of human rights.

One of the results was that I came to be looked upon in some quarters as an advocate of the student cause, willing to condone the excesses of student behavior on the assumption that students had not only special qualities of idealism and imagination but were to be forgiven for such actions as breaking into the office of the president of Columbia University, smoking his cigars, and reading his mail. Some of my former colleagues among the presidents and faculty felt that I had deserted them, changed sides, and was now encouraging the young to go ahead with whatever they had in mind in their attacks on presidents, deans, and other targets for student abuse.

∽

Before the student revolt I had never been very much interested in Columbia University. Aside from what I learned about it from friends there in the faculty and from knowing the president, Grayson Kirk,[5] who had been a colleague at the University of Wisconsin, I didn't know a great deal about the university. My impression was that it had been standing still for much too long and that it had become a congregation of conventional minds engaged in conventional academic practices, a place of middle-aged and older men in an institution which had seen better days when the older men were younger. For forty-three years Nicholas Murray Butler [*president of Columbia University from 1902 to 1945*] had had such a tight grip on the presidency and the university as a whole and such a passionate reluctance to give up the office or any part of it that it began to look as if nothing short of death could clear the way for a new president. It took three years, from 1945 to 1948 with a dutiful all-purpose acting president in charge, before a Butler successor could be found. By that time Butler had become eighty-two, and there had been an intentional postponement of educational initiatives for more than ten years.

Then there was the genial Dwight D. Eisenhower [*president of Columbia University from 1948 to 1953*] whose military aide it was necessary to see for dealing with nearly all university matters and whose appointment to the presidency seemed to indicate that the university was not a serious institution as far as educational leadership and public policy was concerned. Once in a while I went down to Columbia at the invitation of faculty or student groups to talk philosophy and educational issues, or at the invitation of Millicent McIntosh [*dean and later president of Barnard College from 1952 to 1962*] to speak to one of the all-college assemblies of Barnard students which Millicent arranged.

In my experience with Eisenhower as a colleague among the college presidents, I never knew him to stay at whatever academic or educational occasion he had been invited to attend. He swept in, accompanied by his aides, made whatever remarks were called for, and swept out bound for more important things. I remember one Saturday afternoon when Barnard was host to a women's college alumnae conference on education and Eisenhower as president of Columbia and I from Sarah Lawrence sat side by side on the dais, ready to make our speeches. Before the program started Eisenhower had told me, man to man, that Mamie was most unhappy that he had to go to work on a Saturday and she was damned if she would go, and he was to come straight home after he had made his speech.

As we sat there, the only two men in the entire auditorium, Eisenhower leaned toward me and whispered, "What are you going to say?"

I gestured toward the manuscript in the folder on my knees. "I have to think about it ahead of time."

"Got any of it you can spare?"

"Fifty percent of the married people in the world are women. You can have that if you want it."

"Thanks," he said, "I'll start with that."

Which he did, and followed it with five minutes of anecdotes from high school to illustrate his theme that he knew nothing about women or their education. He then went home.[6]

Taylor with Dwight D. Eisenhower, president of Columbia University, and Millicent McIntosh, dean of Barnard College, 1949. Courtesy of Barnard College.

Among other places, my defection from the university and my betrayal of its principles was cited by Sidney Hook in an angry piece in the *Phi Delta Kappan* of October 1969, where Hook referred to my views as a "blueprint for educational disaster," "factually misleading," "scandalous in distortion," "fundamentally confused," "approving of practices which nullify academic freedom," "vagueness and looseness of language," and with a conception of the university which would destroy it as a center of learning.[7] A little later on, in June of 1973, Fred Hechinger, writing in *Change* magazine about "Salvaging the Youth Movement" referred to three of us who spoke at the Columbia University counter-commencement in June of 1968 as "middle-aged gurus who stood on the steps of Low Memorial Library as honorary valedictorians . . . quite typical of the arrogant intellectual spokesmanship that, time and again, embraces fads and factions with uncritical enthusiasm and endows them with unwarranted authority."[8]

The three gurus who spoke at the counter-commencement in June of 1968 were Erich Fromm, Dwight Macdonald, and myself.[9] Mr. Hechinger did not have the advantage of having been present or of talking to the students who arranged it, or of knowing what the speakers said. Nor did Diana Trilling who wrote about it in *We Must March My Darlings*, where she mistook the scattered groups of students and other people gathering at the steps of Low Library for the counter-commencement itself.[10] The crowd which eventually assembled itself was over two thousand in size led by nearly three hundred students who had left the regular commencement at the Cathedral of St. John the Divine, just before Professor Richard Hofstadter began his commencement address, and marched happily up Amsterdam Avenue to the Columbia campus accompanied by a large supply of parents. It was a combination of outdoor picnic, Fourth of July celebration, Labor Day rally, and June festival, with dogs, balloons, children, and passersby all joining in.[11]

There was a mood not so much of protest but of exhilaration. The event had been planned by a group, Students for a Restructured University, who didn't want to see the destructive elements in the student body shut down the commencement by acts of violence and clashes with the police. For these students and the others who supported them, the counter-commencement was not merely their final protest against a university whose character they had come to reject. It was a celebration in honor of the kind of university they wished they had had all along.

Dwight Macdonald spoke of the meaning of the student revolt in Paris and New York. He warned his audience, to the accompaniment of a certain amount of cheerful booing, that if they wanted to make a revolution they should not try to make it on a university campus. The university as a social space was reserved for the development of ideas of all kinds and social strategies to go with them. Don't destroy the university, said Macdonald, we have nothing to replace it. The boos came from those who had spent a lot of their time in the previous months trying to do just that.

Erich Fromm pointed out that in a society if enough citizens become sick, then sickness is assumed to be the norm, and those who denounce the diseases and try to cure them are considered to be dangerous and deranged. The students, said Fromm, by their demonstrations, protests, and rebellions against a political and moral sickness marked by militarism, racism, social injustice, and a failing educational system, were carrying on a form of social therapy which the society badly needed.

I started by saying that "institutions come and go, students come and go, but learning goes on and on, and education is an art that can be practiced anywhere. The mistake is to allow institutions to live a life of their own without regard to the people in them. That is what has happened to universities around the world." I also awarded degrees of whatever kind the members of the audience wished to have to everyone within earshot and expressed the hope that no one in the audience would ever become "addicted to, or corrupted by, the idea that in order to learn what you need to know you have to commit yourself to an institution." I recommend the style of this free form commencement, with or without the march through the streets, and with the addition of chairs for the speakers.[12]

∽

Whatever else was accomplished by the revolt, the students at Columbia and elsewhere made their universities take education seriously and pay attention to their responsibilities to American society at large. The attacks of the Mark Rudds and the speaker-blockers succeeded for a while because they were directed at the soft underbelly of an academic profession which lacked a sense of social and educational responsibility and could exert little influence on a student body it had previously ignored. These were students in a stormy time, having later discovered in the retrospect of the 1970s and 1980s that most of that time they were right, that their government was in fact deceiving them, that millions of lives were being destroyed through the big lie of American political and military ambition. In the absence of political leadership by their elders, they learned through their own initiatives how to take action on behalf of ideal causes.[13]

∽

While Taylor mentions Fred Hechinger's critique in Change *magazine, the more immediate attack of the event occurred five days after the Columbia commencement in Hechinger's June 9th article in the* New York Times, *"The Harsh Legacy of the Class of '68," where he specifically singles out Tom Hayden—who, Hechinger asserts, "masterminded the Columbia rebellion"—and wrote that the "rump commencement" included "the services of some academic and para-academic figures who symbolize the developing trend of camp-followers to the youth* movement."[14] Hechinger identified Taylor as one of the "middle-aged gurus," and Taylor would write that very day, objecting to his portrayal of the event and the student protests in general. In this letter, Taylor refers to his recently published work, The World and the American Teacher.[15]

June 9, 1968

Dear Fred,

Enclosed is what I said at the Columbia counter-commencement. I wish you could have been there. I think you would have enjoyed it and that it would have shifted the emphasis of your June 9th article in the *Times* about the two commencements away from its denunciation of the SDS style of confrontation and over toward the serious efforts of Columbia students to create a better university, for themselves and for their successors.

The counter-commencement was organized, not by the SDS group, or the Student Strike group, each of whom felt that from their point of view that kind of event would be a futile gesture, but by the Students for a Restructured University, a group of serious and informed students who want to put an end to factionalism and inject some positive ideas into the total situation.

I thought very carefully before accepting their invitation, since I felt that any educator who enters the Columbia situation from the outside has a serious responsibility not only toward Columbia University but toward the whole American university system, for some of the reasons developed in your article. My decision to accept the student invitation was based on some of the conclusions I had already reached in *The World and the American Teacher*—that the role of the students in the world's educational system has been badly misinterpreted and misunderstood by the educational authorities who, in my judgment, have abandoned the role of educational and social leadership which is rightfully theirs. I felt that I had a responsibility to do whatever I could do to sustain the idealism of a group of sensible, liberal, and reform-minded students in their efforts to improve higher education. That is why I agreed to speak, and I believe you will find that what I said, and what the students took from it, was helpful to that end.

"Camp-followers to the youth movement?" Taylor? For twenty-eight years, ever since the work we did in the early 1940s in the reconstruction of teaching philosophy at the University of Wisconsin, in the Meiklejohn and Wisconsin–idea atmosphere of that university, I have been doing my best to make new camps for youth and for everyone else, and I think you will find, on analysis, that if there has been any following of camps, it has come from the students who have been influenced by educational thinking and the example of educational programs of a kind which it has been my concern to undertake.

The operative sentences in my remarks at Columbia were: "It is up to the members of the new generation to fill the democratic forms with a new content, derived from those ideals which make a union among all possible and necessary. Democracy is the way men and women confront their common needs in a spirit of compassion and organize themselves in such a way that all have power within the dimensions of their own lives, all can act upon their society to strengthen it, and in so doing, can strengthen themselves."

The dramatic quality and the symbolism in the counter-commencement lay in the fact that the SDS and Strike groups were forced to cooperate with the Students for a Restructured University and that proposals for counter-demonstrations, disruption, and general trouble were not successful. Many of the confrontation advocates came to the counter-commencement, and the small amount of hissing in response to Dwight Macdonald's remark about not using the university as a tool for revolution came from a minority in the audience whose actions and ideas were contrary to his and to mine. Our intellectual independence in a university community in which students have a decisive role in the conduct of university policy is guaranteed, not weakened, by the policies of any university which stands against the mainstream of American society, that is to say, stands against war, racial injustice, and educational deprivation.

It is a simple matter to agree with Arthur Schlesinger when he says that "in the long run, any sane society must rest on freedom and reason." It has been the lack of reason and the lack of freedom for students in educational policy-making which has made American society less sane than it could be. That is what Erich Fromm was saying when he spoke, at the counter-commencement, of the way in which societies become insane while appearing to be sane, by conforming to socially approved norms which in fact condone violence and unreason while claiming to eschew them.

As you know, I hold a deep respect for your qualities as an educator, an educational thinker, a fair-minded analyst of educational trends, and as an editor in the field of education. I am therefore seriously concerned, and in view of our friendship and your personal knowledge of the way I think and act, am hurt by what seems to me to be a sneer at my integrity and a misinterpretation of the intention of those who organized the alternative commencement and those who agreed to address it. Since my views are on record in some detail in a book so recently published as *The World of the American Teacher* and in the text of the commencement address itself, I would prefer to be judged publicly by what I had actually said and done, not on the basis of a quick and inaccurate reference to my role in the student movement.

Yours sincerely,

Harold Taylor[16]

In addition, Taylor drafted a letter, signed by Erich Fromm and Dwight MacDonald, that would be published in the New York Times' Letters to the Editor *on June 17, 1968.*

To the Editor, the *New York Times*, June 12th, 1968

Dear Sir,

Mr. Hechinger's account (*New York Times*, June 9) of the counter-commencement at Columbia University is inaccurate in description and misleading in interpretation. Had Mr. Hechinger been present he would have found the counter-commencement a lively and warmhearted outdoor celebration, attended by two to three thousand persons, many of them undergraduates, others parents of the seniors, faculty members from Columbia and other universities, others from the militant student groups which had previously refused to take part in organizing the event.

The three hundred seniors who left the regular commencement to attend one of their own, did so not to deny Professor Hofstadter's right to be heard nor to reject his idea of the university as the home of "the splendid world of our imagination," but to affirm it, by holding a commencement more in keeping with their ideas about what a university should be—that is, free and open, with a student choice of speakers.

The slight amount of hissing when one of the speakers argued against using the university to fight a revolution was nothing more, nor less, than the expression of a small minority in the audience, perhaps ten to twenty persons, who took this way of expressing disagreement. It was an exuberant commencement.

We who spoke at the counter-commencement are not, in Mr. Hechinger's words, "camp-followers to the youth movement" or "para-academics," nor are we supporters of force and violence against anyone in the conduct of university affairs. We each hold views in social philosophy which we have held for years, some of which are now shared by a growing number of younger people, including the view that the universities, here and abroad, have failed in their mission as centers of humane learning.

Evidence of that failure has simply become more explicit in the recent weeks and months. Part of the evidence lies in the fact that the universities have not been humane enough, imaginative enough, nor democratic enough to gain the respect of their students or to find ways of dealing with them without the help of the police.

    Erich Fromm, Dwight MacDonald, Harold Taylor[17]

On June 20, 1968, Hechinger replied to Taylor's June 9, 1968 letter, including the following excerpt:

Dear Harold:

I am not persuaded by anything that I have read that the counter-commencement at Columbia or the part played in it by those who addressed it has been a very constructive demonstration of either reform or enlightenment. Nor am I persuaded that the best way to foster the free exchange of opinions on a university campus is to walk out on a speaker before he has spoken—even at the prospect of reading the text in *The New York Times* the following day—flattering testimony of faith in this newspaper as this may be.

    It goes without saying that I immediately added my strong recommendation to the editorial department to publish the letter challenging my views at the earliest possible time, so that I could not be accused of turning my back on a different opinion or causing others to be deprived of it.

    At any rate, we can't always agree. As ever,

Sincerely,

Fred M. Hechinger[18]

~

Taylor's and Hechinger's differences would arise again five years later in the pages of Change *magazine where Hechinger would take issue with the intent of the student movement and, while not mentioning Taylor by name, would resurrect his description of "the middle-aged gurus who stood on the steps of Columbia."*[19] *Taylor would respond with the article "Salvaging the Youth Movement from Its 'Enemies' " in* Change *later that year which included the following statement:*

Macdonald, Fromm, and I had not thought of ourselves as aging intellectual, middle-aged gurus, camp-followers of youth, or the contradictory of that—arrogant spokesmen and misleaders of the young—until it was brought to our attention shortly after the commencement in a local New York newspaper by a middle-aged editorial writer who is aging gracefully, detached from the hurly-burly of student life and action, after once serving as a reporter of live events in the field of American education. We were surprised then, as we are now, at Mr. Hechinger's insulting attitude toward the students, who seemed to us during the 1960s to have been getting along very well without gurus and had developed a strong anti-leadership bias as an organizing principle of their movement.[20]

Chapter 12

Unbegun Chapters

Hubert Humphrey, Plagiarism, and Albert Barnes

Harold Taylor's "A State of Mind" would have included three additional chapters: "Hubert Humphrey's Visit," focusing on a group of writers and activists who visited the White House in 1966; "Plagiarism," recounting when a portion of a Taylor speech was plagiarized by the president of Cornell University; and "Three Dancers," describing Taylor's friendships and professional involvement with Agnes de Mille, Martha Graham, and Bessie Schonberg. The "Hubert Humphrey's Visit" and "Plagiarism" entries have been arrayed from Taylor's archival papers and represent a gesture of good will toward his original intentions.

Unfortunately, personal letters and autobiographical accounts do not portray Taylor's involvement as president of the American Ballet Theatre and Agnes de Mille Dance Theatre, vice chair of the Martha Graham School for Contemporary Dance, and friendships with de Mille, Graham, and Bessie Schonberg, who taught dance from 1938 to 1975 at Sarah Lawrence in what was one of the first dance departments at the college level. For this reason, the intended "Three Dancers" chapter is not represented nor any exposition about the importance of the arts in general education, which is somewhat ironic since Taylor may be best known for his 1960 publication, Art and the Intellect: Moral Values and the Experience of Art,[1] a widely distributed monograph that he prepared for New York City's Museum of Modern Art. An autobiographical account of Taylor's interactions with art collector Albert Barnes has been added instead.

Hubert Humphrey's Visit

During the 1960s, Harold Taylor was a leading advocate for peace, calling for the end to the Vietnam War, and served as chair and speaker with Eleanor Roosevelt at the June 1965 Madison Square Garden Vietnam War rally, sponsored by the Committee for a Sane Nuclear Policy. He was also involved in leadership roles with many organizations, including Turn Toward Peace, National Research Council on Peace Strategy, Congress of Scientists on Survival, Committee for World Development and World Disarmament, Institute for International Order, and the Peace Research Institute, among others.

On April 26, 1966, a group of writers traveled to Washington, DC, to present a petition to Vice President Hubert Humphrey urging for a negotiated settlement to the Vietnam War and an immediate halt to the bombing of North Vietnam. The two-page statement, drafted by Taylor, Irving Howe, Alfred Kazin, and Lenore Marshall, was first introduced to the press at the Willard Hotel and later presented to Humphrey in a private meeting at the White House.[2] At the Willard Hotel press conference, Kazin attacked Humphrey, saying that he was suffering from "the Hemingway syndrome: you can never be tough enough, and you have to prove your masculinity." Howe criticized the vice president for using "our traditional (liberal) vocabulary to ends radically different" from the beliefs of the group of writers, also including Lillian Hellman, John Hersey, Anaïs Nin, Muriel Rukeyser, and Edmund Wilson, who represented what they termed the "conscience of the Nation."[3]

Their statement appears below along with excerpts from an April 28 letter from Taylor to Humphrey expressing apologies for his colleagues who "cut loose at the press conference before we had talked with you about the criticism of administration policy and your role in it." Taylor, who served as chair of the Willard Hotel event, had little control over the assorted writers and may not have been necessarily well received by certain members of the group since Kazin would later mention the "dispiriting cheeriness of Harold Taylor" during the Washington gathering.[4]

Presented to Hubert Humphrey on
April 26, 1966, Washington, DC

The undersigned, a group of American writers, are intensely concerned with the increasing military commitment of the United States in Vietnam—in effect, an undeclared war.

We are here to bear witness to our commitment to humanity. Wars are always destructive of the most precious human values; this war bears within itself the seeds of terrible risk, terrible inhumanity, terrible destruction. We are not persuaded that enough effort has been made by our government to press toward a negotiated peace and to convince the rest of the world that it is ready to take the steps necessary for an end to the bloodshed.

It is our conviction that a settlement by negotiation is necessary; that such a settlement must take place in the immediate future, rather than be postponed until presumed changes in the military balance can be effected; and that the U.S. Government, as the proclaimed spokesman for democracy and the most powerful nation in the world, has a special responsibility to take the initiative toward ending the conflict.

Without wishing to prescribe exact political or diplomatic steps, or the sequence in which they should be undertaken, we urge the U.S. Government

To declare as its policy an immediate cessation of bombings in North Vietnam, to remove any real or alleged impediments that bombings may constitute to peace negotiations;

To declare its readiness to negotiate with all interested parties, including the NLF [*National Liberation Front of South Vietnam*], the political arm of the guerrilla forces in South Vietnam;

To declare itself ready to support an agreed-upon international agency, perhaps through the U.N. or the International Control Commission set up by the Geneva Conference, which would supervise an immediate cease fire and a transitional phase leading to free elections;

To declare its intention of abiding by the results of such elections, even if those results are not pleasing to us;

To declare its intention of withdrawing American troops and bases from Vietnam upon the signing of appropriate agreements.

President Johnson, in his Honolulu speech, said that those who oppose his present policy are "blind to experience and deaf to hope." We are not blind to experience and deaf to hope. We know that freedom cannot be secured merely by military victory. We know that hope is possible for the people of Vietnam only if they can face some perspective other than a prolongation of a war which has already devastated their country.

That negotiations cannot easily be achieved in Vietnam and that their outcome may bring unsatisfactory or problematic results for men who desire both peace and democracy, we are ready to acknowledge. But we are also convinced that the prolongation and escalation of the warfare in Vietnam can lead only to disaster—disaster for Vietnam, for ourselves, for the cause of world peace.

Is it not time for the U.S. Government, in the spirit of generosity that ought to accompany its enormous power, to try again for an end to the bloodshed?

—Alan Dugan, Peter Feibleman, Maxwell Geismar, Mitchel Goodman, Barbara Guest, Shirley Hazzard, Lillian Hellman, John Hersey, Irving Howe, H. Stuart Hughes, Alfred Kazin, Denise Levertov, Lenore Marshall, Ira Morris, Anais Nin, Elmer Rice, Muriel Rukeyser, Harvey Swados, Francis Steegmuller, Harold Taylor, Walter Teller, Louis Untermeyer, Edmund Wilson, Marguerite Young[5]

To Hubert Humphrey

April 26, 1966

The Hon. Hubert Humphrey, Vice President of the US

Washington, DC

Dear Hubert,

I am terribly sorry that my companions in the Washington visit cut loose at the press conference before we had talked with you about the criticisms of administration policy and your role in it. Since there was no way that you could possibly pin down a date to see us until the day of the meeting, and we wanted to present our statement to the public as well as to you, the press conference had to be set when it was. Once it started, there was nothing I could do to stop Kazin, Howe, and the others from taking off on their own or from answering the reporters' questions in the particular way they did.

Before coming down, we had had no thought of talking about you to the press, but only to talk with you about our views and yours. But the excerpts from your speech to the publishers in the [New York] *Times* that morning started the boys off, and it was your stated views rather than those of the president which bore the brunt of their criticisms.[6]

I acted as chair at the press conference, and when asked questions about your position, said that I respected your liberalism but disagreed deeply with your position on the war. I said quite explicitly that it was not possible to identify liberals by the single criterion of whether or not they agreed with the government on the war.

On the other hand, your position has indeed shifted to a quite hard line, and there are many people who admire you and respect you who feel that you have shifted your basic political attitude in foreign affairs to one closer to Goldwater than to the former Hubert Humphrey.

I report this as a fact, while respecting your integrity, believing in your serious efforts to obtain peace, to improve the social and economic conditions of the South Vietnamese, and believing in your right to change your mind about the best policy the United States should pursue in Vietnam. The disagreement I and the others have with your reasoning, as revealed in your public statements and in your arguments in our session on Tuesday, is on the question of escalating the bombing and the military action, at the same time expecting that political, social, and economic reform under our supervision will be possible. We believe that what is needed is an internationalizing of the problem, so that our military forces are used to stabilize the situation, guarantee workable free elections, and concentrate on getting a government which genuinely represents the various groups. No matter what the administration says, the president's plan to pursue to its end a military victory before turning to the solution of the political and economic problems assumes that you can bomb people into submission on behalf of an unrepresentative government.

But I do not want to take your time with a repetition of the arguments already made. What I do want to say is that from the bottom of my heart I appreciate your willingness to talk frankly with us in the privacy of your office, and I appreciate more than I can say, after the mix-up yesterday, your final remark, "You are always welcome in this office."

The country is lucky indeed to have a man like you as its vice president, and I deeply wish that I did not have to disagree with you on a matter of such fundamental importance.

With affectionate regards,

Harold Taylor[7]

Taylor and Humphrey continued their correspondence after the April 1966 meeting. Humphrey would respond to Taylor's letter on May 5, 1966, defending his stance and stating that the conflict "cannot be won on the military battlefields. It must be won by a combination of providing security on the one hand, a social revolution for social justice and economic opportunity on the other. We don't disagree on these matters."[8] By July 1966, their letters shifted to discussing Humphrey's NAACP speech as Taylor described his experiences with SNCC workers and, later, Humphrey thanking him for his insights. Taylor, most likely, would have used this chapter to reminisce about his activities with the peace movement.

Plagiarism

The vitality of public statement and leadership in America [is] not to be found in the new Presidential Man, who, having absorbed the conventions and cliches of an uncriticized world, is capable only of repeating them with an air of solemnity whenever the occasion is provided. Ghost-writers, whether from the faculty or from the public relations department, are of help only in preventing the grosser errors which might betray an intellectually sterile past.

—Harold Taylor, "The Task of College Administration," 1950

On September 19, 1951, Deane W. Malott, incoming president of Cornell University, delivered a fifteen-minute address to ten thousand people attending his presidential inauguration. Months later, the New Yorker *printed, in their* Funny Coincidence Department, *a comparison of portions of the address with a speech first delivered by Harold Taylor at Boston University on March 12, 1949, and later published in the* Harvard Educational Review.[9] *A 221-word passage by Malott was compared to two passages totaling 212 words by Taylor, with the two excerpts being "quite similar."[10] Malott was first confronted with this "unhappy situation," as termed by the* Cornell Daily Sun, *by the University of Kansas's* Daily Kansan, *the student newspaper of the institution he had just left after serving as its chancellor for twelve years. He maintained that he drew content from an educational pamphlet he had used many times before Taylor's 1949 speech, a comment made to the* Daily Kansan *that he would later deny. The* Kansas City Star *reported Malott also told the* Daily Kansan *that Taylor must have drawn text from the same source.[11]*

The following account by Taylor is taken from a 1986 oral history session conducted for the Sarah Lawrence College Archives.[12] He, most likely, would have used this chapter as an occasion to address issues of the changing nature of the college presidency.

I had given a speech in 1949 on human relations and the need to make an educational system that paid attention to the necessity of being sensitive to other people's feelings. I argued for colleges with intellectual vitality to act as illustrations of democracy in action. The speech was reprinted in the form of a brochure and sent out to ten thousand on a mailing list by the Council on Human Rights or some such title who could afford to have the speech printed and sent around.[13] It had my picture on the front and the title and my name.

One morning at breakfast, I was reading the *New York Times*, and I came upon passages quoted from Deane Malott, the new president of Cornell.[14] I said to Muriel [*Harold Taylor's wife*], at the opposite end of the table, "This guy sounds pretty good." And I read out a couple of sentences.

Muriel said, "I think that's something you wrote. It sounds very familiar."

So, I looked at it again, and I saw that the main body of the quotation from the *Times* was pretty much my kind of writing, with the particular style that I could recognize as my own.[15] I checked it with my speech when I got up to the office. The phone started ringing with people who knew my work and had read my speech and saw the quotation in the *Times*. One of them looked up my speech and sent it to the *New Yorker*, along with the quotation from the *Times*. The *New Yorker* then sent for my original speech and for Malott's speech and ran the identical excerpts in the Funny Coincidence Department side by side.

The *New Yorker* simply put the dates on the two excerpts. It didn't make any comment at all, just the dates. Mine was made two years before Malott's. All up and down the Eastern Seaboard there were people—a great number of the faculty members at Cornell—calling for Malott's resignation. I had a call from Arthur Dean, the chair of the [*Cornell University*] board of trustees at the time wanting to know if there was any explanation that would make sense that I could give for this use of my speech.

I said, "No. The only explanation I can give is to refer you to your president. He's the only one who knows. It is a speech I made before and it's been reused without attribution."

The students up at Cornell were writing on the board, "Who's cheating now?" They just had a study of cheating on exams by Cornell students. This had become a problem worthy of being studied.

Malott didn't call. Then, he gave a telephone interview to a student out in Kansas, where he'd been chancellor of the university. He said in passing that perhaps I had found this material (he referred to it as "material") in the same place that he did. I couldn't believe it when they called me from the *Kansas City Star* and asked me if I had a statement to make.

I said, "No. I have no statement. I will simply send you a copy of my speech and where it was first given. You already have a copy of Mr. Malott's speech."

So, they ran the excerpts from both speeches on the front page of the *Kansas City Star*. At that point, it was picked up by the *Cornell Sun*, the student newspaper to whom Mr. Malott wouldn't give an interview and wouldn't provide an explanation. So, the students just reprinted the Funny Coincidence section again with the *Kansas City Star* story about what Malott had said. At that point, Malott finally called and I said, "I'd like to put my secretary on the line. She will make notes on this conversation."

He said, "I suppose you saw that squib in the *New Yorker* they ran to embarrass me."

I mean, that's actually what he said. I said, "Yes, I did. I admire your taste in ideas."

He said, "Well, I just want you to know that I wouldn't steal from a New York State colleague." It sounded as if had I come from another state he'd think it would be quite all right. And he said, "I'd never heard of you and I had no idea this was yours."

And I said, "Well, it's hard for me to understand why you would just then assume it was in the public domain—usable without attribution."

He said, "Oh, well, I just want you to know that I wouldn't do a thing like that."

I said, "Well, thank you very much."

It wasn't even an apology. He was implying again that I had found my own speech in the same place that he had.

A lot of people on the Cornell board thought that he should be dropped, but they had spent two years trying to find a president. They thought this thing would blow over. He was in office for twelve years after that.

EXCERPTS FROM THE *NEW YORKER'S* FUNNY COINCIDENCE DEPARTMENT

[From an address delivered by Deane W. Malott at his installation, September 19, 1951, as president of Cornell University]

. . . Emerson . . . best stated the mood of America, at its youthful best, when he asked, "If there is any period one would desire to be born in, is it not the age of Revolution? When the old and new stand side by side and admit of being compared; when the energies of all men are stimulated by fear and hope; when the historic glories of the old can be compensated by the rich possibilities of the new era?"

If our wish is Emerson's, we have it today. The trouble is that for a number of people, the future is a bit too rich in alarming possibilities, and when they take the old and the new side by side, they would much prefer the old. The fearful ones who hate and condemn the liberalism in our colleges never suggest any additions to the store of human knowledge. . . . They want us to leave out all that is interesting and vital, the great current social issues . . . on which they wish neither professor nor students to take sides. Such a course would not mean free minds. We cannot be free and at the same time preserve ourselves only amid "the gentility of the obvious and the tedium of the uncontroversial." Young people, at least, cannot be expected to reserve their greatest enthusiasm for the status quo.

[From "The Student as a Responsible Person" by Harold Taylor]

It is Emerson who states the mood of America at its youthful best, when he asks, "If there is any period one would desire to be born in, is it not the age of Revolution? When the old and the new stand side by side and admit of being compared; when the energies of all men are searched by fear and hope; when the historic glories of the old can be compensated by the rich possibilities of the new era?"

If our wish is Emerson's, we have it today. . . . The trouble is that for many people the future is a bit too rich in alarming possibilities, and when they take the old and the new side by side, they much prefer the old. . . . The fearful ones who hate and condemn the liberalism in our colleges are more anxious to prohibit ideas than to make them grow. They want us to leave out the interesting and vital parts of education, the . . . current social issues . . . and they do not want professors or students to take sides. They want us to be careful what we say. We must not offend anyone. . . . We must preserve the gentility of the obvious, and the tedium of the unconventional. We must reserve our wildest enthusiasms for the status quo.[16]

Even with charges of plagiarism and calls for his resignation, Malott would serve as the sixth president of Cornell University from 1951 to 1963. To explain the "coincidence" between Taylor's and his speech, Malott invited members of Cornell's board of trustees to his study and, from a wall of books, asked the board chair to randomly select a work and to begin reading. Shortly after the opening passage was read aloud, Malott began reciting the following paragraph verbatim. "Malott then said, 'You see my problem gentlemen. I have a photographic memory and I simply cannot recall with confidence whether what I am writing is or isn't original.' "[17] Official plagiarism charges were not raised.

In the September 20, 1951, New York Times article about the presidential induction, Malott was quoted as saying, "We should take a good look at our past failures and not be so cocky about what we're trying to shove down other peoples' throats."[18] Since the alleged plagiarized passages appeared in Taylor's published text, titled "The Student as a Responsible Person," he may have wondered whether President Malott was a responsible person himself. Ironically, three days before the publication of the New Yorker's Funny Coincidence Department column, Taylor was invited to speak at Cornell by a student-sponsored educational and fraternal organization. The planned February 1952 event was cancelled. Yet, in December 1953, the same student organization invited Taylor again to speak at their annual conference, to be held in February 1954. This event, too, was cancelled because, as Taylor later learned, Cornell faculty advisors were fearful that his appearance would be seen as the student organization and faculty seeking to embarrass Malott.[19]

∽

Remembrances of Dr. Barnes

Before you [Harold Taylor] arrived at our Gallery, I had told the attendant to let you sit there for ten minutes before he announced your presence. At the expiration of that time, I appeared, found you lolling in a chair sucking your pipe, totally unaware of what was around you.

—Albert Barnes, correspondence to Harold Taylor, 1950

In recent years, Taylor's interactions with Albert Barnes (1872–1951), the legendary Philadelphia eccentric art collector, have been reported in various

Unbegun Chapters | 205

biographies. I have included personal anecdotes by Taylor about their June weekend visit in 1950 as a way to complete this chapter. While the following account does not reflect Taylor's actual engagement in the arts or his extensive work in aesthetics, on display is his wit, insight, and good-naturedness as well as his narrative, raconteur voice.

Taylor tells of the circumstances leading up to his visit with Barnes to discuss Sarah Lawrence's "involvement"—use of or acquisition of—the Barnes art collection. Neil Rudenstine would describe Taylor in his biography, The House of Barnes: The Man, the Collection, the Controversy, as "perhaps the shrewdest, most decisive college administrator Barnes ever encountered,"[20] and even Barnes was first impressed with Taylor, describing him as "young, alive, full of pep, and with both feet on the ground."[21] Mary Ann Meyers, in Art, Education, and African-American Culture: Albert Barnes and the Science of Philanthropy, refers to their exchange as "cagey on both sides."[22]

Barnes's impressions of Taylor would change drastically after their visit as he proceeded to insult Taylor's intellect and accuse him of dogmatism, writing, "I knew this long ago, and that's why I wanted you to begin your voyage of education by entering our first-year class and learning what education is—but your crust is impenetrable."[23] Barnes was just warming up. By the late autumn, he was mocking, criticizing, correcting, judging, and baiting Taylor and then critiquing a recent publication that he had edited. Taylor's retort to Barnes—"why don't you just relax, enjoy life, and let us go on doing our best"[24]—served only to unleash more of Barnes's ire, in many ways what seemed to have been Taylor's intention, confirming Rudenstine's assessment that Taylor appears "to have been the only president who sized up the situation immediately."[25]

John Dewey called one day and asked me if I could come down for a talk. Since he said I think I may have a $20,000,000 art collection for Sarah Lawrence, I said fine, I will be down. I want to talk to you anyway, but for a $20,000,000 art collection, I'll come a little sooner.

John said that Albert Barnes, who was a friend of his, was a rather eccentric, former semi-professional baseball player who had made a lot of money in Argyrol and became interested in art.[26] He had an influence on Dewey by getting him more interested in painting than he had been before. Barnes had taken a liking to Dewey, and John took a liking to him; it was an amusing relationship of this bluff, outspoken eccentric Barnes and America's greatest philosopher. The relationship between the two men continued through this period.

When I knew Dewey, Barnes was agitating around and had been talking with various people at the University of Pennsylvania—Harold Stassen, when Stassen was president there—about the University of Pennsylvania having the collection.[27] He talked to Katherine McBride at Bryn Mawr and I suppose someone at Swarthmore,[28] but it was a peculiar kind of talk in that he would sort of tease them by suggesting that maybe, if the right circumstances were arranged, they could have the collection. But then he would run off like a coquette and make up some reason, Stassen being a fool or something of that sort, as to why he wouldn't give it to Pennsylvania.

At this stage, John was actually discussing with Barnes what he should do with the collection and, since he had been discussing the possibility of giving it to one of the universities, John said, well, the only person in the country who would really know how to use this in educational terms is Harold Taylor at Sarah Lawrence. John and Robbie [*Roberta Dewey*] and Muriel [*Taylor*] and I were to go to Barnes's place outside Philadelphia for a weekend so that we could all talk it over, John, and Albert, and myself. That was all arranged. But at the last minute, John couldn't go because he wasn't well enough and, when he wasn't feeling absolutely fit, it was just too dangerous for him to go running around the countryside.

So Muriel and I went off for the weekend [*June 10–11, 1950*] to discuss the collection and, of course, letters had gone back and forth between John and Barnes about why this should be done and how important it would be. Barnes arranged to meet us at his museum. We went in, and Barnes wasn't around, so we sat and waited, and finally he came in his bluff, arrogant way and took us around the gallery before going out to his place in the country. We spent two days together talking about philosophy, about Barnes himself, mainly. He had an enormous, inflated ego and was incapable of conducting a conversation for longer than three minutes without bringing it back to himself. If you said it's a nice day, by the time you got through talking, he had you thinking he had made it.

But I was patient and coped with him as best I could. Then we got talking about the specifics and what arrangements could be made since Sarah Lawrence was in Bronxville and the collection was in Philadelphia. I said that I didn't think we would care to move the whole college just to be near the collection, though that was a possibility.

But I felt the atmosphere in Philadelphia would be inhibiting for the free spirit of Sarah Lawrence, and that it would be much preferable if we made some kind of arrangement so that weekly trips of the student body would give direct access to the collection. This would be a central part of the education of the students in the arts, and we would limit it in the beginning to those who are specifically interested in the arts and then, hopefully in the future, we would gather together all sorts of college students for whom the collection would serve as an education in modern art.

Dewey knew that my ideas of education would be consonant with those of Barnes and that we would really use the collection in the way it should be used. Immediately Barnes got into discussion, "Well, then, of course, you would only be able to have a certain limited number of Sarah Lawrence students use the collection." I said, "If you're going to turn the collection over to me and the college, we are going to have to use it in educational terms, in consonance with your ideas of how it should be used, but with more students being educated than just a sprinkling from Sarah Lawrence. It had to be that way. I wouldn't want to be the trustee of such an important collection and not be able to use it fully."

That is when it started getting sticky. Barnes didn't think then that it would be altogether wise to have the collection open. This was a particular neurotic thing he had about people seeing it. By the time we got through the weekend, he said, "Well, of course the first condition is that you will have to come down here every Tuesday for the day and attend my seminar on the collection." He had a course which was all laid out according to his educational theories, and there was a particular way he used the collection. I was to go through this, otherwise I wouldn't understand how to educate people in the arts. I said, "Albert Barnes, I cannot come down here every Tuesday to go through the seminar. I understand your theory and I know enough about contemporary painting to understand how it would work, but I don't think that needs to be a precondition of your assignment of the collection to me since I am not about to become your disciple." It was very clear that's what he wanted—to teach me what to do with this collection. I would then spend the next five years, obviously, of my life just fussing, being his student. He was half out of his mind. I figured while Dewey could handle him because Barnes had such a deep respect for John, it was very clear that a person like myself wouldn't be able to cope with him in any better terms than did Presidents Stassen and McBride. John was the only person whom

Barnes didn't denounce; he denounced absolutely everybody, everyone was a son of a bitch or everyone was untrustworthy. And he wrote quite abusive letters to people. He was really unbalanced.

Barnes should have given the collection to the University of Pennsylvania or Swarthmore, someone nearby. So we ended up then. Barnes said, "Well, of course, if you aren't even interested enough in the collection to come and study it," and I said, "That's not the point, I will come and study it, but I'm not going to be put into a framework of your manufacture because I'm just not built like that. If I'm going to understand this collection, I'll commit myself to understanding it but on my own terms." That had to be very clear because his attitude to everybody within five minutes of meeting them was that they were fools and stupid. Well, he couldn't say that about me because Dewey had denied it by saying this is the only man in the United States who can handle this collection educationally. The problem then was for John to tell him just never mind the conditions—give it to Sarah Lawrence and trust Taylor to handle it, which was what he did say. But Barnes at that point was not the slightest bit interested really in giving it to anybody and, although John did his best, there wasn't anything we could do.

Barnes turned out to be an incredible neurotic who was playing games with all the university and college presidents in his neighborhood, doing this same thing—inviting them over for a weekend. As I said to Dewey after it settled down, I don't think he's ever going to give up that collection. Even when he dies, he'll fix it so that nobody can see it . . . which is about what he did.[29]

After this exchange with Taylor in 1950, Barnes began to develop another complicated and strained relationship with Lincoln University, ending abruptly with Barnes's death in a car accident in July 1951. The Barnes collection remained at his home in Merion, Pennsylvania (a suburb of Philadelphia), under the jurisdiction of the Barnes Foundation and was opened to the general public, with limited attendance, in the early 1960s. With much more litigation and uproar, the Barnes Foundation and art collection ultimately moved to a newly constructed museum, "The Barnes," at Center City Philadelphia in 2012 with full public access to what is considered one of the finest private collections of impressionist, postimpressionist, and modern paintings in the world.

Epilogue

Luck, Fate, Commitment, and Change

> When I look back on those years of my life and find that, without meaning to be, I became president of one of the foremost experimental colleges in the country, I am astonished that it happened and delighted that it did.
>
> —Harold Taylor, interview with Carole Nichols, 1985

Harold Taylor believed that his proximity to New York City and a leadership role at a distinctive, East Coast liberal arts college, where he used the title "former president of Sarah Lawrence College" longer than his actual presidency, offered him a forum to be heard. The Sarah Lawrence position also allowed for an idiosyncratic life after his college duties. While many emeritus presidents during this period continued their careers in some form, few became a host of a national television program, an attendee at Leonard Bernstein's Black Panther–Radical Chic party, and so active on the lecture circuit as to be represented by a leading speakers agency. Yet, with the attention Taylor received from his engaging lectures, still youthful and striking appearance, British veneer,[1] well-known wit and charm, as well as his place among New York City intelligentsia, he still displayed a willingness to help others and a disarming curiosity for the play of ideas—a joy of exploration—unlike an ideologue's pedantic quest to disseminate if not to instigate ideas and policies.

There are few rules for ending an autobiography let alone a posthumous memoir, yet certain patterns do exist. Often a memoirist prepares a manuscript that views life as an occasion to offer advice to readers, and the concluding chapter is filled with a flourish of insights and caveats—life's lessons. Others feel that their stature warrants interest and any concluding statement would prove anticlimactic since the point of reading such a memoir is self-evident and involves interest in the life lived. Those personal accounts merely end, allowing the reader to bask in the satisfaction of having learned about an interesting person.

I am uncertain what would have been Taylor's approach. I suspect he would not have turned his experiences into an object lesson nor would he have written a grand finale, and neither will I. Taylor led a charmed life with much good fortune, albeit with certain disappointments. Openness and the spirit of progressivism guided him from one intellectual adventure to another as well as a fundamental belief that higher educators had abandoned a role of educational and social leadership which was rightfully theirs. Rather than attempting to complete his memoir with a summary or analysis, I instead have prepared a somewhat atypical vignette to supplement his text with descriptions of important-but-unmentioned activities as a way to provide context for his career. Unlike most biographical portrayals, however, I have included large portions of quoted material to allow Taylor to continue to speak for himself.

Compulsory Exposure, General Education, and the Harvard Redbook

> What is wrong with the university as a teaching institution is precisely this: It has no philosophy of education, no unifying principle around which reforms can be made, either to meet the problems of student unrest or to engage the students in their own learning.
>
> —Harold Taylor, *How to Change Colleges: Notes on Radical Reform*, 1971

During the summer of 1945 as Harold Taylor was moving from the Midwest to the East to begin his presidency at Sarah Lawrence, Harvard University published what proved to be the defining statement of the mid-twentieth century for the mission of undergraduate education, including the configuration for curricula at both colleges and secondary schools in America. *General Education in a Free Society*, known as the Harvard

Report (as well as the Harvard Redbook for the hardcover's crimson color), was a national sensation representing two years of committee work by Harvard faculty, and its release was anxiously awaited by secondary and postsecondary educators who were in the process of determining new directions for a post-WWII educational landscape.[2] With the anticipated increase in enrollment of veterans, supported by the GI Bill, and with high school educators searching for standardized curricula during a time of school consolidation and the reorganization of school districts, the Harvard Report provided answers to many looming questions and issues as well as a sense of confidence for educators who would be welcoming a new era with expert guidance from Harvard's faculty. The Redbook's reexamination of the aims of education was said to have provided not only a blueprint for undergraduate programs throughout the United States but, also, an educational philosophy for America.[3]

The Harvard Report took on even more significance with its focus on general education, what is now commonly called core curriculum or, in the broadest sense, what is viewed as liberal education. Colleges and universities, private and public, maintained specific mission statements yet their philosophies were still somewhat generic if not prosaic. General education programs, however, by articulating common learnings and configuring courses, best represented an institution's working philosophy and de facto beliefs, and the term "general education" subsumed issues of curriculum, instruction, and evaluation in what could be seen as the school's basic mission and philosophical orientation.

General Education in a Free Society offered Taylor good fortune during his first year at Sarah Lawrence. As president of an East Coast liberal arts college (and as one who was critical of the Redbook's recommendations), he was invited to participate in an academic conference with some of the country's leading academic philosophers and, most certainly, at a venue that would not have otherwise included an assistant professor from the University of Wisconsin. Taylor took part in a symposium at Columbia University in February 1946, including Raphael Demos of Harvard University (who was a member of the Harvard Report committee), Horace Kallen of the New School, and Sidney Hook of New York University. Papers from this meeting were published later that year in the quarterly journal *Philosophy and Phenomenological Research*, with responses and rejoinders appearing the following year.[4]

The area of philosophy of education was quite distinct from the professional field of philosophy, and professors of philosophy, like Taylor, rarely directed their attention toward schooling as did educational philosophers. He had stumbled upon an entrée—via *General Education in a Free Society*—to critique educational philosophy at the national level and, with the Harvard Report's popularity among both college and high school educators, his audience expanded greatly. With characteristic candidness and disarming honesty, he would write to the editor of the *Philosophy and Phenomenological Research* journal expressing great thanks for this opportunity. "I am surprised that I have enjoyed doing the work and am obliged to you and the journal for having set the condition that I examine my own conclusions about the [*Harvard*] Report. I find that I am now much clearer on a number of things, through having undertaken the analysis."[5] Taylor would recall, "The essays in the Symposium were widely read among the academic people, and I had proved to myself and to educators in general that it was possible to be a college president and a working intellectual at the same time."[6] His critique brought him attention, nationally, as a leading progressive educator and critic of traditional schooling at both the secondary and postsecondary levels.

Taylor objected to the Redbook's curricular recommendations, in what was a "compulsory exposure" approach to liberal education, and would later write that "the mere ability to read and discuss a series of well known books, some of which are tedious to the point of hysteria, has little to do with recreating the ideas of the past in a way which will help understand our present."[7] Taking a characteristic progressive position, his comments were sharp and biting, and he dismissed the Harvard Report committee for perpetuating "the genteel tradition" in higher education, a phrase popularized by George Santayana, where New England intellectuals controlled literary and academic standards. Taylor felt the Redbook reduced general education to an administrative device of course listings, and core curriculum requirements became merely selected and sequenced content rather than an opportunity to forge shared values for an academic community.[8]

Many of Taylor's most basic thoughts about the purposes of higher learning appeared in his analysis of the Harvard Report, beliefs that stayed with him throughout his life:

> The young people whom we are asked to educate have matured considerably during the war, they are much more conscious of the possible roles they could play in society than young people

have ever been before. They have, to a degree which is new in higher education, a set of interests and needs about which they are often articulate and clear. The majority of them are thinking in practical terms. They want either education for a profession and for an occupation, or when they think in broader terms, want their general education to provide them with the means of finding a functional place in society. As a consequence of the lack of contact of the contemporary educator with the young people themselves, these facts have somewhat been missed. A great deal of discussion has accordingly centered itself around the question of whether or not to require a curriculum of basic studies, which always raises the more awkward question of what to require. It is not so much a question of whether or not to compel study of certain kinds of knowledge, but a bigger question of what kind of studies are most likely to fulfill the needs of a new kind of student, more mature, more serious, and more critical of their own education. Or alternately, the question is, what curricular means can we take to develop the kind of socially conscious, enlightened men or women which our country and the rest of the world needs so badly?[9]

The Redbook merely offered another rearrangement of subjects, according to Taylor, and not a new method for young people to discover knowledge. "It is as if education had no spiritual content, offered no joy, no intellectual delight, but were only a matter of subjects to be taken for material reasons and external purposes. Education has become all structure and academic content, when it should in fact provide a rich experience in the enjoyment of ideas and human values."[10] He was more interested in what students learned, not what they were taught, and the enjoyment of ideas and purposes of schooling were to be found in "a common core of liberal values to which the students are committed, rather than in a common core of subjects which each has studied."[11] While Sarah Lawrence never became (nor wished to become) a model for higher education similar to St. John's Great Books program, Columbia College's Contemporary Civilization courses, or Harvard's *General Education in a Free Society*, Taylor expanded the conversation, moving beyond merely identifying high school and college course requirements.

Sarah Lawrence and Progressive, Experimental Education

> Bad education and bad teaching by foolish methods should not be confused with progressive education. It is the quality of the teacher more than anything else which determines the quality of education, and the progressive system requires depth and range in its teachers far beyond the conventional demands.
>
> —Harold Taylor, "Debate over 'the Progressive Idea,'" 1961

Sarah Lawrence College did not originally represent the basic tenets of progressive thought, unlike Bennington College where William Heard Kilpatrick, a John Dewey apostle and chair of its board of trustees, was actively involved in framing the fundamentals of its program. As Taylor has described, Sarah Lawrence grew into, or discovered, its progressive traditions, similar to Taylor himself. His special role, however, stems not as a progressive philosopher expanding the theoretical literature but, instead, as a philosopher-practitioner engaged in a type of middle-range theorizing.[12] Drawing upon his experiences as a teacher at University of Wisconsin and president at Sarah Lawrence, he drew theory *from* practice, rather than putting theory into practice, to broaden the professional literature. Taylor's writings served as an historical bridge between early twentieth-century progressivism to the writings of the "romantic critics" and progressives of the 1960s and 1970s—Paul Goodman, Maxine Greene, Ivan Illich, Herb Kohl, Jonathan Kozol, Deborah Meier, and others.

Taylor was cautious describing the Sarah Lawrence program as an example of mainstream progressive education. Upon arriving at the college in 1945, he noted, "There is no high-sounding philosophy of education under which everyone is heeded. People feel that if you have some good teachers who are talented in their own field and interested in human beings, then the trick is to get the students talking with them often enough to allow some of the knowledge to infect 'em. There are no housemothers, no examinations, no formal curriculum, no nonsense."[13] He carefully used the descriptor "experimental" as he placed Sarah Lawrence within an ongoing tradition of other progressive schools at the college level. His speeches and articles caused some resentment among faculty who objected to him speaking on behalf of the college and, for others, who wished not to have Sarah Lawrence identified with any philosophical point of view or labeled with any type of educational jargon.[14] Taylor, too, was critical of school educators for reducing Dewey's ideas into a collection of standardized methods and, later in his career, felt the term "progressive education" had lost its meaning since the vocabulary of its proponents had become cliché-ridden and public perception of its theory and practices had been so misrepresented by its critics.[15]

Even with the concerns of faculty, Sarah Lawrence held a special place in the history of progressive education, albeit unacknowledged. Before Taylor's arrival, the college participated in the Progressive Education Association's (PEA's) Eight-Year Study as one of the postsecondary institutions, obtaining information about the success of students from progressive high schools.[16] In addition, the college served as the location for the Eight-Year Study's first six-week, summer teacher training program, in 1937, and would host a regional six-week summer workshop in 1938 as well as other Eight-Year Study–affiliated sessions. Yet, with this pedigree there was little if any reference to Sarah Lawrence's own educational research in the progressive education literature prior to Taylor's presidency. In the early 1940s, college faculty published a five-volume educational research report related quite directly to their participation in the Eight-Year Study, describing the faculty's efforts to design exploratory courses for first-year students.[17] Readers of these volumes, however, would be unaware of any connection between Sarah Lawrence and the Eight-Year Study or the PEA. During his fourteen years as president, Taylor connected Sarah Lawrence's practices to the larger professional literature, while stressing overlooked dimensions of education in higher education and bringing greater recognition to the practices of the college.

In 1949, Taylor assessed the state of the field of progressive education:

> In the beginning of the experiments with the new design of education, there were very often mistakes. There was one branch of the movement which mistook education for anarchy and believed with Rousseau that if you left the little dears to do anything they wanted, they would grow up naturally and spontaneously into charming people. They proved to be wrong. . . . Fortunately, these mistakes were usually not repeated, although those who now criticize progressivism in education identify it with the mistakes rather than with the successes. The effort to develop disciplined and well-integrated children by these methods has now gone on for thirty to

forty years, and a large body of tested practice and theory is based on actual experience with children. There are now research studies which show that the qualities of spontaneity, imagination, and independence are developed, along with other desirable human qualities, in higher degree by these methods than by those of the traditional system. We know, from the results of the Eight-Year Study in which a matched sample of students who were educated by progressive methods were compared with those educated by traditional methods, that success in college is not the number, type, or sequence of subjects studied but the way in which students learn to learn. As a consequence, the ideas of progressives are now imbedded in the system of nursery schools, elementary schools and, to a lesser extent, the high schools. The colleges, with a few exceptions such as Goddard, Bard, Reed, Bennington, Antioch, and Sarah Lawrence, have ignored modern educational thinking and have shown little interest in progressive reforms. They have preferred to continue the European tradition of academic discipline.[18]

This excerpt features what could be considered one of Taylor's more important (and subtle) contributions to progressive thought during the 1950s—recognizing that progressive methodology was embedded in practice and much more widespread than assumed, implicitly arguing against what is now a widely held belief that the progressive education movement ended by midcentury with the aftermath of World War II. In essence, he was attempting to shift the discussion away from the Harvard Redbook/core curriculum controversy, maintaining that there "has been a national obsession with the rearrangement of old courses in new clusters. Professors in every university have developed guilt feelings about the courses they have been giving harmlessly enough for years, and have added a great many facts and books from other fields, and seem bound to give the same courses next year under new and more complicated titles."[19] This would lead him to argue for engaging students in their own learning but, also, introducing both secondary school teachers and college professors to the strengths of progressivism.

Later in the 1960s when educators were "deskilling" teachers and preparing teacher-proof curriculum, Taylor became more vocal about the aims and purposes of teacher education and would ultimately view a strength of progressivism not as dispensing a storehouse of knowledge but allowing individuals—well-informed teachers *and* curious students—to explore their commonly related interests and needs. He would always return to this theme that administrators and teachers should not be determining which subjects were to be studied; rather, students working with their teachers should be engaged in their own intellectual lives, a point that would guide his defining book, *Students without Teachers: The Crisis in the University*.

As a national spokesperson for both Sarah Lawrence and progressive education, ironically, Taylor's most widely read passage about the college (if not progressivism, as well) described students as apathetic and unable to conduct their own affairs. In Betty Friedan's legendary *The Feminine Mystique*, published in 1963, Taylor is quoted by name in her chapter "Progressive Dehumanization: The Comfortable Concentration Camp," with four sentences from four separate pages of his 1961, thirty-one-page essay "Freedom and Authority on the Campus."[20] Written not as a critique of contemporary youth or progressive education, Taylor's article actually addressed student morale as a factor in learning and stressed the important transactional aspects of the student-professor relationship, ultimately concluding that the students of the 1960s recognized their responsibility "to make their own way, that their education is in their own hands."[21] Taylor's independent sentences are accurately presented but out of context, and the compilation was not the best portrayal of his work, especially to such a widespread readership.

Harold Taylor and Social Justice

> Each college must therefore take active leadership in breaking down barriers to Negro, Jewish, foreign, and underprivileged students.
>
> —Harold Taylor, "Education as Experiment," 1949

Harold Taylor's call for gender equity and social justice could appear self-righteous and pious since his pronouncements were coming from the office of the president of an elite, predominantly white women's college with the then-highest tuition in the United States. He did not necessarily seem guilt-ridden by serving as president of Sarah Lawrence since, at that time, male leadership was common at women's colleges. During his early years at Sarah Lawrence, Taylor criticized state universities and liberal arts colleges for not making a serious effort to provide for the special interests and needs of women. He found most coeducational institutions and many women's colleges furthering stereotypes of the American coed that illustrated negative class and racial consciousness, social snobbery, and materialistic values. "Our college women have adapted themselves to the conventional requirements of education and social behavior [and] are given inadequate aid from liberal education for the kind of life they could lead if their college studies dealt with the matters most relevant to their major interests."[22] He believed that women's education was merely conforming to patterns for men, typically fostering competition for success rather than personal satisfaction.[23] The college experience, asserted Taylor, should allow women to become as intellectually and emotionally mature and to engage them to be academically involved in their own schooling, in what would become another foundational belief for his later writings to transform higher education.

Taylor and the topic of race is more curious. He was not uninvolved; yet, neither was he a crusader although, throughout his career, he recognized and addressed racial inequities and injustices. When the *Brown v. Board of Education* decision was announced on May 17, 1954, the *New York Times* education editor, Benjamin Fine, requested a statement from him that appeared in his May 18th column, implying that Taylor had some credibility and insight on the topic of school desegregation.[24] Bothered by the low number of enrolled Black students at Sarah Lawrence, as noticed during his 1945 interview for the presidency, he would obtain scholarship funds from Sarah Lawrence board of trustee member Marshall Field and the United Negro College Fund while also initiating a short-term student exchange program between Sarah Lawrence and Bennett College, an historic Black college in North Carolina.[25] During the 1960s, he funded SNCC projects as grants coordinator of the Eleanor Roosevelt Memorial Foundation, organized formal hearings for Mississippi residents to testify about racial atrocities, and helped to stage and served as master of ceremonies for a Freedom Riders benefit concert with Pete Seeger, Ossie Davis, and Ruby Dee.[26]

A defining moment for Taylor occurred in 1947 when he was invited to serve as vice chair of the New York State Committee for Equality in Education. In conjunction with the American Jewish Congress, the

Taylor with Pete Seeger, from an informal session at a private party in 1980. In 1962, Taylor and Seeger played together at a benefit concert for the Freedom Riders. Courtesy of the Taylor family.

committee supported legislation for fair educational practices in the state of New York, including forbidding prejudicial practices in college admissions based on race, religion, color, or national origin and citing, as evidence, the quota system and the use of discriminatory application forms. From this organizational role, Taylor did more than assist the work of the committee. He openly criticized the Association of Colleges and Universities of the State of New York for denying that there was no discrimination among New York State colleges and questioned its claim that any proposed legislation to ban admission quotas would undermine the freedom of colleges.[27] In a 1948 editorial, he acknowledged bigotry toward African Americans and Jewish students, criticized extant and tacit quotas, and noted "an appalling lack of vision as to the function of education and the moral values of the educator, for if ever there was a problem that touches the roots of social evils in the world today, it is this one."[28] He concluded that educators have a moral obligation for the sake of a better society to overcome the public pressures of discrimination at the college level.

Thus, the 1983 article in *Commentary* by Louise Blecher Rose, "The Secret Life of Sarah Lawrence," proved disconcerting for Taylor with its criticism of him and the college. Rose accused Sarah Lawrence of a Jewish quota and criticized its request for race and religious information on the admissions form. In her article, Rose felt Taylor was using a euphemism, "geographical diversity in admissions," for the quota system and ridiculed his comments during her research interview: "Taylor's replies, by contrast, were classic Sarah Lawrence productions, full of high-minded outrage at the suggestion that Sarah Lawrence could possibly be discriminating against Jews 'either by geographical quota or any other means.' Such a suggestion, Taylor said at one point, was actually 'insulting to those of us who are trying for the sake of the quality of education to select a diverse and talented student body from everywhere in the country.'"[29]

Taylor would write to then–Sarah Lawrence president Alice Stone Ilchman, after the release of the article, objecting to Rose's characterization of the college and describing his early years as president when Bronxville residents were angry at the school for being unfair not to Jews but to Christians and for not allowing Episcopalian student clubs to organize. "By the 1950s, the college began to be so well known for its liberalism and honest treatment of social issues that Jewish applications from all over the country increased markedly. The proportions of Jewish to non-Jewish students increased accordingly. The college had developed a warm-hearted and mellow environment in which Jews, non-Jews, and every other category of humans felt at ease."[30] Taylor's comments certainly do not dismiss Rose's claims and, in 2026, when the original Sarah Lawrence source materials used for "The Secret Life of Sarah Lawrence" become available for review, historians may be able to confirm or question the viability of her charges and his defense as well as other accusations raised during that period.[31] Rose does write in her *Commentary* article that "Taylor must have known he was in any case not telling the truth."[32] His professional papers indicate quite clearly that he believed he was telling the truth—perhaps misinformed, perhaps deluded—nonetheless, he felt her accusations of discriminatory admissions practices during his presidency were false and unjust.

Taylor at his New York City/West Village home office, 1985. Courtesy of Craig Kridel.

An Itinerant, Uninstitutionalized, Active Intellectual

> It was very much like the way I decided what to do with my life in the earlier times. I decided I would decide nothing except to cut loose from all the responsibilities I had been carrying for fourteen years, and that I was once more back to my basic situation. I was an uninstitutionalized musician/scholar who loved teaching and living the life of an active intellectual.
>
> —Harold Taylor, interview with Carole Nichols, 1985

Harold Taylor has already described in this memoir the meeting in 1959 with Alvin Eurich of the Ford Foundation when, after being asked about his retirement plans, replied "that I didn't know and that I wasn't going to decide anything until I had spent some time, possibly a year, free from any responsibilities or obligations either for writing or for running any kind of organization."³³ The Ford Foundation offered open-ended support for international travel during which time Taylor met with dignitaries, educators, and political and cultural figures. Upon returning in February 1960, his future was still unclear, even with job offers for professorships, deanships, and presidencies; however, he received an invitation to speak at a student-organized conference at Yale University in March that proved quite fortuitous. Joined by Barry Goldwater, Thurgood Marshall, and Philip Randolph, Taylor participated in an intercollegiate event, the Challenge Conference, attended by 1,500 students where he presented the opening address, "The Crisis in Liberal Democracy."³⁴

Informing students that he had just returned from travels abroad to find America in an aimless and confused state bordering on anarchy, Taylor's speech roamed among the topics of McCarthyism to the works of Kierkegaard to insights of Asian and Soviet countries while examining the apathy of the American general public. He concluded with what must have been a moving call for domestic equity, equal opportunity, and social agency in the quest for a more liberal and humane world order. Stemming from this single presentation, Taylor received so many invitations to speak that he would become a client with the Harry Walker Agency. During the conference, Taylor saw students form into what he described as twenty new activist organizations. "This was a really fresh and new thing to encounter, and I find that a spirit does exist on the campuses far different from the one I left last year."³⁵ Thus began a new chapter of his career as campus lecturer, author, project director, public intellectual, and social and educational activist. He would later recall, "Once I got loose on that world trip it has been awfully hard to get me tied up again, even if I could stand being house-trained inside a department as an institutionalized philosopher."³⁶

Taylor never fully accepted the term "public intellectual," although this label was used regularly, as I have done, to describe him after leaving Sarah Lawrence. Writing in 1953 to his friend and former University of Wisconsin colleague Merle Curti, Taylor stated, "I think that even using the term intellectual as if this were a special breed of cat involves a lot of dangers which can and should be avoided. As I see it, the term itself is a function of a class society in which the intellectual is a person who thinks up ideas for workers and other people to put into action."³⁷ After his return from world travels, he followed his own advice, being one of those workers who put ideas into practice. He was constantly forming experimental programs, developing social projects, and organizing educational communities while living the life of an itinerant, uninstitutionalized, active intellectual.

Any list of Taylor's many activities between 1960 until 1982 would be quite chaotic. Writing to Ruth Field in 1962, he admitted, "I've got so many interests that I could fly apart with them, and I also can't seem to hold back when there's some action I'd like to get into. Right now the danger is that I'll continue to lecture, write, run around putting out some fires and starting others, and God knows what else, and not build the whole thing into a coherent pattern which will gather strength as it goes along."[38] Establishing and chairing the Peace Research Committee of the Institute for International Order; participating with the Peace Research Institute, Congress of Scientists on Survival, and Turn Toward Peace; organizing the National Research Council on Peace Strategy; and cochairing and speaking at the May 1960 National Committee for a Sane Nuclear Policy (SANE) Madison Square Garden Rally for Peace and the December 1966 SANE Madison Square Garden Vietnam Rally were merely a few of his many activities.[39]

In the 1960s, he was also engaged in many disparate programs—leading research projects for the American Association of Colleges of Teacher Education and Unitarian-Universalist Associates and serving as host for *Meet the Professor* in 1962–1963, an ABC-TV program introducing university professors and their interests and works to the general public. He cofounded with Agnes Meyer and served as vice chair of the National Committee for Support of the Public Schools, a project attributed to helping the passage of Lyndon Baines Johnson's 1965 Elementary and Secondary Education Act. His administrative work in the arts flourished, including serving as president of the board for the American Ballet Theatre, where he wrote and received funding from the National Council on the Arts (later to become the National Endowment for the Arts) in what would be "the first grant ever issued by the Federal Government in direct support of the arts."[40]

Among the many activities with various arts and peace organizations, he also coordinated an exchange program with American Russian poets and authors, organized a poetry competition with the *Nation* (the Lenore Marshall Poetry Prize, now overseen by the Academy of American Poets), while also presenting numerous lectures, writing articles, and publishing eight books. His close friendship with Norman Cousins, editor of the *Saturday Review*, provided him with a standing invitation to contribute to that magazine, and he continued working as an elder statesperson for 1960s student activists while also stressing the need to restructure colleges and universities in his publications *Students without Teachers: The Crisis in the University* and *How to Change Colleges: Notes on Radical Reform.*

One programmatic theme, a direct outgrowth of Taylor's 1960 Ford-funded international travels, evolved into "a coherent pattern that gathered strength" and lives on to this day—namely, his efforts to establish international education centers for students. In speeches and articles as well as his books—*The World and the American Teacher*, *The World as Teacher*, *The United Nations University*, and *A University for the World*—he wrote about the importance of cross-cultural and international experiences in postsecondary settings.[41] Taylor, as he noted as early as 1948, maintained, "The three years I spent in England and the chance to travel around Europe on a cruising liner while working in the orchestra, was one of the deepest educational factors in my youth. The chance to learn about a different culture, the necessity of making my way without help of any kind from family, and the necessities of existence in a foreign country taught me a great deal about philosophy, life, education, politics, and personal relations."[42] His efforts, however, were much more than encouraging and celebrating the act of travel. Taylor's various projects attempted to establish on-site educational settings where groups of faculty and students of different nationalities would come together to search for new understandings of global issues.

In 1963, Taylor directed a six-week, experimental project—a world college—with an array of international faculty. Twenty-four United Nations countries were invited to select and fund one student to participate in the program, with general sponsorship from the Friends World College Committee. Focusing on the themes of world history, cultures, colonialism, and disarmament as a method to develop international perspectives, the curriculum was developed by students to educate for a world order free from war. Taylor writes,

> It was an extraordinary event. One of the most moving experiences of the whole session occurred on the last day when two SNCC students, recently released from jail in the front-line action, came to visit us. They met the World College students, played games, sang, gave some freedom demonstrations on the lawn, and then joined our seminar

for an hour, during which each of the visitors talked about the experiences he or she had had in Alabama, Georgia, Mississippi and Virginia. Students were absolutely astonished with the gallantry, simplicity and honesty of the visitors, and of course immediately identified with them as fellow-workers in the big struggle. At the end of the meeting we all rose and sang together *We Shall Overcome*. The man on my right was the Counsellor from the Polish Mission to the U.N., a sophisticated Marxist and long-time party member, the man on my left was from SNCC, and I can tell you that by the time we were through there was not a dry eye in the house.[43]

The World College became the Friends World Institute, then the Friends World College, merging with Long Island University in 1991, renamed the Global College in 2007, and then rebranded as Long Island University Global in 2012, continuing to the present.

Accompanying his work with the World College, Taylor collaborated with administrative staff at the United Nations as founder and chair of the United States Committee to establish the United Nations University. This project sought to couple the activism from the international student movement to those efforts for peace, justice, and world unity. His intent was not to develop another university program for student fieldwork and foreign studies. Rather, the United Nations University, founded in 1973 by the United Nations General Assembly, formed a world community of scholars to create educational programs in the humanities, social sciences, and natural sciences designed to address global problems. Through the organizational structure of the United Nations, Taylor sought to establish a global educational network collaborating with colleges and universities that would develop a sense of unity among student activists worldwide and, in so doing, give voice to the young. "The United Nations is the only organization with the capacity to bring the world's youth together on a world scale and to create an international system through which youth can join in building a world community."[44] The United Nations University, headquartered in Japan since its founding, continues today with research and educational programs, introducing global thinking and action research toward world problems.

Postscript

The Play of Ideas

> I have never set up a specific set of goals and then arranged my life so that I could achieve them. For example, I had never intended to be a professor of philosophy, or a college president, or a research psychologist, or a tennis coach, or a band leader, or television performer. I simply went ahead doing the things I enjoyed doing. I did them as well as I could—and each of them led to the next thing. But as I look back, I would say that the center of it all was the fascination I had for literature, the arts, and the play of ideas. I thought of myself as a young writer and musician. But I didn't think specifically or consciously about being "a writer" and "a musician." I simply read and wrote and played music and everything worked out beautifully.
>
> —Harold Taylor, interview with Carole Nichols, 1985

During a series of interviews with Michael Rossman,[1] Harold Taylor recognized an unselfconsciousness about his career and readily admitted that his life consisted of moving from one interest to the next—"the gratuitous character of the life that has played itself before me. . . . I went along welcoming the next day as it turned up after the previous day."[2] Taylor joked with Rossman about the apparent carefree aspect of his career, and Rossman would later describe, when in 1974 considering and ultimately declining the invitation to become his biographer, "an oddness—half accidental, half direct," to Taylor, more like "an amiable smart lad blundering fortunately through life."[3] A life filled with luck . . . a

Taylor at Brushwood, 1989. Courtesy of Craig Kridel.

career guided by fate . . . The accidental and unselfconscious aspect of Taylor's career could be viewed in another way—one rooted in a Deweyan belief that the educational worth of an experience is its ability to lead to other experiences. His life defines progressivism, welcoming ideas and guided by interests and needs and, notably, with a commitment for building community and engaging in service to and with others. As he said of Dewey who showed through his thoughts and actions that "the world can be made to respond to the demands of reason and the imperatives of justice," Taylor did not need a pattern or plan to his life; he just needed "to go on trying."[4]

Luck and fate aided Taylor's career considerably as did his charm, enthusiasm, curiosity, thoughtfulness, and his ability to inspire the young into action. Yet, what may have served more to further his success and commitment to activism was his openness to experimentation and the play of ideas. His work emerged not with predefined expectations or predetermined outcomes. Taylor was in a constant state of programmatic exploration while maintaining his faith in democratic discourse. "The distinctive aim of experimental education is to develop ways of creating in youth such a deep attachment to humane moral values that the life of each becomes intuitively liberal and the action of each constantly helpful to the total community of human interests."[5] Perhaps his career may have appeared half accidental and half direct; however, he welcomed whatever experiences occurred, maintaining faith in a common good and the power of community and discourse to lead ultimately to fruitful outcomes. Standing alongside his mentors, he continued to see the university as an intellectual center for society—displaying a more thoughtful and humane way of behaving rather than reflecting and instilling traditional mores. Working for a better social order, he believed, "has no end, but only new beginnings . . . pressing upon all institutions and testing their capacity for alteration and survival."[6] Taylor was always searching for those new beginnings.

∽

Taylor's memoir is not a desolate story of hardship or regret, nor does his writing reflect sentimentality or narcissism. He was more than willing to compliment the accomplishments of others and to criticize his own efforts. He approached his work with good cheer while aware of his successes and limitations. His luck—bad luck—was that he never finished this memoir. Much has been omitted . . . by fate and by his own choosing. Similarly, as the editor and arrayer of this publication, I have left certain topics unattended that otherwise would have been explored in an intellectual biography. This is all to say that as was the case in 1974 is still the case today. Harold Taylor is in need of a sensitive biographer who will examine his life and career and bring attention to an important-yet-not-fully-recognized college president of the mid-twentieth century.

Appendix
Sample Schedule for Harold Taylor, May and June 1965

May 2, 12:00 p.m. Fairmont Hotel, San Francisco, address to Annual Conference of California Mental Health Association

May 3, 12:30 p.m. WETV Television lectures: (1) What Is Progressive in Education? (2) Progressive Ideas in Action, for Los Angeles teachers' in-service education program

May 5, 12:30 p.m. San Francisco State College, Honors Day Address to students and faculty

May 6, 12:15 p.m. Luncheon with president, faculty, and students; 3:00 p.m. Queens College, lecture to students and faculty, "The American Student"

May 7, 6:00 p.m. Teachers College, Columbia University, lecture in students' series, "The Teacher in a Mass Society"

May 13, 3:00 p.m. Queens College, lecture to students and faculty, "The Student in a Mass Society"

May 14, 12:00 p.m. Address to *Herald Tribune* Book and Author Luncheon, with Russell Lynes, Hoagy Carmichael, "Reading, Writing and Thinking," Hotel Statler Hilton, New York City

May 15, 6:00 p.m. With Jules Feiffer, Robert Lifton

May 16, 9:30 a.m. to 5:00 p.m. Cochair, conference sponsored by National Research Council on Peace Strategy and Scientists on Survival, "Alternatives to Present Policies in S.E. Asia," Hotel Roosevelt, New York City

---

Speaking Schedules; HTA B1:F_Speaking Schedules.

May 17, 9:00 a.m. University of Wisconsin, Conference Center, address to National Conference on the Role of Universities in the Musical Arts, "The Musical Arts in America," Madison, Wisconsin

May 18, 8:30 p.m. Concord Hotel, Address to New York State Association for Curriculum Development, "The Transformation of Education," Lake Kiamesha, New York

May 19, 12:30 p.m. Yale Club, with Dr. Howard Reed, "Education and World Affairs"

May 20, 12:15 p.m. Queens College, luncheon with administration, faculty, and students; 3:00 p.m., lecture to students and faculty, "Education and Social Change"

May 22, 10:00 a.m. Putney School, meeting, Board of Trustees, Putney, Vermont

May 24, 3:00 p.m. Shady Hill School, seminar, apprentice-teachers, Cambridge, Massachusetts

May 26, 4:00 p.m. Presentation, Tennis trophy, Sarah Lawrence College

May 27, 7:00 p.m. With Mr. and Mrs. Albert Hirschfeld

June 2, 12:15 p.m. Overseas Press Club, luncheon for WBAI, New York City

June 3, 10:00 a.m. American Jewish Committee; seminar in human rights, with speaker Louis Sohn; 8:00 p.m. WNEW television program *New Voices on the American Campus*

June 4, 11:00 a.m. Sarah Lawrence College commencement

June 5, 8:00 p.m. Westport, Connecticut, Freedom Ball

June 8, 3:00 p.m. Clinton, New Jersey, commencement address to Women's Reformatory; 7:00 p.m. Cochair, Madison Square Garden, SANE rally on Vietnam

June 11, 11:00 a.m. Putney School, Putney, Vermont, commencement address

June 17, 8:00 p.m. Raymond College, address to students, Stockton, California

June 18, 6:00 p.m. Address to dinner for Peninsula School, San Francisco, California

June 19, 6:00 p.m. University of California, Berkeley, dinner with Chancellor Meyerson

June 21, 8:00 p.m. University of Northern Colorado, address to students, Greeley, Colorado

June 22, 8:00 p.m. State University of Colorado, address to students, Fort Collins, Colorado

June 23, 7:30 p.m. University of Colorado, address to students, Boulder, Colorado
June 24, 8:00 p.m. University of Iowa, address to students, Iowa City, Iowa
June 26, 27 Mt. Kisco, New York, with Mrs. Eugene Meyer
June 28, 11:00 a.m. National Committee for the Support of the Public Schools, Executive Committee meeting, Mt. Kisco
June 30 Leave for R.F.D. Ashland, New Hampshire, for months of July and August

Notes

Abbreviations

HTP   Harold Taylor Papers, RG 2.1.3, Sarah Lawrence College Archives, Bronxville, New York

HTA   Harold Taylor Papers, RG 2.1.3 Addendum (accessioned in 2020), Sarah Lawrence College Archives, Bronxville, New York

Foreword

1. Clark Kerr, *The Uses of the University: The Godkin Lectures on the Essentials of Free Government and the Duties of the Citizen* (Cambridge, MA: Harvard University Press, 1963).

2. Erich Fromm, *Escape from Freedom* (New York: Farrar & Rinehart, 1941); David Riesman with Nathan Glazer and Reuel Denney, *The Lonely Crowd* (New Haven, CT: Yale University Press, 1950); Paul Goodman, *Growing Up Absurd* (New York: Random House, 1960).

Preface

EPIGRAPH

Page xxi: Michael Rossman, Interview with Harold Taylor, 4B (July 1974, Holderness, NH); HTA B5:F_Rossman.

1. Taylor, Correspondence to Jessica Mitford (August 16, 1982); HTA B4:F_Mitford.

2. "A State of Mind" was mentioned by Taylor in Correspondence to C. Y. Tung (August 4, 1977) and Ronald Bross (August 29, 1977); HTA B6:F_1977.

3. In 1993, days after Taylor's death, his professional papers were in jeopardy. The Taylor family asked if I would travel to New York City, pack the documents from his West Village brownstone, ship them to University of South Carolina, and house them at the Museum of Education, a small research facility where I served as curator. I did this; however, I always assumed that someday the papers would be housed at their rightful place—Sarah Lawrence College.

4. Taylor, Correspondence to Michael Rossman (July 14, 1975); HTA B5:F_Rossman.

5. Jessica Mitford, *The American Way of Death* (New York: Simon & Schuster, 1963).

6. Taylor, Correspondence to Mitford (November 9, 1982).

Chapter 1. The Day Duke Died

1. Taylor, Correspondence to Alastair Reid (July 24, 1975); HTA B5:F_Reid. Taylor, Correspondence to Michael Rossman (July 14, 1975); HTA B5:F_Rossman.

2. "The orchestra missed out Britain on this tour because of a ban by the Musician's Union on American instrumentalists, which was to last too long." Derek Jewell, *Duke: A Portrait of Duke Ellington* (New York: Norton, 1977), 66.

3. Michael Rossman, Interview with Taylor, 2A (July 1974, Holderness, NH); HTA B5:F_Rossman.

4. Christina Baade, "'Something We Cannot Get in England': Hearing Anglo-American Difference in America Dances," *American Music* 33, no. 3 (Fall 2015): 307–344. Christopher J. Wells, "'Go Harlem!' Chick Webb and His Dancing Audience during the Great Depression," PhD dissertation, University of North Carolina, 2014. Kristin A. McGee, *Some Liked It Hot: Jazz Women in Film and Television, 1928–1959* (Middletown: Wesleyan University Press, 2009), 158.

5. Gordon Parks (1912–2006) was a renowned photographer as well as composer and writer. Harry Carney (1910–1974) became Ellington's baritone saxophonist beginning in 1926 and lasting for the rest of his life, becoming the longest serving member of the Ellington band.

6. Rex Stuart (1907–1967) was Ellington's trumpeter from 1934 to 1945. Stuart and Taylor's friendship lasted for the remainder of Stuart's life, and he visited Taylor periodically at Sarah Lawrence and at Taylor's West Village brownstone in New York City.

7. Billy Strayhorn (1915–1967) was a composer, arranger, pianist, and lyricist who collaborated with Duke Ellington from late 1938 until his death.

8. Robert Maynard Hutchins (1899–1977) was president of University of Chicago, Clarence Dykstra (1883–1950) was president of University of Wisconsin, and James Bryant Conant (1893–1978) was president of Harvard University.

9. In the original manuscript, Taylor wrote, "It was this combination of making severe demands on himself and holding to an image of what a true jazz musician should be that finally led Bill to take his own life. He had become tired of traveling with bands and had settled down in New York as a staff pianist for CBS, playing occasional recording dates and living in a house designed by Frank Lloyd Wright in the hills of New Jersey. Suddenly one day he decided that this was not the life he should be leading, gave up his CBS position, his Wright house, took an apartment in New York, and gave lessons in jazz piano.

"By the time he realized that this was a grotesque mistake and that he had thrown away his career, it was too late for him to come back. In the late 1950s in New York there were no jobs for small groups, big bands, or solo engagements which measured up to Bill's idea of the kind of music he should be playing. He gave up the struggle to find the right kind of work and went to sea in the orchestra of a cruising liner. In my case when I had done that in England back in 1937, it was a beautiful interlude for a young man who had never travelled in Europe. For Bill it was banishment to sea with mediocre musicians. His only comfort was that nobody knew who he was. One night after the band finished playing, he jumped overboard." Taylor, "A State of Mind," unpublished manuscript; HTA B23.

Chapter 2. A Student's Journey

EPIGRAPH

Page 33: Taylor, "Why Go to College?," written for *Woman's Home Companion* but not published, September 13, 1951, 1; HTA B14.

1. Michael Rossman, Interview with Taylor, 1A (July 1974, Holderness, NH); HTA B5:F_Rossman. "We were fairly poor—not destitute, but we were lower income people all the way through. When I was twelve I started working, with a paper route, an ice route, and with a weekend job carrying boxes around in a grocery store." Carole Nichols, Interview with Taylor, SLC Oral History Collection (June 26, 1985), 9; HTA B2:F_Oral History. "Most of us [had] no sense of consciousness about being poor; no sense of disenfranchisement as children." Rossman, Interview with Taylor, 2B.

2. Rossman, Interview with Taylor, 1A.

3. Rossman, Interview with Taylor, 2B. Northrop Frye (1912–1991) would criticize Taylor, rather harshly, about his assessment of his college education at University of Toronto in a review of Taylor's essay "The Private World of the Man with a Book," in *Saturday Review*, January 7, 1961, 17–19. Northrop Frye, "Autopsy on an Old Grad's Grievance," *University of Toronto's Varsity Graduate* 9, no. 1 (Spring 1961): 30–33.

4. Jack Kent Cooke (1912–1997) made his fortune in broadcasting and professional sports, owning the Washington Redskins, the Los Angeles Lakers, and the Toronto Maple Leafs. Cooke would write to Taylor on May 30, 1945, congratulating him for his new post at Sarah Lawrence. "Dear Harold, You can hardly imagine my surprise and pride at seeing your picture in this morning's *Globe and Mail*. I'm pleased as Punch to learn that you are getting on so well. . . . Congratulations on your success and my bests wishes for the future. Kindest personal regards. Yours truly." Jack K. Cooke, Correspondence to Taylor (May 30, 1945); HTA B6:F_1945.

5. T. H. Green (1836–1882) was a British philosopher-idealist.

6. George Sidney Brett (1879–1944), Taylor's official tutor at Victoria College who was educated at Oxford University, was a scholar of the history of psychology and guided him toward study in England. Fulton Henry Anderson (1895–1968) was a professor of philosophy from 1926 to 1966. Herbert John Davis (1893–1967), an expert on eighteenth-century philosophy, would later become president of Smith College from 1940 to 1949, overlapping with the early years of Taylor's presidency at Sarah Lawrence, and would, during his 1937 sabbatical at University of London, lend Taylor tuition money for the first year of his doctoral program.

Chapter 3. Coming Down from Cambridge

EPIGRAPH

Page 35: Taylor, "Thinkers Who Influenced Me," in *Moments of Personal Discovery*, ed. R. M. MacIver (New York: Institute for Religious and Social Studies, Harper & Brothers, 1952), 133.

1. Jan Wilbanks, *Hume's Theory of Imagination* (The Hague: Martinus Nijhoff, 1968).

2. John MacMurray (1891–1976) was a professor at University of London from 1928 to 1944 and then taught at University of Edinburgh until his retirement in 1958.

3. Lizzie Susan Stebbing (1885–1943) was a leading British analytic philosopher between the World Wars and is thought to be the first woman to hold a professorial chair in philosophy in the United Kingdom.

4. In 1927, Bertrand and Dora Russell founded the Beacon Hill School, located near the West Sussex–Hampshire border, with Bertrand leaving the school in the early 1930s.

5. Taylor played on the *Lancastria* in 1937. Three years later, after the RMS (Royal Mail Ship) *Lancastria* was requisitioned by the British government for World War II service, the ship was sunk (on June 17, 1940) while evacuating

troops and civilians in what was then considered to be one of the greatest single ship disasters in the maritime history of the British Isles.

6. Carole Nichols, Interview with Taylor, SLC Oral History Collection (June 26, 1985), 40; HTA B2:F_Oral_History.

Chapter 4. The Wisconsin Years

EPIGRAPH

Page 55: Michael Rossman, Interview with Taylor, 5A (July 1974, Holderness, NH); HTA B5:F_Rossman.

1. "I didn't have any enormous drive to go to the United States but just thought it would be a good idea to be affiliated at an institution, teaching, and that is what I really meant about being a writer." Rossman, Interview with Taylor, 2B.

2. Carole Nichols, Interview with Taylor, SLC Oral History Collection (June 26, 1985), 40; HTA B2:F_Oral_History.

3. Alain Locke (1885–1954), philosopher, first African American to receive a Rhodes Scholarship, and often described as the "Father of the Harlem Renaissance," was invited by Max Otto in June 1945 to teach Taylor's aesthetic class in the Department of Philosophy for the next year, spring 1946. Jeffrey C. Stewart, *The New Negro: The Life of Alain Locke* (New York: Oxford University Press, 2018), 837.

4. Rossman, Interview with Taylor, 2B.

5. "I played clarinet in the symphony orchestra and got up early sometimes to play with the students before the day started. I coached the tennis team and acted as the assistant dean of men. And I took the Pro Arte (string) Quartet around the state in the president's eight-passenger Buick to play for children in the elementary schools in the mornings and for their parents at night. The four members of the Pro Arte Quartet were professional musicians from Europe, and they spoke no English. They'd been stranded by the war. I had to introduce them wherever we went because most of the people around Wisconsin thought they were going to hear four singers when the quartet was announced. I had to explain that these poor dears were Belgians who couldn't speak any English and played string instruments." Taylor, "Sarah Lawrence College in the Fifties," Sarah Lawrence College Metro Area Alumnae/I, November 6, 1985; HTA B10.

6. Max Otto (1876–1968) was a professor of philosophy at University of Wisconsin from 1921 to 1947, serving as served as chair of the philosophy department from 1936 to 1947. He was a close friend and colleague of John Dewey.

7. Taylor worked on an applied psychology project as a University of Wisconsin staff member under the jurisdiction of the National Defense Research

Committee, preparing a test and training program for US Navy radar operators. The program was housed in Florida where he and his family lived from autumn 1943 to early winter 1945. "Our task was to develop a training program through which radar operators could develop their talents faster and could become more accurate in the radar tracking of enemy aircraft. We used the methods of the research psychologist to test the equipment by which the radar operators worked. We developed a new curriculum, having discovered that most of the required courses which had been in effect before we studied the program were irrelevant to the work which the operators actually did. We also developed new methods of training the operators in the manipulation of the controls and cut the time required to learn the process by two to three months." Taylor, Correspondence to Mary Ann Wighman (December 13, 1962); HTA B6:F_1962.

8. Text has been arrayed from the following sources: Nichols, Interview with Taylor, 53, 54, 56–57, 86–87, 89. Taylor, Correspondence to Charles Muscatine (August 2, 1965); HTA B6:F_1965. Taylor, "Thinkers Who Influenced Me," in *Moments of Personal Discovery*, ed. R. M. MacIver (New York: Institute for Religious and Social Studies, Harper & Brothers, 1952), 137–138. Taylor, "'Quo Vadis': Another View," in *Proceedings, Thirteenth Annual Meeting, Western Association of Graduate Schools*, Newport Beach, CA (February 28–March 2, 1971), 103–104; HTA B10. Herald Tribune Book Review, autobiographical sketch (August 1953); HTA B1:F_Biographical material. Taylor, Correspondence to Shirley Kast (December 8, 1948); HTA B6:F_Wisconsin. Taylor, "Sarah Lawrence College in the Fifties," Sarah Lawrence College Metro Area Alumnae/I, November 6, 1985; HTA B10. Taylor, "Society, the Seventies, and Higher Education," University of Wisconsin, Madison (no date; circa spring 1970), 1, 8; HTA B7.

9. Taylor, "Progressive Education—What It Is and What It Isn't," Education Writers Association, Atlantic City, NJ (February 12, 1965), 3; HTA B10.

10. Rossman, Interview with Taylor, 3B. Harold Taylor and Grace Muriel Thorne Taylor would have two daughters, Mary E. Taylor Lehner and Jennifer Thorne Taylor Tuthill.

11. The Wisconsin Idea represented an early twentieth-century position, initiated by University of Wisconsin president Charles Van Hise with support from Robert La Follette, governor of Wisconsin, that education should extend beyond the classroom to help the general public through service and social action in the state of Wisconsin.

12. Taylor, "The Philosopher in Society," *Antioch Review* 4, no. 1 (Spring 1944): 111.

13. Taylor, "What Good Is Philosophy Today?," *Humanist* 2, no. 4 (1942): 124.

14. Taylor, Correspondence to Max Otto (May 25, 1945); HTA B4:F_Otto.

15. Rossman, Interview with Taylor, 3A. Taylor, "What Is Progressive Education," In-Service Education, Los Angeles County Superintendent of School, Los Angeles, CA (May 3, 1965), 1; HTA B10.

Chapter 5. Sarah Lawrence Remembrances

EPIGRAPHS

Page 63: Taylor, Correspondence to Lenore Sagalyn Cohen (March 18, 1946); HTA B3:F_Cohen.

Page 64: Carole Nichols, Interview with Taylor, SLC Oral History Collection (June 26, 1985), 72; HTA B2:F_Oral_History.

Page 66: Burton Fowler, Correspondence to Taylor (May 11, 1945); HTA B3:F_Fowler.

Page 72: Taylor, "Sarah Lawrence Reconsidered," *Sarah Lawrence Alumnae Magazine*, February 1958, 4.

Page 74: Bob Wool and Charlotte Brooks, "Conversation with Harold Taylor," *Look*, February 20, 1958, 3; HTP Series II:5 Publicity-Look Magazine Articles, 1958.

Page 81: Taylor, "A Garland for Mrs. Stone," Riverside Church Chapel, New York, NY (October 14, 1973), 3–4; HTA B10. Helga Houmere, a Lab Nursery School staff member, remembers that Wright "was impatient, could not wait until the procession started. He was at the head of it, of course, walking next to Harold Taylor. He sat down on a chair next to him. Then the ceremonies proceeded. Harold Taylor got up to speak to the graduating students. He had not talked more than two minutes, when Frank Lloyd Wright got up, marched away, and went into the building. Harold Taylor stopped his speech and went after him. In a minute he was back, grinning. Our guest was neither ill nor did he have to go to the bathroom, he just didn't like to listen to other people's speeches!" Helga Houmere, *Learning from a Lost Childhood* (Barrington, RI: Brie Gull, 2006), 112.

Page 82: Taylor, "The Task of College Administration," in *Democracy in the Administration of Higher Education*, ed. Harold Benjamin (New York: Harper & Brothers, 1950), 40.

Page 86: Taylor, "College President—Not Just a Fund-Raiser!," *Overview*, pilot issue, September 1959, 68.

1. Taylor, "Sarah Lawrence College in the Fifties," Sarah Lawrence College Metro Area Alumnae/I, November 6, 1985; HTA B10.

2. Lucy Greenbaum, Manuscript for the *New York Times* (circa 1946); HTA B1:F_Interviews.

3. Beatrice Doerschuk, Correspondence to Taylor (June 14, 1945); HTA B3:F_Doerschuk.

4. Theodor Mommsen (1817–1903) was rector of the University of Berlin, and Charles Richard Van Hise (1857–1918) was president of University of Wisconsin.

5. Taylor, Correspondence to Beatrice Doerschuk (June 14, 1945); HTA B3:F_Doerschuk. The chair of the board of trustees, Burton P. Fowler, would

write to Taylor noting his amusement at the "friendly tilt" between Doerschuk and Taylor and expressing his support for Taylor's suggested conference as well as his appointment. Fowler, Correspondence to Taylor (June 23, 1945); HTA B3:F_Fowler. Doerschuk would respond by agreeing with Taylor's suggestion for a conference and underscoring that she supported him expressing his own convictions. Doerschuk, Correspondence to Taylor (June 20, 1945); HTA B3:F_Doerschuk.

      6. Taylor, Correspondence to Max Otto (October 22, 1945); HTA B4:F_Otto.

      7. "College President: Thirty-Year-Old Harold Taylor Is the New Head of Sarah Lawrence," Life, September 24, 1945, 95.

      8. "A Birthday among Friends" (compiled by Jane Smart), Time, November 5, 1945, 92; HTA B24:F_1945 Clippings-SLC presidency.

      9. Taylor, Correspondence to Horace Fries (September 18, 1945); HTA B3:F_Fries.

      10. Taylor, Correspondence to Mrs. George C. Sellery (November 13, 1945); HTA B5:F_1945.

      11. Taylor, Correspondence to Rita Smith (December 19, 1945); HTA B5:F_1945.

      12. Constance Warren, *A New Design for Women's Education* (New York: Frederick A. Stokes, 1940).

      13. Wool and Brooks, "Conversation with Taylor," 3.

      14. Michael Rossman, Interview with Taylor, 5A (July 1974, Holderness, NH); HTA B5:F_Rossman.

      15. For Sarah Lawrence's donning program, a professor was designated as a student's don to serve as advisor and mentor and to guide her through experiences at the college, similar to the role of dons at British universities. Taylor would describe the don as an intellectual friend and academic advocate for the student in what was, in essence, a personal dean. Sarah Lawrence integrated field work—"systematic observation, participation, and research carried on outside the college"—into its academic program for certain areas of study, notably the social sciences and the arts. Helen Lynd, *Field Work in College Education* (New York: Columbia University Press, 1945), ix. The first-year studies seminar was developed with a 1930s grant from the General Education Board and designed to offer exploratory general education experiences that would introduce students to new and different knowledge so that they could explore freely ideas and discover their own intellectual and emotional interests. Esther Raushenbush, *Literature for Individual Education* (New York: Columbia University Press, 1942), vi.

      16. Wool and Brooks, "Conversation with Taylor," 3.

      17. Henry Noble MacCracken (1880–1970) served as president of Vassar College from 1915 to 1946.

18. William Heard Kilpatrick (1871–1965) was a professor of educational philosophy at Teachers College and a self-proclaimed disciple of John Dewey.

19. A curricular program that included studying an "essential" collection of books that represented the foundations of Western European culture.

20. Alexander Meiklejohn (1872–1964) was president of Amherst College (and will be featured in this memoir). Stringfellow Barr (1897–1982) was president of St. John's College, and Scott Buchanan (1895–1968) was dean of St. John's College. Robert M. Hutchins (1899–1977) was president of the University of Chicago.

21. Text has been arrayed from the following sources: Nichols, Interview with Taylor, 96–98. Taylor, Correspondence to Edward J. Bloustein (July 8, 1965); HTA B6;F_1965. Wool and Brooks, "Conversation with Taylor." Taylor, Correspondence to Benjamin Wright (March 18, 1950); HTA B5:F_Wright, B. Taylor, Correspondence to Gladys Chang (May 7, 1947); HTA B6:F_1947. Taylor, "Sarah Lawrence Reconsidered," 4–5. Taylor, "An Approach to Education," in *Achievement in the College Years*, ed. Lois B. Murphy and Esther Raushenbush (New York: Harper & Brothers, 1960), 18–19.

22. Rossman, Interview with Taylor, 4B.

23. See Wayne J. Urban, *Scholarly Leadership in Higher Education: An Intellectual History of James B. Conant* (London: Bloomsbury Academic, 2020), 189–201.

24. Kenneth Duckett, Interview with Taylor (April 8, 1966, Center for Dewey Studies, University of Southern Illinois, Carbondale, IL), 27–30; HTA B1:F_Interviews.

Chapter 6. Assault on a Small College

EPIGRAPHS

Page 89: FBI File: Correlation Summary–Harold Taylor, 100-356042-8 (November 30, 1956), 13; HTA B2:F_FBI.

Page 91: Taylor, *On Education and Freedom* (New York: Abelard-Schuman, 1954), 252.

1. Carole Nichols, Interview with Taylor, SLC Oral History Collection (July 9, 1985), 284, 291; HTA B2:F_Oral_History.

2. https://www.sarahlawrence.edu/archives/exhibits/mccarthyism/

3. Taylor was well recognized as one of the few presidents who was willing to fight such charges and accusations. In 1953, Harold Larrabee's essay, "Sarah Lawrence vs. the Legion," began with the opening sentence: "At a time when so many college presidents are so fearful of adverse publicity that they spend hours in boasting about the conservatism and orthodoxy of their faculty mem-

bers instead of defending those few whose opinions happen to be unpopular, it is refreshing to be able to record one example, at least, of an effective defense of academic freedom by a president and board of trustees against the combined assaults of reactionary and clericalist attackers." Harold A. Larrabee, "Sarah Lawrence vs. the Legion," *Humanist* 13, no. 4 (1953): 149. Larrabee proceeds to describe the tensions between Taylor and the American Legion and concludes with, "At least one college president and board of trustees have shown that the sound and effective way to meet them is not to run for the nearest cover, but to stand up and fight for some of those American principles of freedom which the American Legion does not seem to understand." Larrabee, "Sarah Lawrence vs. the Legion," 153.

4. Mary Collins, "Political Attitudes of Sarah Lawrence Students" (January 31, 1955), 2, 6; HTA B12:F_Freedom and Authority on the College Campus Survey, 1952–53.

5. Kitty Minns Gellhorn, ed., *The Reminiscences of Esther Raushenbush* (New York: Oral History Research Office, Columbia University, 1973), 330; SLC Archives Raushenbush Papers RG 2.1.6. Kitty Minns Gellhorn, ed., *Reminiscences of Helen Lynd* (New York: Oral History Oral History Research Office, Columbia University, 1973), 2:15; SLC Archives Lynd Papers RG 10.4. Mary Reynolds, Interview with Alastair Reid (New York, NY; July 15, 1998), 18; SLC Archives, Oral History Collection, Box 2. In the 1952 issue of the *Progressive*, Arnold Serwer stated, "The most classic defense of academic freedom to be made in many years is now in its seventh month at Sarah Lawrence College" and applauded Taylor and Sarah Lawrence for their courageous actions in response to accusations of indoctrinating students and the attacks by the American Legion of the college allegedly employing communists. Arnold Serwer, "The Contagion of Courage," *Progressive* 16, no. 5 (May 1952): 26.

6. Text has been arrayed from the following sources: Taylor, memoir manuscript pages 51C and 60; Taylor, "A State of Mind," unpublished manuscript; HTA B23. Taylor, Notes from the November 2, 1951, meeting with members of the Americanism Committee of the Westchester County American Legion (November 3, 1951); HTP Series II:2 Academic Freedom—American Legion, Bronxville, 1949–1956. Taylor, Correspondence to the Board of Trustees re. Paul Aron (April 2, 1953); HTA B3: F_Aron case. Taylor, Correspondence to Elmer Davis (April 6, 1953); HTP Series II:2 Academic Freedom—Letters from Various Colleges and Universities, 1953–1954, 1959. Taylor, Correspondence to the Board of Trustees, dictated (April 9, 1953); HTP Series II:2 Academic Freedom—Paul Aron and Jenner Committee, 1953. Taylor, Correspondence to the Committee on Academic Freedom of the Board of Trustees (October 20, 1953); HTP Series II:2 Academic Freedom, F10. Taylor, Correspondence to Buell G. Gallagher (October 8, 1953); HTA B3:F_Gallagher. Carole Nichols,

Interview with Taylor, SLC Oral History Collection (July 9, 1985), excerpts from 279–314; HTA B2:F_Oral_History.

7. On March 21, 1947, President Harry Truman signed Executive Order 9835, the "Loyalty Order," as a way to investigate suspected communists in the US federal government. The Loyalty Order led to the release, on April 3, 1947, of the "Attorney General's List of Subversive Organizations."

8. Nicola Sacco and Bartolomeo Vanzetti were accused of murder in 1920, convicted in 1921, and executed in 1927. The case attracted national and international attention and exposed the strong anti-radical, anti-communist, anti-immigrant feelings and biased legal system in America.

9. Albert F. Canwell (1907–2002) served in the Washington state legislature from 1947 to 1949. Canwell chaired the state of Washington's Joint Legislative Committee on Un-American Activities, known as the Canwell Committee.

10. J. Robert Oppenheimer (1904–1967), a theoretical physicist, is considered the "father of the atomic bomb." During the McCarthy era, he was accused of being associated with communists and, later, being a Russian spy.

11. Taylor, "Should Communists Be Allowed to Teach in Our Colleges?," Town Hall, New York, New York (March 1, 1949), ABC *Radio Town Meeting: Bulletin of America's Town Meeting of the Air* 14, no. 44 (March 1, 1949): 5; HTA B13.

12. Serwer noted that the three antagonists who raised charges against Sarah Lawrence—Louis Budenz, Rabbi Benjamin Schultz, and Alfred Kohlberg—all lived with a few miles of the college. "Here was a test case at their doorstep which they could prosecute with convenience. They have done so with unflagging zeal." Serwer, "Contagion of Courage," *Progressive*, 27.

13. Francis E. Walter was a member of the US House of Representatives from 1933 to 1963, a member of the House Un-American Activities Committee from 1951 to 1963, and served as its chair from 1955 to 1963.

14. Euphemia (Micky) Virden Hall worked in the Washington, DC, office for the TASS News Agency from 1948 to 1951.

15. Victor S. Navasky, *Naming Names* (New York: Viking Press, 1980), 364.

16. Telford Taylor (1908–1998) was a lawyer and law professor who had been general counsel for the prosecution at the Nuremberg trials and would later defend many individuals accused of being communists. Arthur Garfield Hays (1881–1954) was cofounder and general counsel for the American Civil Liberties Union. Lloyd Garrison (1897–1991) was former dean of the University of Wisconsin Law School and a Wall Street lawyer who was involved with the defense of Langston Hughes and Arthur Miller, both of whom who were accused of communist connections. Harrison Tweed (1885–1969) was an important New York lawyer and trustee of Sarah Lawrence.

17. Irving Goldman and his counsel, Arthur Garfield Hays, developed the calculated contempt defense—"the best way to reconcile one's conscience without harming his college was speaking openly about personal activities, refusing to testify about others." William M. Beccher, et al., "Education and the Fifth Amendment: Old Privilege Seeks New Meaning in Wake of Legislative Probes," *Harvard Crimson*, June 10, 1953, https://www.thecrimson.com/article/1953/6/10/education-and-the-fifth-amendment-pno/.

18. James M. Minifie, "Witness Says He Woke Up Not a Red," *Washington Post*, March 25, 1953, 8. Minifie set the tone of the article with his opening sentence: "A novel angle was introduced into the routine refusals to admit Communist Party membership when a college professor swore yesterday that he was not a Communist when he woke up last Friday, but refused to say whether he was last Thursday."

19. Taylor, "To the Board of Trustees Re: Paul Aron" (April 2, 1953), 11, 12.

20. "Report of Advisory Committee on Appointments Concerning Mr. Aron's Resignation" (April 14, 1953); HTP Series II:2 Academic Freedom—Paul Aron and Jenner Committee, 1953. Paul H. Aron (1921–1991) would become a portfolio advisor for the Dreyfus Corporation, emerging as a leading economist and authority on American-Japanese investments.

Chapter 7. On Being Written About

EPIGRAPH

Page 107: Taylor, Correspondence to Carl Bogholt (May 4, 1955); HTA B3:F_Bogholt.

1. Mary McCarthy, *The Groves of Academe* (New York: Harcourt, Brace, 1952). Randall Jarrell, *Pictures from an Institution* (New York: Knopf, 1954). Mary McCarthy (1912–1989) was a novelist and literary critic; Randall Jarrell (1914–1965) was a poet and literary critic.

2. In 1952, Jarrell would write to his mentor, John Crowe Ransom, describing the Taylor-Robbins similarities in his draft. A portion of the letter is quoted here: "My Dwight Robbins' appearance, perpetual youngness, perfect adjustment to his surroundings, are modeled on Taylor's (Taylor's conversation is quite unlike Robbins, Robbins talks ordinary President-banalities, Taylor likes to sound as cultivated as possible, as versatile as possible, like [a] Renaissance Man being pals with Stephen Spender). In other words, I think Taylor is like my Dwight Robbins (except for a few particulars like curly hair, ingenuous sincerity) only insofar as he's like the general type of such Boy Wonder executives, he was mostly a point of departure for me, but I did take several steps before departing. . . . My Dwight Robbins is so different from Taylor . . . but

Taylor seems to me a smarter, more disingenuous, more unpleasant man." Mary Jarrell, ed., *Randall Jarrell's Letters* (Boston: Houghton Mifflin, 1985), 366, 367. On another occasion, Jarrell shows similar feelings about Taylor. Writing in personal correspondence in November 1951: "There was a wonderful picture of Harold Taylor in the *Herald-Tribune*—entirely *true* but otherwise libelous. You know, he really isn't a bit older than he was in 1946. He's like that wheat from Egyptian tombs—I'll bet if they buried him for three thousand years and then exposed him to limelight he'd begin to make a speech on civil rights." Jarrell, *Randall Jarrell's Letters*, 288.

3. Suzanne Ferguson, "To Benton, with Love and Judgment: Jarrell's *Pictures from an Institution*," in *Critical Essays on Randall Jarrell*, ed. Suzanne Ferguson (Boston: G. K. Hall, 1983), 272.

4. Ferguson, "To Benton, with Love and Judgment," 282.

5. Jessica Mitford, Correspondence to Taylor (February 18, 1982); HTA B4:F_Mitford. Mitford adds, "I've been reading *Pictures from an Institution* for the first time. I thought it a bit disappointing—especially in view of the absolutely ecstatic blurbs on the jacket by all sorts of illustrious folks. Am really longing for your riposte to all that, so do hurry up with it."

6. Michael Wreszin, ed., *A Moral Temper: The Letters of Dwight Macdonald* (Chicago: Ivan R. Dee, 2001), 216.

7. William F. Buckley Jr. (1925–2008) was a conservative author, host of the television program *Firing Line*, and founder of the *National Review*.

8. Frances Kiernan, *Seeing Mary Plain: A Life of Mary McCarthy* (New York: W. W. Norton, 2000), 284, 681.

9. Dates have been corrected in this chapter. William H. Pritchard in *Randall Jarrell: A Literary Life* suggests that Jarrell and McCarthy were both teaching at Sarah Lawrence in 1947 (New York: Farrar, Straus and Giroux, 1990), 153. Similarly, David Leeming in *Stephen Spender: A Life in Modernism* maintains that Spender's Sarah Lawrence colleagues in autumn 1947 included McCarthy and Jarrell (New York: Henry Holt, 1999), 168. Records indicate, however, that while Jarrell was at the college in spring 1947, moving to Greensboro in autumn 1947, McCarthy taught during the spring of 1948. Faculty Appointment Administrative Form–Jarrell; *Bulletin of the Woman's College of the University of North Carolina*, Greensboro, NC: UNCG Campus Publications (1947–1948), 14. Martha Blakeney Hodges Special Collections and University Archives, the University of North Carolina at Greensboro. Faculty Personnel Sheet–Mary McCarthy, December 18, 1947; Faculty File, Sarah Lawrence College Archives, Bronxville, NY.

10. Randall Jarrell coached Kenyon College's tennis team in the late 1930s. J. A. Bryant, Jr., *Understanding Randall Jarrell* (Columbia: University of South Carolina Press, 1986), 1. Taylor served as coach of the University of Wisconsin tennis team during his years as a faculty member in the early 1940s.

11. Theodore Roethke (1908–1963) would teach at the University of Washington from 1947 to 1963.

12. While *Pictures from an Institution* was published in 1954, a draft was written in 1952. Jarrell biographer William H. Pritchard writes, "Its [*Pictures*'] oddity can be measured by comparing it with Mary McCarthy's *The Groves of Academe*, which was published in 1952, by which time Jarrell had written his book in its earlier form. He read McCarthy's novel soon after it appeared—and was shocked to find his own name in the list of poets who weren't invited to the poetry conference at McCarthy's mythical Jocelyn College." Pritchard, *Randall Jarrell*, 234. J. A. Bryant maintains that Jarrell produced the work during 1952–1953. Bryant, *Understanding Randall Jarrell*, 102.

13. "Tales would come back of her telling stories about her students to people in New York. In those days at Sarah Lawrence, we took pains to help students who weren't doing well—whatever their weaknesses were, we tended to try to help them. Mary would also talk about her students with other students. It tended to undermine the confidence of the students in a way. She made fun of the college. For certain students who were prone to take the same posture, she worked out very well. She liked bright lively young people. Whereas the philosophy at Sarah Lawrence was you take them as they come. Her psychological distance from the college, her wish not to be identified with its sloppy progressivism, her seeing it as something to be made fun of along with the students and president, were all apparent." Taylor quoted in Kiernan, *Seeing Mary Plain*, 283.

14. Jarrell, *Pictures from an Institution* (New York: Farrar, Straus and Giroux, 1954), 8.

15. In the 1980s, when contacted by McCarthy biographer Frances Kiernan, Taylor would write, "I was looking at *The Groves of Academe* last summer because I'm doing my autobiography. I was redoing the chapter on Randall and Mary. I read the book again and it's very good. It's packed with authentic detail. She's caught the attitude of the softhearted liberal. Randall Jarrell's book doesn't have the intricacy of Mary's observations about the liberal faculty members in a progressive environment. I don't think there's anybody who has better caught the flavor of an intellectual community where everything is permitted." Kiernan, *Seeing Mary Plain*, 335.

16. Jarrell, *Pictures from an Institution*, 28–29.

17. These final four sentences have been inserted from Carole Nichols's Interview with Taylor, SLC Oral History Collection (July 2, 1985), 202; HTA B2:F_Oral_History.

18. Taylor would describe the 1967 *Firing Line* "encounter": "After a while I began to think that he was nothing but a sinister face in front of a fairly empty mind, and that he now comes on as an entertainer with a reputation for right wing ideology but without much conviction. After the program I told him that before he went on again to talk about students or education, he should get to

know a little more about them both, since he seemed to me to be talking as if he had never left the Yale of 1950." Taylor, Correspondence to Seymour Fersh (March 31, 1967); HTA B3:F_Fersh.

19. Sarah Gibson Blanding (1898–1985) was Vassar College's first female president and served in that position from 1946 to 1964.

20. Vassar College Student Forum on Liberalism and Conservatism in Education: A Discussion with William Buckley Jr. and Harold Taylor, Poughkeepsie, NY, January 27, 1962; HTA B9:F_ Vassar College Student Forum. While there is no audio or video recording of the Taylor-Buckley 1962 debate at Vassar, Taylor's appearance on Buckley's *Firing Line* in 1967 to discuss academic freedom may be suggestive of their 1962 exchange and is accessible as "Academic Freedom and Berkeley," *Firing Line*, January 16, 1967, Episode 042; https://www.youtube.com/watch?v=7juxJPrSKVI.

21. Taylor, "Opening Statement," Vassar College Student Forum on Liberalism and Conservatism in Education, 1, 2.

22. Jarrell, *Pictures from an Institution*, 220, 221–222.

Chapter 8. Dewey, Meiklejohn, and the 1950s

EPIGRAPHS

Page 125: Taylor, "Thinkers Who Influenced Me," in *Moments of Personal Discovery*, ed. R. M. MacIver (New York: Institute for Religious and Social Studies, Harper & Brothers, 1952), 142–143.

Page 127: Taylor, Correspondence to Margaret Marsh (September 9, 1955); HTA B4:F_Marsh.

1. Opened to students in 1934, the San Francisco School of Social Studies, a community-based adult education program, focused upon the Great Books and addressed contemporary social problems in America. The school continued until 1940.

2. Adam R. Nelson, *Education and Democracy: The Meaning of Alexander Meiklejohn 1872–1964* (Madison: University of Wisconsin Press, 2001), 233–260.

3. George Dykhuizen, *The Life and Mind of John Dewey* (Carbondale: Southern Illinois University Press, 1973).

4. Text has been arrayed from the following sources: Kenneth Duckett, Interview with Harold Taylor (April 8, 1966, Center for Dewey Studies, University of Southern Illinois, Carbondale, IL); HTA B1:F_Interviews. Taylor, *Students without Teachers* (New York: McGraw-Hill, 1969), 191–192. Taylor, "Thinkers Who Influenced Me," 142. Another version of Taylor's 1987 speech appeared as "Meiklejohn and Dewey in the 1950s" in *Teaching Education* 2, no. 1 (1988): 20–29.

5. William Allan Neilson (1869–1946) was president of Smith College from 1917 to 1939.

6. Taylor's thoughts toward Barr and Hutchins were similar to Algren's feelings about Adler. Taylor described Barr as "an aggressive Rotarian business man who is clubbing his way through the educational crowd with a few advertising slogans and a muscular aggression." Taylor, Correspondence to Sidney Hook (September 28, 1945); HTA B4:F_Hook. Upon hearing that Hutchins was receiving support from the Ford Foundation, Taylor was reported as saying, "This is a great opportunity. Tell Paul Hoffman [president of the Ford Foundation] that the best thing he could possibly do for the welfare of this nation is to give Hutchins a million dollars on the condition that he live in Afghanistan the rest of his life, and get him the hell out of here." Harry Ashmore, *Unseasonable Truths: The Life of Robert Maynard Hutchins* (Boston: Little, Brown, 1989), 326–327.

7. Roberta Dewey, officially a companion when Taylor first visited, married John Dewey in 1946; their adopted children were siblings, John Jr. and Adrienne.

8. Frederick James Eugene Woodbridge (1867–1940) was a professor of philosophy at Columbia University, dean of the faculties of political science, philosophy, and pure science, and founder of the *Journal of Philosophy, Psychology and Scientific Methods*. Woodbridge attracted a highly regarded faculty in the Department of Philosophy while at Columbia University between 1902 and 1937.

9. Hyman Rickover (1900–1986) was a Navy admiral who would lead a movement in the United States criticizing the decline of educational standards in the public schools.

10. As Taylor recounts, "Prime Minister Nehru, who was in the country at that time and who was being entertained at a dinner in his honor, was so desperately sorry that his own dinner conflicted with the one for Dewey that he sent word that he would come over to the dinner if he finished his in time without insulting his guest." Duckett, Interview with Taylor (April 8, 1966), 15–16. Jawaharlal Nehru (1889–1964) was a leader of the Indian nationalist movement and served as the first prime minister of India.

Chapter 9. Thoughts on Leaving Sarah Lawrence and Life Thereafter

EPIGRAPHS

Page 144: Taylor, *On Education and Freedom* (New York: Abelard-Schuman, 1954), 57.

Page 145: Taylor, Correspondence to Millicent McIntosh (September 7, 1959); HTA B6:F_1959.

Page 152: Taylor, Correspondence to Alastair Reid (March 13, 1973); HTA B5:F_Reid.

1. Taylor, "College President—Idea Man or Money Man?," *New York Times Magazine*, April 12, 1959, 84.

2. See Taylor, Correspondence to Agnes Meyer (November 29, 1956); HTA B4:F_Meyer. Taylor, Correspondence to Harry Hawthorn (November 27, 1956); HTA B4:F_Hawthorn. Taylor, Correspondence to Helen Lynd (July 1, 1956); HTA B4:F_H_Lynd.

3. Kenneth Duckett, Interview with Taylor (April 8, 1966, Center for Dewey Studies, University of Southern Illinois, Carbondale, IL), 27–30; HTA B1:F_Interviews.

4. Taylor, Correspondence to Lloyd K. Garrison (January 2, 1959); HTA B1:F_Resignation-correspondence.

5. Taylor, "Some Thoughts on Leaving Sarah Lawrence," *Sarah Lawrence College Alumnae Magazine*, Spring 1959, 2, 3, 17.

6. "Activities of Harold Taylor after Leaving Sarah Lawrence College on August 1st, 1959"; HTA B1:F_Biographical Material 1960s–1980s.

Chapter 10. Adlai Stevenson and the 1960 Presidential Campaign

EPIGRAPH

Page 155: Norman Mailer, "Superman Comes to the Supermart," *Esquire* 54, no. 5 (November 1960): 119.

1. Marshall Field III (1893–1956) was an investment banker, publisher, philanthropist, and grandson of department store businessman Marshall Field. Taylor, no doubt, would have also had some contact with Stevenson through his close friend and colleague Lloyd Garrison (1897–1991), Sarah Lawrence trustee, lawyer, and president of the National Urban League, who traveled around the world with Stevenson on various occasions. Ruth Field (1908–1994) was a philanthropist for race relations projects and child welfare programs and wife of Marshall Field III. Agnes Meyer (1887–1970) was a journalist and civil rights advocate, mother of Katharine Graham, and wife of Eugene Meyer, owner of the *Washington Post*. Eleanor Roosevelt (1884–1962) met Taylor in 1945 during his first week at Sarah Lawrence. Taylor recounts, "She called up the college and invited me up to have a conversation with her at her place in Walhalla at Val-Kill Cottage. I went up and spent a whole day with her and we talked about everything. She had read about me in the *Times* and she wanted me to come up to just discuss education. She was interested in Sarah Lawrence in particular and its progressive ideas, and we became fast friends from that point on." Michael Rossman, Interview with Taylor, 5A (July 1974, Holderness, NH); HTA B5:F_Rossman.

2. "Notes on Conversation with Adlai Stevenson at 990 Fifth Ave. with Ruth Field and Stuart Brown, Prepared by Harold Taylor, March 28th [1960]"; HTA B5:F_Stevenson, A. "Brown-Taylor Piece on Adlai Stevenson," July 13, 1961; HTA B5:F_Stevenson, A. Stuart G. Brown (1912–1991) was professor of citizenship and American culture at Syracuse University from 1947 to 1965 and a campaign aide to Stevenson.

3. Theodore White, *The Making of the President 1960* (New York: Atheneum, 1961); Arthur M. Schlesinger, Jr., *A Thousand Days: John F. Kennedy in the White House* (Boston: Houghton Mifflin, 1965); Stuart Gerry Brown, *Conscience in Politics: Adlai E. Stevenson in the 1950s* (Syracuse: Syracuse University Press, 1961).

4. Taylor, Correspondence to Stuart Brown (July 13, 1961); HTA B5:F_Stevenson, A. Thomas Finletter (1893–1980) would become ambassador to NATO for the Kennedy administration.

5. Taylor, Correspondence to Brown (July 13, 1961).

6. Dulles-Eisenhower policy represented a harsh anti-communist stance with threats of "massive retaliation," in essence a position of either containment of or resistance to any gesture suggesting communist expansion.

7. William Attwood (1919–1989) was a journalist and campaign aide to both Stevenson and Kennedy and would serve as an ambassador to Guinea and Kenya for both the Kennedy and Johnson administrations.

8. The estate of Marshall Field III, Caumsett, was located on Lloyd's Neck in the village of Lloyd Harbor, New York. Marietta Peabody Tree worked as a campaign aide for Adlai Stevenson and became a companion. She would later represent the United States on the United Nations Commission on Human Rights during the Kennedy administration. Ronald Tree, married to Marietta Tree, was a grandson of Marshall Field. Elizabeth (Buffie) Stevenson Ives was Adlai Stevenson's sister.

9. Taylor, "The Crisis in Liberal Democracy," Intercollegiate Conference of Challenge, Yale University, New Haven, CT (March 11, 1960); HTA B19. Ruth Field gave a copy of the manuscript to Stevenson who then requested to meet with Taylor and, subsequently, invited Taylor to write for him. Taylor, Correspondence to Marc Slonim (June 1, 1960); HTA B5: F_Slonim. This speech also led to Agnes Meyer writing to Taylor: "After reading your wonderful speech at Yale University, I decided that you are one of the few people who could help write some speeches for him [Stevenson] and for me." Agnes Meyer, Correspondence to Taylor (March 23, 1960); HTA B4:F_Meyer.

10. Willard Wirtz (1912–2010), speechwriter for Stevenson, would become secretary of labor in the Kennedy and Johnson administrations.

11. Eleanor Roosevelt, My Day, Saturday, June 11, 1960.

12. Eleanor Roosevelt, My Day, Monday, June 13, 1960.

13. Wayne Phillips, "Stevenson: Not Candidate; Mrs. Roosevelt: Yes, He Is," *New York Times*, June 13, 1960, 1.

Chapter 11. The Student Revolt Revisited

EPIGRAPH

Page 173: "An Interview with Harold Taylor," *Media and Methods* 6, no. 1 (September 1969): 62.

1. Tom Hayden, *Reunion: A Memoir* (New York: Random House, 1988), 107. Robert Westbrook also notes Taylor's influence on Hayden in *John Dewey and American Democracy* (Ithaca: Cornell University Press, 1991), 549. In 2010, I gave a copy of the original fragment of Taylor's chapter to Tom Hayden during his visit to my campus. The next day he told me how much he liked Harold's account and his writing style.

2. Tom Hayden describes tensions during the Port Huron conference and notes that he and Robert Alan Haber (who would become the first president of Students for a Democratic Society) were suspended from their League for Industrial Democracy posts (with accusations posed by Michael Harrington): "Within months, however, our positions were restored through the intervention of principled individuals like Harold Taylor and, surprisingly, Norman Thomas, who chastised the LID for their rigid behavior." Hayden, *Reunion*, 91.

3. Taylor mentioned that parts of the Port Huron Statement were drafted by Hayden and others on the dining room table at his NYC West Village brownstone. "Since the boys were from Michigan, there was nowhere else they could find a place to write at that time in New York." Taylor, "Society, the Seventies, and Higher Education," University of Wisconsin, Madison (no date; circa spring 1970), 15; HTA B7.

4. Taylor, "The Student Revolution," University of New Mexico, Albuquerque, New Mexico (February 25, 1970); HTA B10.

5. Grayson Kirk (1903–1997) was president of Columbia University from 1953 to 1968.

6. A writer for Barnard's alumnae association reported, "During the deep silence which followed [Eisenhower's introduction], President Eisenhower made his brief welcoming address. . . . He said, "you are one-half of the population and, unless we attend to the education of women, we can have, at best, only a half-educated country." Marjorie Herrmann Lawrence, "The General Meeting," *Barnard College Alumnae Magazine*, February 1949, 6.

7. Sidney Hook, "The Architecture of Educational Chaos," *Phi Delta Kappan* 51, no. 2 (October 1969): 68–70. Hook also viewed Taylor's position as

being "mealymouthed nonsense," "and when not confused, mistaken and likely to generate mischievous consequences," "of dubious value," and justifying if not actually encouraging "the violence and lawlessness that have disrupted so many American campuses."

8. Fred Hechinger, "Students of the Sixties: Salvaging the Youth Movement," *Change: The Magazine of Higher Learning* 5, no. 5 (1973): 34.

9. The outdoor Columbia University counter-commencement staged on June 4, 1968, included an invocation by Rabbi A. Bruce Goldman, benediction by Reverend William Starr, and speeches by Erich Fromm, Harold Taylor, and Dwight Macdonald. Richard Hofstadter served as the commencement speaker for the official ceremony at Columbia University where it is said that the students walking out during his speech led to his turn toward conservatism.

10. Diana Trilling, *We Must March My Darlings* (New York: Harcourt Brace Jovanovich, 1977), 139.

11. Murray Schumach, "An Audience of 2,000 Applauds Rump Columbia Commencement," *New York Times*, June 5, 1968, 34.

12. I wish to take an endnote indulgence to underscore the phrase "and with the addition of chairs for the speakers" as an example of Taylor's characteristic subtle wit and irony—the Taylor touch.

13. Text has been from Taylor, *Students without Teachers: The Crisis in the University* (New York: McGraw-Hill, 1969), 37–41.

14. Fred Hechinger, "The Harsh Legacy of the Class of '68," *New York Times*, June 9, 1968, E11.

15. Taylor, *The World and the American Teacher* (Washington, DC: American Association of Colleges for Teacher Education, 1968).

16. Taylor, Correspondence to Fred Hechinger (June 9, 1969); HTA B4:F_Hechinger.

17. Erich Fromm, Dwight MacDonald, and Harold Taylor, "Commencement at Columbia," Letters to the Editor, *New York Times*, June 17, 1968, 38.

18. Fred Hechinger, Correspondence to Taylor (June 20, 1968); HTA B4:F_Hechinger.

19. Hechinger, "Students of the Sixties," 31–35.

20. Taylor, "Salvaging the Youth Movement from Its 'Enemies,'" *Change: The Magazine of Higher Learning* 5, no. 8 (October 1973): 10.

Chapter 12. Unbegun Chapters

EPIGRAPHS

Page 201: Taylor, "The Task of College Administration," in *Democracy in the Administration of Higher Education*, ed. Harold Benjamin (New York: Harper & Brothers, 1950), 31.

Page 205: Albert Barnes, Correspondence to Taylor (September 5, 1950); HTP Series II:3 Correspondence—Albert Barnes, 1949–1950.

1. Taylor, *Art and the Intellect: Moral Values and the Experience of Art* (New York: Museum of Modern Art, 1960).
2. John W. Finney, "24 Writers Urge New Steps for Vietnam Peace," *New York Times*, April 27, 1966, 6.
3. Richard Cook, *Alfred Kazin: A Biography* (New Haven, CT: Yale University Press, 2008), 270. Geoffrey A. Wolff, "Humphrey's Viet Role Attacked by Writer," *Washington Post*, April 27, 1966, A12.
4. Richard Cook, ed., *Alfred Kazin's Journals* (New Haven, CT: Yale University Press, 2011), 356. Kazin would refer to the "gallant and uninspiring group" and described a "good" press conference where he attacked "our great and immortal vice-president like anything, and sure enough, when we called on the great man as per appointment, he expressed indignation."
5. Undersigned, a group of American writers (April 26, 1966); HTA B4:F_Humphrey.
6. Homer Bigart, "Humphrey Urges Hard Line in War," *New York Times*, April 26, 1966, 1, 38.
7. Taylor, Correspondence to Hubert Humphrey (April 28, 1966); HTA B4:F_Humphrey.
8. Hubert Humphrey, Correspondence to Taylor (May 5, 1966); HTA B4:F_Humphrey.
9. Taylor, "The Student as a Responsible Person," *Harvard Educational Review* 19, no. 2 (1949): 71.
10. Funny Coincidence Department, *New Yorker*, November 10, 1951, 102.
11. "President Issues Public Comment about Inaugural," *Cornell Daily Sun*, November 30, 1951, 1, 12. "Kansas 'Star' Reports on Western Coverage," *Cornell Daily Sun*, November 30, 1951, 1–2.
12. Carole Nichols, Interview with Taylor, SLC Oral History Collection (July 2, 1985), 195–200; HTA B2:F_Oral_History.
13. Taylor's speech was published in a Community Relations Service pamphlet on May 14, 1949.
14. Warren Weaver Jr., "Malott Installed as Cornell's Head," *New York Times*, September 20, 1951, 6.
15. The phrase that would have caught Taylor's attention in the September 20th *New York Times* article is the following: "The future is too rich in alarming possibilities, and when they take the old and the new side by side, they much prefer the old."
16. Funny Coincidence Department, 102.
17. Stuart P. Green, "Plagiarism, Norms, and the Limits of Theft Law: Some Observations on the Use of Criminal Sanctions in Enforcing Intellectual Property Rights," *Hastings Law Journal* 54, no. 1 (November 2002): 180. Available at: https://repository.uchastings.edu/hastings_law_journal/vol54/iss1/3.

18. Weaver, "Malott Installed as Cornell's Head," 6.

19. Harley Frank, Correspondence to Taylor (November 7, 1951); HTA B6:F_1951. Paul Arca, Correspondence to Taylor (December 1, 1953); HTA B6:F_1953. Mary Milligan, Memo: Arrangements for Mr. Taylor's Talk at Cornell (January 5, 1954); HTA B6:F_1954.

20. Neil L. Rudenstine, *The House of Barnes: The Man, the Collection, the Controversy* (Philadelphia: American Philosophical Society, 2012), 140.

21. Albert Barnes, Correspondence to Jon Longaker (July 7, 1950); HTP Series II:3 Correspondence—Albert Barnes, 1949–1950. Howard Greenfeld, in *The Devil and Dr. Barnes*, also notes Barnes's initial respect for Taylor. *The Devil and Dr. Barnes: Portrait for an American Art Collector* (Philadelphia: Camino Books, 2006), 280.

22. Mary Ann Meyers, *Art, Education, and African-American Culture: Albert Barnes and the Science of Philanthropy* (New Brunswick, NJ: Transaction, 2003), 266.

23. Barnes, Correspondence to Taylor (September 5, 1950).

24. Taylor, Correspondence to Albert Barnes (November 20, 1950); HTP Series II:3 Correspondence—Albert Barnes, 1949–1950.

25. Rudenstine, *The House of Barnes*, 140.

26. Albert Coombs Barnes (1872–1951) marketed the antiseptic, Argyrol, beginning in 1901. Before the introduction of antibiotics, Argyrol was a compound of silver and protein that proved to be the most successful topical drug to combat localized infections. Argyrol's success was said to have depended largely on its being adopted as the standard anti-venereal treatment of the French army. By 1912, Barnes was devoting his life to collecting art. Greenfeld, *The Devil and Dr. Barnes*, 3.

27. Harold Edward Stassen (1907–2001) served as president of the University of Pennsylvania from 1948 to 1953.

28. Katherine Elizabeth McBride (1904–1976) served as president of Bryn Mawr College from 1942 to 1970.

29. Text has been arrayed from the following sources: Kenneth Duckett, Interview with Taylor (April 8, 1966, Center for Dewey Studies, University of Southern Illinois, Carbondale, IL), 19–23; HTA B1:F_Interviews. Nichols, Interview with Taylor, 92.

Epilogue

EPIGRAPHS

Page 211: Carole Nichols, Interview with Taylor, SLC Oral History Collection (June 26, 1985), 79; HTA B2:F_Oral History.

Page 212: Taylor, *How to Change Colleges: Notes on Radical Reform* (New York: Holt, Rinehart and Winston, 1971), 67.

Page 216: Taylor, "Debate over 'the Progressive Idea,'" *New York Times Magazine*, November 26, 1961, 123.

Page 219: Taylor, "Education as Experiment," *Antioch Review* 9, no. 2 (Summer 1949): 234.

Page 223: Nichols, Interview with Taylor, 347.

1. Jack Lyons, Correspondence to Taylor (November 4, 1946); HTA B4:F_Lyons.

2. Committee on the Objectives of a General Education in a Free Society, *General Education in a Free Society* (Cambridge, MA: Harvard University Press, 1945).

3. Daniel Bell maintained that the Harvard Report sought "to formulate a complete educational philosophy for American Society." Daniel Bell, *The Reforming of General Education* (New York: Columbia University Press, 1966), 38.

4. "A Symposium on Educational Philosophy: Some Problems in the Philosophy of Education" appeared in *Philosophy and Phenomenological Research* 7, no. 2 (December 1946): 187–292. Taylor, "Philosophical Aspects of the Harvard Report," *Philosophy and Phenomenological Research* 7, no. 2 (December 1946): 226–239. Taylor, "Some Questions and Answers," *Philosophy and Phenomenological Research* 7, no. 3 (March 1947): 446–452. The symposium was held on February 14, 1946, at Columbia University.

Taylor would also appear on a panel, The Contribution of Education to Philosophy, with Raphael Demos and the dean of St. John's College, Scott Buchanan, later that same year, December 28, 1946, at an American Philosophical Association meeting at Yale University. Taylor's comments are not preserved from this 1946 session. Four months later, however, Taylor, in correspondence with John Dewey, would describe Demos as having "a simple-mindedness which can see no problems of any serious kind in either training the intellect or conceiving the universe." Taylor, Correspondence to John Dewey (April 26, 1947); HTA B3:F_Dewey.

5. Taylor, Correspondence to Marvin Farber (June 1, 1946); HTA B6:F_1946.

6. Carole Nichols, Interview with Taylor, SLC Oral History Collection (June 26, 1985), 40; HTA B2:F_Oral_History.

7. Taylor, "What Is Progressive in Education," Athenaeum, Summit, NJ (March 9, 1950), 16; HTA B8.

8. Taylor, *Students without Teachers: The Crisis in the University* (New York: McGraw-Hill, 1969), 13.

9. Taylor, "Some Problems in the Philosophy of Education," A Symposium on Educational Philosophy, Columbia University (February 14, 1946), 13; HTA B7.

10. Taylor, "College President—Idea Man or Money Man?," *New York Times Magazine*, April 12, 1959, 23, 84.

11. Taylor, "Progressive Philosophies in Higher Education," New School, NYC (November 13, 1950), 7; HTA B9.

12. Middle-range theorizing involved drawing theoretical insights from practice and then implementing those insights as a way to enhance and refine further practice. Taylor wrote about his distaste for the purely theoretical and "for all abstractions and for all ideas which are advocated loosely with no indication that the advocate has any clue as to how they can be carried out. Conversely, I have learned to cherish ideas which are helpful and interesting, and can be put into practice. I have never believed in the separation of thought and action, or the idea that educators and intellectuals should simply produce thoughts which it is the duty of the rest of the world to act upon." Taylor, *On Education and Freedom* (New York: Abelard-Schuman, 1954), 12–13.

13. Taylor, Correspondence to Jack Lyons (August 29, 1945); Box 4:F_Lyons.

14. Taylor, Correspondence to Helen Lynd (June 23, 1945); Box 1-Inauguration (1945).

15. Taylor, *Students without Teachers*, 193.

16. The Eight-Year Study involved thirty progressive secondary schools nationwide who were invited to reconceive their curriculum, instruction, and evaluation practices; their graduates, subsequently compared with graduates from traditional high schools, were followed into specified participating colleges. The Progressive Education Association's project is considered one of the more important educational research projects of the mid-twentieth century. See Craig Kridel and Robert V. Bullough Jr., *Stories of the Eight-Year Study: Reexamining Secondary Education in America* (Albany: State University of New York Press, 2007).

17. Sarah Lawrence College Publication series: No. 1: Esther Raushenbush, *Literature for Individual Education* (New York: Columbia University Press, 1942); No. 2: Esther Raushenbush, ed., *Psychology for Individual Education* (New York: Columbia University Press, 1942); No. 3: Ruth Learned Munroe, *Teaching the Individual* (New York: Columbia University Press, 1942); No. 4: Lois Barclay Murphy and Henry A. Ladd, *Emotional Factors in Learning* (New York: Columbia University Press, 1944); No. 5: Helen Lynd, *Field Work in College Education* (New York: Columbia University Press, 1945).

18. Taylor, "What Is Progressive in Education," 12.

19. Taylor, "Education as Experiment," 220.

20. Betty Friedan, *The Feminine Mystique* (New York: W. W. Norton, 1963), 284. Friedan selected quotes by Taylor that were referring to student comments from a 1948–1953 Sarah Lawrence College research project.

21. Taylor, "Freedom and Authority on the Campus," in *The American College*, ed. Nevitt Sanford (New York: John Wiley, 1961), 804.

22. Taylor, "Women in College," Bronxville Women's Club, Bronxville, NY (January 15, 1946), 2; HTA B8.

23. Taylor, "New Curricular Needs of Women," *Association of American Colleges Bulletin* 44, no. 1 (March 1958); HTA B13.

24. Benjamin Fine, "School Leaders Applaud Decision," *New York Times*, May 18, 1954, 14.

25. Bennett College is a private, African American liberal arts college for women in Greensboro, North Carolina. Nichols, Interview with Taylor, 244–248.

26. Taylor chaired a "panel of citizens," including Robert Coles, Paul Goodman, and Joseph Heller, who met in Washington, DC, at the National Theatre on June 8, 1964, to hear testimony from Mississippi residents about civil rights atrocities. Taylor wrote to President Lyndon B. Johnson on June 11, 1964, calling for law and order and specific and immediate actions. Taylor, Correspondence to Lyndon B. Johnson with Summary of Major Points in Testimony by Citizens of Mississippi; HTA B4:F_Johnson, L.

The Freedom Riders benefit concert was staged on March 18, 1962, at Scarsdale High School; this event was picketed by Westchester County residents who felt the participants were communists, and litigation was filed, with the support of the Scarsdale American Legion, to block the event, thus becoming a news item reported in the *New York Times*. Merrill Folsom, "Suit Seeks to Bar Scarsdale Show," *New York Times*, March 16, 1962, 33; "40 in Scarsdale Picket Concert," *New York Times*, March 19, 1962, 31.

27. Alvin Johnson, cofounder and former director of the New School, invited Taylor to serve as vice chair. Alvin Johnson, Correspondence to Taylor (May 21, 1947); HTA B19:F_Equality in Education. The Association of Colleges and Universities of the State of New York, "The State Commission to Examine into the Need for a State University" (October 20, 1947); see New York State Committee for Equality in Education materials; HTA B19:F_Equality in Education.

28. Taylor, "Moral Principles and Racial Discrimination," *College and University Business* 4, no. 5 (May 1948): 1.

29. Louise Blecher Rose, "The Secret Life of Sarah Lawrence," *Commentary* 75 (May 1983): 56.

30. Taylor, Correspondence to Alice Stone Ilchman (August 11, 1983); HTA B4:F_Ilchman. In correspondence earlier in his presidency, Taylor mentioned that he instructed all questions of religion to be removed from the college's application form and stated that "in every meeting of this [the admissions] committee which I have attended, no mention has ever been made of the religion or race of the applicant." Taylor, Correspondence to Evelyn Forman (March 6, 1947); HTA B6:F_1947.

31. "History of Sarah Lawrence College—Publications on SLC-Rose. Louise Blecher-The Secret Life of Sarah Lawrence and Responses-1983"; Sarah

Lawrence College Archives RG 11.2, Box 1. "Office of the President-Admissions—Quotas-Jewish Students, 1932–1956"; Sarah Lawrence College Archives, uncatalogued.

32. Rose, "The Secret Life of Sarah Lawrence," 56.

33. "Activities of Harold Taylor after leaving Sarah Lawrence College on August 1st, 1959" (circa 1982), 1; HTA B1:F_Biographical Material 1960s–1980s.

34. Taylor, "The Crisis in Liberal Democracy," Yale University (March 11, 1960). At the time of the Challenge Conference, Barry Goldwater (1909–1998) was a senator from Arizona; Thurgood Marshall (1908–1993) was Director-Counsel of the NAACP Legal Defense and Education Fund; and Philip Randolph (1889–1979) was a civil rights activist and past president of the National Brotherhood of Workers of America.

35. Taylor, Correspondence to Charles Frankel (n.d.; 1966); HTA B3:F_Frankel.

36. Taylor, Correspondence to Herbert Davis (November 4, 1964); HTA B3:F_Davis.

37. Taylor, Correspondence to Merle Curti (December 12, 1953); HTA B3:F_Curti.

38. Taylor, Correspondence to Ruth Field (August 13, 1962); HTA B3:F_Field.

39. Taylor served as master of ceremonies of the SANE Madison Square Garden Rally for Peace on June 19, 1960, and, after an introduction from Eleanor Roosevelt, presented the first speech, with other presentations by Walter Reuther, Norman Thomas, Norman Cousins, and others. Taylor reported that twenty thousand people were in attendance with another five thousand outside listening on loudspeakers. Taylor, Correspondence to Slonim (June 1, 1960); HTA B5: F_Slonim]. On June 8, 1965, Taylor would chair and present opening remarks for the SANE Madison Square Garden Vietnam Rally.

40. "Roger L. Stevens, Hubert Humphrey, and Dr. Harold Taylor at the White House," *American Ballet Theatre Friends Newsletter* 41 (March 1966): 1.

41. Harold Taylor, *The World and the American Teacher* (Washington, DC: American Association of Colleges for Teacher Education, 1968); Harold Taylor, *The World as Teacher* (Garden City, NY: Doubleday, 1969); Harold Taylor, *The United Nations University* (Washington, DC: American Council on Education, 1973); Harold Taylor, *A University for the World: The United Nations Plan* (Bloomington, IN: Phi Delta Kappa Education Foundation, 1975).

42. Taylor, Correspondence to Vernon Pope (October 6, 1963); HTA B6:F_1948.

43. Taylor, Correspondence to Sandra (Casey) Hayden (September 8, 1963); HTA B4:F_S_Hayden.

44. Taylor, *A University for the World*, 27; Taylor, *The United Nations University*.

Postscript

EPIGRAPH

Page 229: Carole Nichols, Interview with Taylor, SLC Oral History Collection (June 26, 1985), 12; HTA B2:F_Oral History. Harold Taylor, "Career statement," Harold Taylor Exhibition, Museum of Education, University of South Carolina, Spring 1989.

1. Michael Rossman (1939–2008) was one of the leaders of the UC Berkeley 1964 Free Speech Movement and worked as a research associate on a teacher education project with Taylor.

2. Michael Rossman, Interview with Taylor, 2B (July 1974, Holderness, NH); HTA B5:F_Rossman.

3. Michael Rossman, Correspondence to Frank Taylor (July 23, 1974); HTA B5:F_Rossman. Taylor did not find Rossman's assessment objectionable and, in fact, was interested in discussing his suggestion that they write co-autobiographies. Taylor, Correspondence to Michael Rossman (August 27, 1975); HTA B5:F_Rossman.

4. Taylor, introduction to *The Life and Mind of John Dewey* by George Dykhuizen (Carbondale: Southern Illinois University Press, 1978), xxv.

5. Taylor, "Education as Experiment," *Antioch Review* 9, no. 2 (Summer 1949): 235.

6. Taylor, *Students without Teachers: The Crisis in the University* (New York: McGraw-Hill, 1969), 319.

Index

academic freedom, 89, 90, 93, 97
Academy of American Poets, 225
activism, xxii, xxvii, 56, 173, 183, 231
Adler, Mortimer, 137; Algren's description of, 131
Adventures in Ideas (Whitehead), 31
Agnes de Mille Dance Theatre, 195
Algren, Nelson, 131
Allen, Raymond, 92–94
American Association of Colleges of Teacher Education, 225
American Ballet Theatre, 195, 225
American Civil Liberties Union, 92, 130
American Legion, x, xxii, 89–91, 95–99, 104, 106, 118
American Legion Magazine, 90, 95
Amherst College, 128–129
Anderson, Fulton Henry, 31, 240n6
Antioch College, 76, 218
antisemitism, 220–222
Aron, Paul, 90, 91, 100–101, 103–105
Art and the Intellect (Taylor), 195
Attwood, William, 161, 163–164, 165, 254n7
Auden, W. H., 32

Babs, Alice, 2
Baldwin, Roger, 92, 93, 94
Bard College, 109, 116, 218
Barnard College, 185
Barnes Albert, 195, 205–209, 258n26
Barnes, Joseph, 95, 96
Barr, Stringfellow, 77, 131, 245n20, 252n6
Bennett College, 220
Bennington College, 75, 76, 77, 112, 134, 216, 218
Benton, William (Bill), 153
Bergson, Henri, 25, 29, 30, 32, 32, 35, 37, 39, 41, 53, 136
Bernstein, Leonard, 211
Bigard, Barney, 4, 10, 14
Black Mountain College, 76, 77, 116
Black Panther-Radical Chic Party, 211
Blanding, Sara, 121, 251n19
Boatwright, McHenry, 2
Brebner, Adele, 100
Breit, Harvey, 109
Brett, George S., 31, 240n6
Brooklyn College, 102
Brown v. Board of Education, 220
Brown, Stuart, 156, 254n2
Brushwood (Holderness, NH), 61, 170–171, 179

Bryn Mawr College, 207
Buchanan, Scott, 77, 245n20
Buckley Jr., William F., 108; debate with Taylor, 121–124, Taylor's description of, 121, 250n18
Budge, Donald, 111
Butler, Nicholas Murray, 128, 184–185

calculated contempt defense, 102
camp-followers of the youth movement, 174, 188, 190, 192, 194
Campbell, Joseph, 66, 109, 110
Camus, Albert, 57
Canwell, Albert, 93
Carney, Harry, 3, 7, 9, 11, 238n5
Catledge, Turner, 153
Challenge Conference, Yale University, 153, 224
Clifton, Bill, 13, 239n9
College of Staten Island, 154
Columbia University, 102, 125, 128, 139, 174, 184, 185, 188, 189–193, 213
Columbia University Counter-commencement, 187–193
Commager, Henry Steele, 163, 165
Committee for World Development and World Disarmament, 196
communist, 89, 90, 93, 94, 95, 97, 99, 100, 101, 116, 118, 121, 123, 125
Communist Party, 85, 89–90, 94–98, 101, 102, 103–104, 116, 121, 177
Conant, James Bryant, 9, 87
Congress of Scientists on Survival, 196, 225
Contemporary Civilization courses, Columbia University, 215
Cooke, Jack Kent, 26, 240n4
Cooper, Jane, 109
Cornell University, 201–203, 205

Cornell University *Daily Sun*, 201
Counterattack, 90
Cousins, Norman, 225
CUNY–Staten Island, 154
Curti, Merle, 64, 224

Dance, Stanley, 2, 6
Dartington School, 43
Davis, Herbert J., 31, 240n6
Davis, Ossie, 220
de Mille, Agnes, 195
Dee, Ruby, 220
Demos, Raphael, 213, 259n4
Descartes, Rene, 25
Dewey, John, 19, 35, 59, 60, 64, 68, 125–128, 131–143, 174, 180, 206–209, 216, 217, 231; birthday celebration, 139–140; Hutchins, view of, 137–138; progressive education, misinterpretation of, 133–134, 136–138; Rickover, view of, 137–138; Russell, view of, 133
Dewey, Roberta, 132, 207
Doerschuk, Beatrice, 67–71
Dos Passos, John, 108
Dykhuizen, George, 126
Dykstra, Clarence, 9, 238n8

Eight-Year Study, 217–218
Eisenhower, Dwight D., 139, 156–162 passim, 174, 185, 186
Eleanor Roosevelt Memorial Foundation, 155, 220
Elementary and Secondary Education Act of 1965, 225
Ellington, Duke, 1–15, 32; assessment of Taylor's playing, 1–2, 9; funeral, 3–4; leadership, 4–5; Sarah Lawrence College job advice, 9–10; Sonata on A (Duke Ellington Duo), 10; stage presence, 10–11

Ellington, Ruth, 4, 6
Elmhirst, Dorthy and Leonard, 43
Essay concerning the Human Understanding (Locke), 44, 49
Eugene Meyer College, 146
Eurich, Alvin, 152, 223

Feminine Mystique, The (Friedan), 219
Field, Marshall, 155, 220, 253n1
Field, Ruth, 155, 156, 163–165, 225, 253n1
Fine, Benjamin, 220
Finletter, Tom, 156, 165
Firing Line, 121, 250n18, 251n20
Fitzgerald, Ella, 2
Fitzgerald, Robert, 109
Ford Foundation, 152–153, 223–224
Fowler, Burton P., 66
Frank, Glenn, 129
Frank, Lawrence K., 170
Frankfurter, Felix, 131
Freedom Riders, 220, 221, 261n26
Freedom Schools, 142, 183
Friedan, Betty, 219
Fromm, Erich, xii, 187, 191–194
Frost, Robert, 126, 128, 130; Taylor's description of, 135
Frye, Northrop, 18

Galbraith, Kenneth, 165
Garrison, Lloyd, 101, 146–147, 247n16
Garth, David, 164
General Education in a Free Society (Harvard Redbook), 212–215
Gensel, John, 2, 6
Genteel tradition, 214
Goddard College, 76, 218
Goldman, Irving, 100, 102–103, 104, 248
Goldwater, Barry, 199, 224, 262n34

Goodman, Benny, 13
Goodman, Paul, xii, 216
Graham, Martha, 5, 195
Grant, Madeleine, 100
Great Books program, 76, 77, 124, 131, 215
Green, T. H., 27
Greene, Maxine, 216
Gregory, Horace, 100, 109, 110
Groves of Academe, The (McCarthy), 107, 108, 114, 116, 117, 119, 120; Taylor's description of, 117, 120, 250n15

Haber, Robert Alan, 255n2
Hamilton, Jimmy, 4, 14
Hampton, Lionel, 13
Harry Walker Agency, 224
Harvard University, 87, 176, 212–213, 214, 218
Hayden, Tom, 174, 177, 178, 179, 180, 181, 188
Hays, Arthur Garfield, 101, 247n16, 248n17
Headstart, 142
Hechinger, Fred, 174, 186, 187, 188–194
Hellman, Lillian, 108, 196
Hersey, John, 196
Hines, Earl, 2, 12
Hodges, Johnny, 2, 9, 11, 14
Hofstadter, Richard, 187, 192
Hook, Sidney, 68, 93, 186, 213
Houmere, Helga, 245p81
House Committee on Un-American Activities, of the United States (House Un-American Activities Committee, HUAC), 90, 98, 130
How to Change Colleges (Taylor), 212, 226
Howe, Irving, 196, 199

Hume, David, 25, 35, 36, 41, 42, 44, 49, 60
Humphrey, Hubert, 195, 196–200
Hutchins, Robert M., 9, 77, 82, 87, 131, 136–137, 138, 238n8, 252n6

Ideology and Utopia (Mannheim), 41
Ilchman, Alice Stone, 222
Illich, Ivan, 216
improvisation, 5, 13, 14, 22
Institute for International Order, 110, 196, 225

James, William, 35, 59, 136; rules for lecturing, 14
Jarrell, Randell, 107–110, 112, 113, 114, 119, 121, 123–124, 248n1–2; Taylor's description of, 109, 113, 119
Jenner, William, 100, 105
Johnson, Lyndon B., 197, 225
Jones, Jo, 2

Kallen, Horace, 213
Kansas City Star, 201, 202, 203
Kant, Immanuel, 35
Kazin, Alfred, 136, 196, 199
Kefauver, Estes, 160
Kennedy, John F., 156, 157, 161, 163–169
Kerr, Clark, ix
Kilpatrick, William Heard, 75, 216, 245n18
Kirk, Grayson, 184, 255n5
Kirkpatrick, Theodore, 90
Kitchener Primary School (Toronto), 17
Kohl, Herbert, 216
Kozol, Jonathan, 216
Krupa, Gene, 13

Laidler, Harry, 139

Lancastria ocean liner, 48, 49, 50, 52, 240n5
Lawrence, William Van Duzer, 148
League for Industrial Democracy, 174, 180
Lenore Marshall Poetry Prize, 225
Life magazine, 72, 73, 85, 119, 136
Lincoln University, 209
Locke, Alain, 56, 241n3
Locke, John, 42, 44, 47, 48
Loewenberg, Bert, 95, 96, 100
Logan, Arthur, 6
Luce, Henry, 136
Lund, Art, 15
Lynd, Helen, 65, 91, 95, 96, 100, 170

MacCracken, Henry Noble, 75, 76, 244n17
Macdonald, Dwight, 108, 187, 190, 191, 193, 194
MacLeish, Archibald, 152
MacMurry, John, 39, 41, 42, 44, 46, 47, 48–49, 52, 53
Malott, Deane W., 201–205
Malraux, André, 57
Mannheim, Karl, 41–44
Mansell, Kathryn, 100
Marshall, Lenore, 196, 225
Marshall, Thurgood, 224
Martha Graham School for Contemporary Dance, 195
McBride, Katherine, 207, 208, 258n28
McCarthy, Joseph, 120, 122, 123, 131
McCarthyism, xxii, 90, 92, 123, 224
McCarthy, Mary, 89, 107–109, 114, 116–120, 248n1, 250n13, 250n15; Taylor's description of, 114
McIntosh, Millicent, 145, 185, 186
Meet the Professor, 211, 225
Meier, Deborah, 216

Meigs, Louise Lawrence, 148
Meiklejohn, Alexander, 125, 128–131, 190; Experimental College, University of Wisconsin, 128–130; Frost's description of, 130; relations with Amherst College faculty and alumni, 128–129; view of college athletics, 129
Melody Maker, The, 2, 7, 46
memoir, conventions of, xxiii–xxiv, 211–212
Meyer, Agnes, 155, 156, 161, 163, 164, 167
middle age gurus (camp-followers to the youth movement), 186, 189, 190, 194
middle-range theorizing, 216, 260n12
Mills, C. Wright, 57
Mitford, Jessica (Decca), xxii, xxvii, 108
Mommsen, Theodore, 70, 243n4
Moore, G. E., 40
Moss Scholarship, University of Toronto, 28
Morris, Robert, 100, 102, 103, 105
Murphy, Lois, 100, 170
Murrow, Edward R., 152

NAACP, 200
Nabokov, Vladimir, 114
Nance, Ray, 2
Nation, The, 109, 114
National Committee for a Sane Nuclear Policy (SANE), 196, 225, 262n39
National Committee for the Support of the Public Schools, 225
National Committee to Abolish the House Un-American Activities Committee, 130
National Council for American Education, 120

National Council on the Arts, 225
National Research Council on Peace Strategy, 196, 225
National Student Association, 178
Navasky, Victor S., 99
Nehru, Jawaharlal, 139, 140
Neill, A. S., 43
Neilson, William Allan, 127, 252n5
New York Times, 67, 72, 145, 152, 153, 164, 166, 174, 188, 189, 191–193, 199, 202, 205
New Yorker, 109; Funny Coincidence Department, 201, 202, 203, 204, 205
Newsweek, 119
Nin, Anaïs, 196
Nixon, Richard M., 156, 161, 162, 184
Northwestern University, 177

Oppenheimer, Robert, 93, 151, 152, 247n10
Otto, Max, 58, 61–62, 72, 125, 126, 131, 241n6; teaching cheer, 138–139

Parks, Gordon, 3, 238n5
Peace Corp, 142
Peace Research Institute, 196, 225
Phillips, Wayne, 166
Philosophy and Phenomenological Research, 213–214
Pictures from an Institution (Jarrell), 107, 108, 114–115, 119, 120, 123; Taylor's description of, 119; Taylor's summary, 117
plagiarism, 201–205
play of ideas, 229
Port Huron Statement, 174, 177, 178–180, 255n3
Potter, Paul, 181

Pro Arte Quartet (University of Wisconsin), 65, 241n5
progressive education, 43, 60, 64, 67, 79, 108, 126, 133, 136, 138, 142, 174, 216–219; left-wing progressivism, 76–77; right-wing progressivism, 76–77
Progressive Education Association, 217, 260n16
public intellectual, xxi, xxvii, 61–62, 87, 224

Queen Mary ocean liner, 46, 49

Randolph, Philip, 224, 262n34
Ransom, John Crowe, 248n2
Raushenbush, Esther, 91, 105
Reid, Alastair, 31, 121, 139
Richmond Community College, 184
Rickover, Hyman, 136, 137, 138, 252n9
Riesman, David, xii
Roethke, Theodore, 108, 112–113, 250n11
Roosevelt, Eleanor, 151, 152, 155, 156, 165–167, 196, 253n1
Rose, Louise Blecher, 222
Rossman, Michael, 91, 229, 263n1
Rosten, Leo, 164
Rukeyser, Muriel, 196
Russell, Bertrand, 24, 40, 41, 43, 124, 126, 133, 136; Dewey's impressions of, 133
Russell, Pee Wee, 14

Sacco-Vanzetti case, 93, 127, 247n8
School of Social Studies, San Francisco, 125
Sane Nuclear Policy (SANE), 225, 262n39
Santayana, George, 132, 133, 136, 214

Sarah Lawrence College Archives, 90
Sarah Lawrence College: aims and purposes, 77–78, 79–80; curriculum, 78, 80; donning system, 75, 78–79, 244n15; educational philosophy, 148, 216; faculty structure, 78, 79; field work, 75, 244n15; first-year studies seminar, 75, 217, 244n15; instruction, 78; origins, 75–76; practices, 74, 75, 78, 80, 83, 150, 177–178; social idealism, 80; student council, 80, 83–84; testing, 78
Sartre, Jean-Paul, 57
Savitt, Richard, 111
Schlesinger, Arthur Jr., 156, 163, 165, 191
Schonberg, Bessie, 195
Schuman, William, 72
Seeger, Pete, 220, 221
Senate Subcommittee to Investigate the Administration of the Internal Security Act, of the United States (Senate Internal Security Subcommittee, SISS, Jenner Committee), 89, 90, 100, 101, 103, 104, 105, 106, 126
Slonim Marc, 100, 104
Smith College, 127
Smith, T. V., 92, 93, 94
Spender, Stephen, 30, 108, 248n2
St John's College, Cambridge, 36
St. John's College, Annapolis, 76, 77, 215
Stassen, Harold, 207, 208, 258n27
Stebbing, Susan, 40–46, 49, 240n3
Stephens College, 79
Stevenson, Adlai, 155–169; Draft Stevenson, 156, 157, 161, 162; indecisiveness, 157–158, 159, 162, 167, 168; New York Times interview, 166, 167

Stewart, Rex, 7, 9, 10
Strayhorn, Billy, 5, 6, 7, 8, 238n7
Student League for Industrial Democracy, 180
Student Non-Violent Coordinating Committee (SNCC), 142, 177, 200, 220, 226–227
Students for a Democratic Society (SDS), 174, 176–177, 178, 179, 180, 182, 189, 190, 255n2
Students for a Restructured University, Columbia University, 187, 189, 190
Students without Teachers (Taylor), 126, 173, 174, 219, 226
Sullivan, Maxine, 15
Summerhill School, 43
Swarthmore College, 177, 181, 207, 209

Taggart, Genevieve, 109
TASS, 99, 247n14
Taylor, Billy, 2
Taylor, Charles W. (father), 17, 19, 33
Taylor, Elizabeth H. Wilson (mother), 17, 19–20
Taylor [Neilson], Gladys (sister), 17
Taylor, Harold: administrative style, 82–85; athletics, 21–24; Barr, Stringfellow: description of, 252n6; boy wonder, 72–73, 75, 82–85; Dewey, John: description of, 134–136; Duke Ellington band, description of, 10–11; Duke Ellington duo, 10; collegiate education (Victoria College, University of Toronto), 17–18, 24–27, 33; educational reform, 147–148; educational values, 69; fatherhood, 60, 61; Harvard Report, critique of, 214; Hutchins, Robert M.: description of, 252n6;

inauguration, 66–72; individual character, idea of, 15; instruction, basic beliefs, 58–59; intellectual awakening, 18, 27; interviewing for the presidency, 64–66; jazz at sea, 46–53; leaving St John's College, 36–38; liberalism, defined, 122; MA student, 28–29, 30–32; Methodist Church, 11, 17, 18, 30; Moss Scholarship, 28–29; musician, learning to become a, 11–14, 18–19; personal philosophy, 60, 82–83, 85; primary school education (Kitchener Primary), 17, 21; PhD student, 37, 39–44; progressive school practice, 126, 142; purposes of higher education, 175, 214–215; resignation, 64, 87, 145–147, 152; secondary school education (Riverdale Collegiate), 17, 21; social justice, 219–222; social reform, 57; state of mind, a, xxiv, 32, 35, 45, 53; Stevenson, description of, 157–158; teaching at University of Wisconsin, 8, 58–60; tennis with Jarrell, 110–111; tennis with Roethke, 112; tonsils and adenoids, removal of: 19–20; World War II, 55, 59, 241–242n7
Taylor [Tuthill], Jennifer T. (daughter), 60, 61
Taylor [Lehner], Mary E. (daughter), 60, 61
Taylor, Muriel Thorne (wife), 56, 108, 202, 207
Taylor, Telford, 101, 247n16
Teacher Corps, 142
tennis, 56, 65, 110, 111–112, 114, 129, 130, 152
Thayer, V. T., 68
Thomas, Norman, 180, 181

Index | 271

Time magazine, 72, 109, 119, 136
To the Lighthouse (Woolf), 27
Town Meeting of the Air, 90, 92, 95, 117, 118
Trilling, Diana, 187
Trilling, Lionel, 109
Truman, Harry, 92, 159–160, 162, 164
Turn Toward Peace, 196, 225
Tweed, Harrison, 91, 100, 101, 104, 106, 247n16

Unitarian-Universalist Associates, 225
United Nations University, 226, 227
United Nations University, The (Taylor), 226
United Negro College Fund, 220
University for the World, A (Taylor), 226
University of Colorado, Boulder, 174, 182
University of Kansas, 201, 202, 203
University of Kansas *Daily Kansan*, 201
University of Michigan, 148, 178, 181
University of New Mexico, 174, 182–183
University of Pennsylvania, 207, 209
University of Toronto, Victoria College, 17, 24–26, 27
University of Washington, 92, 93
University of Wisconsin, 8, 9, 29, 36, 53–62, 65, 73, 82, 125, 127, 128, 129, 130, 138, 152, 184, 190, 213, 216

Van Hise, Charles R., 70, 243n4
Vassar College, 75, 116, 121, 123–124
Vietnam War, 173, 177, 196–200
Virden Hall, Euphemia (Mickey), 247n14
Vista, 142
Voltaire, 42

Walter, Constance (Connie), 128, 129
Walter, Francis, 128–129
Warren, Constance, 102, 104, 106
Whitehead, Alfred North, 31, 35, 59, 135, 136
Williams, Joe, 2
Williams, Mary Lou, 2
Wilson, Edmund, 196
Wirtz, Willard, 165, 254
Wittgenstein, Ludwig, 36, 37, 40
women's education, 75–76, 79, 220
Woodbridge, Frederick J. E., 132, 252n8
Woolf, Virginia, 27, 28, 29, 30, 31, 32, 38, 39, 53
World and the American Teacher, The (Taylor), 189, 191
World as Teacher, The (Taylor), 226
World College, 226–227
World War II, 54, 59, 83, 126, 218, 241–242n7
Wright, Frank Lloyd, 81, 243p81

Yale University, 82, 98, 121, 224
Yale Conference, 153, 224

Zoll, Allen, 120

www.ingramcontent.com/pod-product-compliance
Lightning Source LLC
Chambersburg PA
CBHW032049230426
43672CB00009B/1528